The History and Philosophy of

the Metaphysical Movements

in America

The History and Philosophy

of the

Metaphysical Movements

in America

by

J. Stillson Judah

THE WESTMINSTER PRESS · PHILADELPHIA

LIBRARY OF CONGRESS CATALOG CARD No. 67–11672

PUBLISHED BY THE WESTMINSTER PRESS®

PHILADELPHIA, PENNSYLVANIA

PRINTED IN THE UNITED STATES OF AMERICA

Contents

Foreword

THIS BOOK DEALS with certain religious philosophies that are of increasing importance in the United States as well as abroad. If a superficial observation shows vast differences among some of these movements, a more careful examination of their basic philosophies discloses sound reasons for treating them as closely related. Moreover, all these groups have a lineal descent from a common cultural origin which shows their doctrinal kinship and illumines more clearly the nature of this relation.

For the above reasons the writer was perplexed concerning the proper term to cover this family of sects. He finally solved the problem by extending the more specialized meaning of " metaphysical movement " to apply in the plural to the groups treated in these chapters. Understood in the special sense intended here, " metaphysical " seems to be the best word for this relationship, especially since each organization speaks of its philosophy as being metaphysical in the sense to be elaborated. And none objects to the application of this word denoting its belief.

Therefore, when one tries to assess the impact of these movements upon traditional Christianity it is not quite correct to regard their force as that of many small, unimportant, individualistic sects or cults, but rather as that of one movement with many expressions. Also, one should not measure their power by the number of members each may claim as its own, for indeed most of these sects are small. On the contrary, it would be more appropriate to include thousands who, in addition to membership in traditional Christian churches, also attend the services of the metaphysical organizations. An even greater number read avidly their books and periodicals, for example, the *Daily Word* of the Unity School of Christianity. Even Protestant ministers have been influenced by their philosophies and practices, as we shall observe.

William James once referred to the potentiality of some of these groups. He prophesied that New Thought and Christian Science would eventually constitute a spiritual movement as significant as the Reformation was for its time.[1] In a similar vein was the correspondence from a Methodist minister who expressed the hope and belief that the future of the ecumenical movement would be church union through teachings like those of the Unity School of Christianity. He believed also that a person like Norman Vincent Peale might be an important agent in this accomplishment. In order not to create a misunderstanding, however, one must add that whereas Dr. Peale's techniques of positive thinking are like Unity's, his theology differs.

In the past, the metaphysical movements as a whole have been largely treated as separate entities whose individual differences have been stressed. This work will endeavor additionally to make plain the common features and heritage as products of American religious culture, and of influences, one group upon another. Finally, it will try to show in a small way their impact upon organized Protestant Christianity. That much more could be said about these movements, their thought and origins, will be evident from the start. The author therefore begs the reader's indulgence for the foreshortening that must be made due to the nature and scope of this work.

He has tried to approach his task with objectivity and yet with sympathetic understanding. He, himself, has not always been a Protestant, but was once a student of many of these movements. Having become dissatisfied with the fundamentalism of a Sunday school teacher, he left the Christian church to become a " seeker of truth." At the age of twelve he began

---

[1] Charles S. Braden, *These Also Believe: A Study of Modern American Cults and Minority Religious Movements* (The Macmillan Company, 1949), p. 130.

studying Theosophy, which led to the practice of Yoga under the tutelage of the Sikh teacher, Dr. Bhagavat Singh Thind. While still pursuing these teachings, he spent a summer with the noted Hindu teacher, Krishnamurti; later found time to attend the Truth Center of Mrs. Nettie Holmes to learn the practices and philosophy of New Thought; was enticed to the lectures of the Ballards, when the "I Am" movement skyrocketed to popularity for a short time; studied Spiritualism, attended séances, etc.

As the writer became acquainted with other sojourners milling to the same lectures of various groups, two facts became significantly apparent. First, these metaphysical pilgrims had little difficulty reconciling with their own views most of what each leader taught. To be sure, there were distinctive characteristics, but the similarities were greater than the incongruities. Secondly, many attending these meetings regularly owed allegiance first to one of the traditional Christian churches.

Although the writer gradually returned to the Protestant fold during his undergraduate days, he has never felt animosity toward any leader of the metaphysical groups who sincerely taught what he honestly believed. Quite to the contrary, it was with very great pleasure and gratitude that the author received a Sealantic Fund grant to study further these movements during the academic year 1957–1958. In this work he has tried to present as fairly as possible the religions of these leaders, to most of whom he is indebted for splendid cooperation and printed materials. What may seem to be at variance with this intent in some places should be considered as constructive criticism offered in the same spirit in which the writer has also criticized the Protestant churches. It should be noted, however, that most of such passages reflect the opinions of those who are leaders in these movements rather than the author's.

Deep gratitude should be expressed to the American Association of Theological Schools and to the Sealantic Fund, whose fellowship made this research possible; to my former colleague, Jan Christiaan Beker, who offered valuable suggestions; to my present colleagues: Charles McCoy, who read through the manuscript and offered his constructive criticism and insights;

and finally, Conrad Bonifazi, who read through two editions of the work and labored long with me on points of style. I, however, take full responsibility for the contents.

To my wife goes a special expression of gratitude for her enduring patience during the writing of this book.

I wish also to thank the leaders of the various metaphysical groups, too numerous to list singly, who have given freely their publications and their time; the Trustees of the Church of Christ Scientist for their permission to quote many passages from the works of Mary Baker Eddy; and Foster Bailey of the Arcane School for permission to quote from the works of Alice Bailey. To one and all I express my gratitude.

S. J.

Pacific School of Religion
Berkeley, California

Introduction

THE WORD " METAPHYSICS," as applied to the metaphysical movements, has a different connotation from the one customarily associated with a division of philosophy. In the words of one of its exponents, it " stands for the deeper realities of the universe, the things which are external — which stand above and beyond the outer phenomenal realm." He then adds the distinguishing words, " It especially concerns itself with the practical application of that absolute Truth of Being in all the affairs of our daily and hourly living." " Metaphysics," then, as used in this work, applies to a practical type of philosophy. It is considered to be both scientific and religious.

By denotation, the term " metaphysical movement " first refers to the New Thought movement, which emerged from the philosophy and experiences of Phineas P. Quimby about the middle of the nineteenth century. It comprises a number of small autonomous groups loosely held together by an organization called the International New Thought Alliance. Akin to New Thought, however, some organized metaphysical churches have developed, such as the Church of Divine Science, the Church of Religious Science, and the Unity School of Christianity.

The term " metaphysical movements " will be used generically to include other groups whose goals differ from those of New Thought, but whose philosophies have similar sources and characteristics. Among these are the Spiritualists, the Theosophists, and later proliferations, which often combine views from several metaphysical sects.

We may reasonably seek a common ground for all of these, since the seeds of the basic philosophies were briefly and swiftly sown between 1840 and 1875, in an area stretching no farther than from Maine to New York. Much of their foundation was the extreme liberalism of American transcendentalism, which first began in the 1830's and produced the influential philosophy of Ralph Waldo Emerson.

These early metaphysical leaders were uniquely syncretistic as a whole. Besides transcendentalism various ingredients of their potpourri of thought are found in Emanuel Swedenborg's philosophy, which entered through his followers, or through the works of Emerson and other transcendentalists. There was seasoning from Indian monistic thought, which influenced again both transcendentalism and the metaphysical movements after the translation of certain Hindu works in the nineteenth century. To the more occult groups like Theosophy, a generous portion of Hermetic and Kabbalistic philosophy gave an accented flavor that was not entirely absent from many mental healing groups. Rather closely associated with this occultism was the philosophical ragout of Anton Mesmer and his followers, whose practice of hypnotism supplied the basis for the trance state in Spiritualism and led to both Davis' and Quimby's experiments in healing. Mesmer's contribution thus added that savor which distinguishes the metaphysical direction most sharply from transcendentalism.

Since all these various groups originated in the United States and therefore have contributed to and fitted into American culture, their strength and growth is partly due to their becoming a mirror of the hopes, thoughts, and aspirations of a large part of the American people. They form one side of our culture's profile. Let us now indicate their pervasive characteristics, some of which are suitable reasons for their growing popularity now.

1. As allies of the transcendentalists, these "metaphysicians" revolted against the creedal authority of organized Protestant churches to find their solace in a new freedom of individualism exemplified by Emersonian self-reliance, and as

a result each person sought his own salvation without needing the Christian church. They lashed out against a conservative Calvinism and its doctrine of predestination, according to which some souls were destined to be damned, and preferred to believe that salvation is for all.

All the present-day metaphysical organizations consider themselves to be creedless, as evident opposition to orthodox creeds, although most have developed statements of principles. Apparently unknown to many of their adherents is the fact that Protestantism itself has also developed a more liberal wing. Certainly an eighteenth-century sermon of Jonathan Edwards depicting unsaved babies burning in hell would now bring incredulous smiles to many Protestant faces. Nevertheless, a great number of these metaphysical followers have told me that one of their reasons for leaving the Protestant Church was that they could not accept an orthodox creed, especially the belief in a hell.

2. Nearly all became united in the central belief that the inner, or real, self of man is divine. Each has his spark of divinity. Thus they dissented from the common Christian view that man is a creature of God, created in his image, but not sharing his divine nature.

3. Although speaking of God in a personal way, as such terms as Divine Mind or Universal Mind might indicate, they have not generally wanted to be considered as theists. Instead, they have preferred the concept of an impersonal God, a God of science, often called by such names as Christ Principle, Infinite Principle, etc. Therefore, all consider their philosophies to be scientific as well as religious. They seek to be united with their God as Principle or Law through the understanding and utilization of spiritual or psychic laws. By their use they believe they can gain health, prosperity, peace of mind, or inner occult development according to their respective goals. The claim to be scientific allures many Americans to their fold.

4. Most groups have conceived of God as being related to man and the world in a quasi-gnostic or dualistic manner. More commonly, however, this apparent dualism gives way to a monistic doctrine of God, who is all and in-all. The natural

world of so-called matter is an error of our minds or is mind
itself and really one with God, the Divine Mind.

The belief that God is completely immanent and readily
available as the law of man's being offers a type of reassurance
that is attractive to many. This stress upon God's immanence
may be contrasted with the emphasis of much current Protestant theology upon God's transcendence and even his absence.

The metaphysical sects arrive at a type of humanism in
which man becomes the master of his fate. He is believed capable of creating his own conditions for his progression through
the knowledge and utilization of God's laws.

5. Some metaphysical groups consider themselves to be
Christian, while others do not, but all make place for some of
the moral teachings of Jesus. Jesus, the man, however, is usually separated in their thought from the Christ or Christ Principle, which is one with God and is every man's inner nature.
Jesus is the way-shower, one who was more aware of his divine nature than others, and who therefore has pointed out the
path.

6. These movements revolted against a traditional Christian
view that man is a sinner, standing under God's judgment and
in need of repentance and forgiveness, so that the Christian
doctrines of grace and atonement are generally absent. Where
such terms are used they are not recognized in any traditionally
Christian context.

7. As God is regarded as being all, in-all, and all good, so
evil, including sickness, is often considered to be unreal or the
absence of good; it is an error of our minds or due to the ignorance of our true nature or its laws. One may contrast this
belief with the more ordinary Christian recognition and concern with evil and sin as a reality to be dealt with both indi-
vidually and through social action.

8. All metaphysical philosophies are pragmatic. One is asked
less to believe than to test the principles to be demonstrated in
his experience. Since the methods often seem to produce results, they strengthen the belief in the validity of their underlying philosophy. Indeed, our American pragmatism, popularized by William James and applied to educational systems

by John Dewey, is reason for many to test the metaphysical claims.

9. By equating salvation with the discovery of a higher reality and utilization of its laws, the metaphysical leaders tend to place their emphasis upon self-realization, knowledge, or spiritual science instead of upon faith or works.

10. All these movements try to demonstrate the scientific validity of different kinds of religious experience as proof of their philosophy which gives meaning to life. In some cases it may be through spiritualistic phenomena or the development of hidden powers. In others it is the amelioration of health or material conditions. This need for meaning through experience attracts many whose faith is insufficient for these times of crisis, who lack security occasioned by the increasing depersonalization and secularization of our culture, and who see the rapid advancement of science threatening their cherished values and bringing them to the brink of annihilation.

It is again not surprising that monistic allies such as Zen Buddhism and Vedanta are in vogue. They too offer a religious experience of reality. Nor can one depreciate the importance of the mystical experience often obtained through such drugs as mescaline and lysergic acid. All these offer an experiential demonstration to support one's belief and one's will to believe.

Just as the monistic philosophies of India nurtured the growth of transcendentalism in the nineteenth century, so have these metaphysical legatees made fallow the soil for the growth and resurgence of these Oriental importations in the twentieth. The metaphysical philosophies are closer in thought to the Hindu Absolute of Vedanta than to the transcendent personal God of Christian orthodoxy. If transcendentalism may be said to have risen, flourished, and passed away in the nineteenth century, its spirit has been partially resurrected in the current metaphysical movements.

Even though neo-orthodoxy has revolted against the liberalism of the late nineteenth and early twentieth centuries by attempting to reinterpret and make efficacious many theological doctrines, the overt question of personal salvation through a meaningful experience of conversion — a problem that concerned our Puritan forefathers — has now, by and large, been left to the fundamentalists, Pentecostals, and more conservative Protestant churches. Their rapid growth and the success of such evangelists as Billy Graham testify to an unsatisfied need of many people. The appearance of glossolalia recently in churches of the more staid denominations and the greater concern for spiritual healing must also be viewed in a similar context. All these phases disclose the widespread need for experience demonstrating that God is still in the world and one's belief is valid.

11. Like Yoga and Zen Buddhism, most metaphysical sects offer a psychological approach to reality. If they have not captured the attention of Carl Jung, Erich Fromm, and other analytical psychologists to the same extent as Yoga and Zen, they profit by the interest Americans have shown in their theories. The late Carl Jung, for example, so popular among many of the American intelligentsia, has often spoken in favor of the monistic philosophies and has indirectly helped the metaphysical cause by setting aside the idea of a theistic God as a " Western archetype." He has posited, instead, the " universal archetype " of Hindu monism, even though the latter has also made a place for theism. Therefore, metaphysical organizations that offer a type of monistic, religious psychotherapy for self-fulfillment and health influence increasingly the American upper-middle class.

12. The metaphysical movements are highly optimistic. They stress the love of God without making explicit his judgment, and man's goodness instead of his propensity to sin. Besides their emphasis upon practical benefits awaiting man in *this* life, they have a strong belief in immediate personal immortality after death. Eventual salvation is the lot of all through continual progression in the heaven worlds or through reincarnation and its law of karma. These alternative beliefs exclude the Christian doctrines of evil, grace, and providence. Therefore, man's state would depend upon understanding his real nature and upon the proper use of spiritual laws.

Conversely, not even all Protestants now have a doctrine of personal immortality. Many ministers hold that the concept of a separate immortal soul is the product of reading Greek philosophy into the New Testament words of Paul and others. While recognizing the Greek influence in terminology, they would prefer the Hebrew view of man suggested by the Old Testament, which recognizes the unity of soul and body. Because of such problems many Protestant ministers only allude to man's future state in a hazy way on Easter. This is not so with the metaphysical sects, although their belief in universal personal immortality and salvation contrasts strangely with the need for salvation preached by conservative evangelists such as Billy Graham. Yet both will play their roles to many in this atomic age who desire to strengthen their faith in personal survival.

13. Particularly among groups associated with New Thought the acquisition of pleasant things under the guise of prosperity has become important. They believe that God gives freely to all who realize their unity with him by using his laws. Moreover, without the recognition of evil as real, they tend to become ethically hedonistic, seeking that which is pleasant as their good and avoiding that which causes pain.

Although the American people have shown themselves capable of sacrifice and suffering, has not our wealth often made the criterion of success depend upon one's ability to acquire material and pleasant things? To this degree will be the inducement of metaphysical philosophies which promise such benefits.

14. Most metaphysical groups have a belief in an inner meaning of words beyond their dictionary definition — a meaning that cannot be discovered empirically from the standpoint of usage or etymology, but that is revealed intuitively. This is known by a variety of terms, such as the spiritual, metaphysical, or occult interpretation. Each leader of one of these sects may have his own special definitions which often disagree with explanations of others. A particular metaphysical sect may make use of the Bible, but its exegesis does not exhibit any awareness of studies in historical and literary criticism, nor does its interpretation show any dependence upon orthodox theology past or present. To one not acquainted with this in-

tuitional or inspirational method, the interpretation would appear to be allegorical. For the adherent of the metaphysical sect, however, it offers the key to a higher truth, through which the Bible appears in agreement with his particular interpretation.

15. All these movements make healing through the mind or spirit a part of their mission. Although the *modi operandi* may vary greatly from sect to sect, nevertheless, particularly those organizations closely related to New Thought do have a modicum of success by using principles recently associated with psychosomatic medicine.

Beginning with Freud, the depth psychologists have made us realize that ideas and emotions can affect our mental and physical health. Moreover, in the last few years Hans Selye, a Viennese doctor, has helped to revolutionize theories of medical science by his important discoveries about the effects of stress. Even the definition of disease has been changed in the *New Gould Medical Dictionary*, a standard volume in many medical schools. It says that disease is " 'the failure of the adaptive mechanisms of an organism to counteract adequately the stimuli or stress to which it is subject, resulting in disturbances in function or structure of any part, organ, or system of the body.' " [1]

According to Selye: " If a microbe is in or around us all the time and yet causes no disease until we are exposed to stress, what is the ' cause ' of our illness, the microbe or the stress? I think both are — and equally so. In most instances disease is due neither to the germ as such, nor to our adaptive reactions as such, but to the inadequacy of our reactions against the germ." [2]

If stress is a factor leading to the onset of many diseases, there should be some practical benefits in techniques that relieve stress, such as those used by the healing sects. Peace of mind and faith are beneficial to health. Still, a life without stress would be an uninteresting existence. Carried to an ex-

---

[1] Quoted in Hans Selye, *The Stress of Life* (McGraw-Hill Book Company, Inc., 1956), p. 221.
[2] *Ibid.*, p. 204.

treme, there would be little concern for anyone except one-self, because a loving care for others involves the stress of pity and the pain of sacrifice. However, pain, suffering, and death are the inevitable lot of all, even for metaphysical healers. The Christian still is not without reward. From his perspective, suffering may be the way to one's regeneration into a spiritual life. Man's anguish, though uninvited, can often be catalytic to great creativity and insight into life's meaning, as some of our greatest literature demonstrates.

Nevertheless, every Christian should relieve pain whenever possible, and even though one may criticize the healing sects for exaggerated claims, their growth and increasing influence testify to some success. Therefore, before the first stone is cast, the Christian churches should become aware of their own deficiencies in not giving more attention to a ministry to the sick. Perhaps what John Sutherland Bonnell once said concerning the healing sects is true: " To some extent we may regard their very existence as a judgment on the Christian church for decades, for failing to follow the Master's injunction to exercize a ministry of healing; for this failure we are now reaping the consequences." To the extent that the Christian churches have failed, many more will be attracted to the metaphysical organizations or will be influenced by their literature.

I

The Mirror of American Culture

THE VERY FACT that the metaphysical movements have originated in the United States and have fitted so well and un-critically into American culture has doubtless added to their power and influence. Perhaps they offer more of what many Americans want than what a Galilean almost two thousand years ago would have prescribed for their needs, but certainly this criticism may apply also to the Protestant Church. More-over, these sects lack that prophetic spirit of the ancient He-brews who criticized themselves and their culture. With few exceptions they fail to protest except against traditional Chris-tian beliefs.

Although their goals may sometimes differ, the metaphysi-cal movements exhibit a common philosophical core with in-dividualistic variations that increase proportionately to the proliferation of sects. Still they are like branches of a single tree growing out of the cultural soil that produced American transcendentalism.

When one thinks of nineteenth-century American litera-ture, the works most generally known are not those of Protes-tant theologians. Probably few schoolboys know their names, but the works of transcendentalists such as Emerson, Thoreau, Whitman, Alcott, and others may be familiar. These men re-volted against the Protestant theology of their day and created a type of religious culture in which the metaphysical leaders participated. Emerson, in particular, through his many lectures and his written works became the topic of discussion throughout the northeastern part of the United States. While the transcendentalists, however, were linked to the earlier Puritan culture indirectly, as will be shown, so were the metaphysical leaders by their orientation toward the environment of transcendentalism. To say that any particular prenineteenth-century idea influenced directly either of the first metaphysical progenitors, Andrew Jackson Davis and Phineas P. Quimby, would be dangerous. These believed their philosophies were revealed and rarely cited past authorities. It will be sufficient to show that many basic metaphysical concepts were already existent in prenineteenth-century American thought, were reinforced in the nineteenth century, and formed a cultural milieu which has continued as a part of the American scene to the present.

The following common metaphysical ideas and others were part of the American heritage in the early years of these movements: a God who is all and in-all and good, implying that evil is unreal; the scientific deity, whose most emphasized attribute is law; a utilitarian deity, who grants the desires of one who recognizes and uses his spiritual laws; a God who, as a Divine Mind, includes the world made from himself as a corresponding yet lesser reality or shadow; the concept of man sharing the divinity of God. I shall now sketch in related portions of American cultural history, in order to delineate a common milieu for these doctrines and the reasons for the origins of these movements.

Growth of Freedom of Belief

Nineteenth-century America reaped the first great harvest of the universal freedom of belief established in the preceding period, and it became an era of new revelations.

The New England Puritan government had been a theocracy ruled over by an oligarchy of magistrates, who were God's representatives on earth. In Massachusetts, for example, suffrage was generally limited to the elect, those chosen by God for salvation. As members of the church, they had testified to their faith and to their covenant with God. Since there was at that time no effective separation of religious doctrine and social solidarity, and since both ministers and magistrates were protectors of their orthodoxy, dissenters such as Roger Williams and Anne Hutchinson were exiled. The Puritans soon had their problems. Many of their children did not join the church by making a declaration of their faith. Therefore, a halfway covenant relation was allowed to those who would still promise to lead Christian lives.

The state supported the dominant faith or faiths in all the colonies except those of Pennsylvania, Rhode Island, New Jersey, and Delaware. In New York, state support was given to both Anglican and Dutch Reformed Churches.[1]

Two factors nurtured the establishment of ubiquitous freedom of religion and the separation of church and state: the revivalism of the Great Awakening and the philosophy of deism. The great influence upon the religious revivals was the forceful preaching of Jonathan Edwards and George Whitefield, who became catalysts to a period of revivalism that ran through most of the churches. It was a period when experience and proper living rather than creedal theology became important for most of the revivalists who lacked the theological interests of Jonathan Edwards. Their attitude set the stage for transcendentalists and metaphysicians who preferred experience to Christian orthodoxy.

Some Presbyterians, Anglicans, and most Congregationalists challenged the revivalists. They believed their theology had to be expounded, and that the influence upon society should be through the state support of the church, a view opposed by the revivalists.

The philosophy of deism was embraced in varying degrees by such political leaders as Benjamin Franklin, Thomas Jefferson, George Washington, and others who were not sympathetic to traditional Calvinism and demanded religious freedom. So after the United States was founded in 1789 with the ratification of the Federal Constitution, the Bill of Rights' first amendment forbade Congress to make laws establishing re-

[1] Jerald C. Brauer, *Protestantism in America: A Narrative History* (The Westminster Press, 1953), pp. 80–82.

ligion or abridging its freedom.[2] This presaged the great burst of freedom seen in development of transcendentalism, the metaphysical and other movements in the nineteenth century.

This spirit of freedom, expressing itself later in the individualism of the new movements, was further enhanced by the spirit of the French Revolution, which began in 1789. The earlier writings of Rousseau, which extolled individual liberty with enthusiasm, helped fan the flames for freedom. He pictured nature, man, and God as all good, but society as the corruptor of his goodness, which would be revealed when he followed the goodness of nature of which he was a part.

New Revelations

The transcendentalists picked up his cry. In his essay on " Nature," Emerson wrote, " Man is born free, but he is everywhere in chains." [3] The reality of nature and natural man as opposed to man molded by creeds and institutions of his making marked the difference between essential man and existential man for the transcendentalists. From nature they would seek new revelations and a basis for a new age. They would fling away the old traditions. As Harold C. Goddard has reminded us, " The transcendental spirit partook to an extraordinary degree of that distrust of the past, that optimistic faith in the future, that confidence in the efficacy of a formula for solving the problems of mankind." [4]

How well indeed these words apply also to the temper of the early leaders of the metaphysical movements! Seizing this new freedom, these founders of new faiths cut themselves from the changing but continuing witness of the church to the past. They built new foundations upon new revelations, selecting elements from the changing culture as building blocks for their philosophies.

Thus from the middle of the nineteenth century onward the new revelators grew in number. Andrew Jackson Davis,

[2] *Ibid.*, pp. 82–88.
[3] Harold C. Goddard, *Studies in New England Transcendentalism* (Hillary House Publishers, Ltd., 1960), p. 185.
[4] *Idem.*

believing he had received divine disclosures from God, the Sensorium, issued a revealed philosophy of Spiritualism. Phineas P. Quimby, forefather of the mental science healing groups, thought his intuitional Wisdom was that of God. Mary Baker Eddy claimed a divine revelation as the source of her Christian Science. But in the same period there were other theophanies outside the context of the metaphysical philosophies. Joseph Smith received a revelation that produced two Mormon sects, the Latter-day Saints and the Reorganized Church of the Latter-day Saints, as well as many splinter groups. Following the revelations of Ellen White, the Seventh-day Adventists and the Christian Adventists came into being.

Therefore, revivalism, deism, and the confluence of other circumstances occurring in the eighteenth century played their part in weakening the belief in doctrinal theology. Even though the metaphysical leaders may have been unacquainted with the philosophy of deism, they were allied with the transcendentalists and deists in opposing creedal theology including the belief in Jesus Christ as Savior. They considered him as a way-shower and teacher of morals.

The metaphysical movements teach universal salvation and consequently no eternal punishment for the damned. Such beliefs were held by the Universalists, whose first church in Gloucester, Massachusetts, in 1778, preceded Unitarianism here by thirty years. By 1870 there were already over sixty Universalist societies in Vermont alone,[5] and Universalists were numbered among those interested in the new metaphysical philosophies. Andrew Jackson Davis, although never a member of the Universalist Church, had attended its services as well as those of the Methodist Episcopal Church. His closest friend and amanuensis of the first book that he claimed to have received clairvoyantly had been a Universalist minister.

[5] Francis P. Weisenburger, *Ordeal of Faith: The Crisis of Church-Going America, 1865–1900* (Philosophical Library, Inc., 1959), pp. 259–260; also Brauer, *op. cit.*, p. 126.

Growth of Idealism and the Mechanistic Deity

The influence of Emanuel Swedenborg cannot be underestimated as one source for the seeds of idealism that blossomed forth in transcendentalism and in the metaphysical movements. Like Swedenborg, Emerson and the metaphysical leaders believed that intuition rather than the senses revealed a spiritual reality and a spiritual science transcending the natural science of the physical world. Emerson was quoting a Swedenborgian article when he wrote: " Socrates says, ' The laws below are sisters of the laws above.' So really are the material elements of close affinity to the moral elements. But they are not their cousins, they are themselves. They are the *same laws* acting on superior and interior planes. On the lower plane it is called *Heat*, on the higher, *Love*. Whenever you enunciate a physical law, I hear in it a moral rule." [6]

The concepts of God as Universal Law or Principle and also as a Divine Mind owe something to such syntheses as Jonathan Edwards and others made of Newtonian thought and Puritanism. Indeed, certain aspects of Edwardian philosophy excised of its Calvinism could be acceptable to both transcendentalists and metaphysical leaders. Perry Miller and other scholars have already shown the connection between the thought of Edwards and the transcendentalists. Let us outline the development.

Newtonian science of the eighteenth century had declared the universal reign of law. The universe became one vast machine operating strictly according to a cosmic constitution lying at the heart of nature. The deists believed God could become an onlooker of a self-regulating world, when once created. Others thought God could express himself immanently in law as one of his emanations. In the latter case, it was but a step farther to regard him as an abstract force without personality. So many came to believe God existed only as a mathematical principle in an abstract scheme of universal law.[7]

[6] Bliss Perry, *Emerson Today* (Princeton University Press, 1931), pp. 82–83.
[7] Richard D. Mosier, *The American Temper: Patterns of Our Intellectual Heritage* (University of California Press, 1952), pp. 99–101.

The metaphysical leaders thought of God as abstract Principle, all and in-all, but also as having gradations. Like Emerson, they made a dichotomy between the natural and spiritual worlds, while considering the natural world to be only the shadow of the higher spiritual one.

In his *Treatise on Optics*, Newton stated that even though we learned only from experience, we were actually cut off from reality by a screen. The question then arose whether man was simply mirroring nature and was caught in his own egocentric predicament. For, according to Newton, man could only know the world outside through his senses, but that which he saw did not reflect the *reality* known to mathematical science. It was only the *appearance* of nature. The vibrations of sounds and colors striking the media of the senses were transmitted to the mind, but the real world was hidden behind these phenomena. From his theory of light Newton believed his experiments had eliminated color as a quality of objects, because outside the brain it had no real existence. The attributes of matter we believe we see were only the contribution of the knower, and the qualitative uniqueness of the universe was therefore only the product of subjectivity.[8]

Jonathan Edwards made a synthesis of ideas from seventeenth-century Puritanism and Newtonian theories, creating the milieu for transcendentalism. The Puritans in the seventeenth century had been well aware of the new principles of science and sought to reconcile them with their theological views. They conceived of God as extended substance underlying the sensible appearance of inert matter. Whatever attributes a thing had were in essence those of God, and extension was its chief quality. God, being omnipresent, was absolute extension.

Jonathan Edwards built upon this view: " It is self-evident I believe to every man, that Space is necessary, eternal, infinite, and omnipresent. But I had as good speak plain: I have already said as much as that Space is God."

Since everything existing would have to exist in absolute space and time, Edwards believed the conception of this could

[8] *Ibid.*, pp. 103–106.

occur only in a mind that was equally absolute — namely, the mind of God. As he declared again: "Deprive the world of light and motion and the case would stand thus with the world, there would be neither white nor black, neither blue nor brown, bright nor shaded pellucid . . . nor wet nor dry, hard nor soft, solidity nor extension . . . nor body, nor spirit, what then is to become of the universe? Certainly it exists nowhere but in the *Divine Mind*."

Although the Puritans could postulate that the world would perish without mind,[9] they regarded it as an imperfect copy of ideas, whose real essences lay in the mind of God. They believed these existed latently in the human mind, and the soul contained the seminal, intuitive knowledge of these truths, which might be shared partly through reason or divine grace.[10]

In the history of eighteenth-century American religious culture, it has not been difficult to find precedents for the ideas of a monistic, mechanistic, and impersonal deity; also a world of appearance, whose true reality in the Divine Mind is to be known only through man's higher mind or intuition.

These ideas became part of the common transcendentalist environment in which the metaphysical movements constructed their idealism. Andrew Jackson Davis, like Emerson, was able to say that God was a Divine Mind, was all and in-all; that all reality was in some sense mind.

Mary Baker Eddy, the founder of Christian Science, believed also that God was the Divine Mind, who was all and in-all. Though denying the reality of matter, she taught that only God and his ideas were real; the world and man were ideas in the Divine Mind.

The Utilitarian Deity

The God of these movements has been regarded as a utilitarian deity, who grants the desires of those who follow and use his spiritual laws. One can point to a similar pragmatism and optimism in American orthodox Christianity stemming from the Puritan period and continuing through the nine-

<hr>

9 *Ibid.*, pp. 61–64.   10 *Ibid.*, p. 67.

teenth century. The Puritan deity was a utilitarian God. The Puritans believed not only that there was a relationship between sin and illness, but also that their growing prosperity in abundant America was a sign of the grace of God and proof of their election. Many felt supported in the latter belief by the fact that the prosperous were more often church members than were people of the lower working classes. As late as 1887 it was asserted that the New York churches had become a kind of " exclusive ecclesiastical club, designed for the accommodation of persons of ten thousand dollars a year, and upward." Like many metaphysical leaders, there were also ministers in this period who were able to defend wealth not only as a blessing of God but as a reward for following his laws. Other ministers, however, were concerned about such conditions, and about the churches' failure to minister to the poorer class. In the late 1800's, Lyman Abbott, a noted Congregational preacher and writer, became worried about the migration of churches from downtown areas. He estimated that less than ten percent of the working class in New York City were regular attendants at any Protestant church.[11]

The growth of republicanism out of deism also contributed to the transformation of God into a benevolent, utilitarian deity. His Puritan absolutism had been changed by Edwards into an arbitrary constitution, with faith in the universal reign of law. The sovereignty of God had to be limited so that it would not interfere with the natural divine rights of man, which had been given him. This tended to shift the emphasis from the sovereignty of God to the sovereignty of man and inferred man's freedom of will as separate from God's sovereignty.[12]

The republican philosophy, which has exerted its influence to the present day, taught that one's happiness and welfare were dependent upon following man's laws, as representatives of the cosmic constitution. Analogously, the metaphysical leaders taught that through the intuitive discovery and utilization of God's spiritual laws, they could reap the rich rewards

[11] Weisenburger, op. cit., p. 42.
[12] Mosier, op. cit., pp. 72–79.

that were God's will for them. Since man's inner self was believed to be divine, so his measure of success and happiness would be proportional to the realization of his inner nature.

Early republicanism, however, was opposed by many churches, and revivalism spread to combat its principles. Timothy Dwight and Lyman Beecher fought against the new federal party of Jefferson, arguing that it was an irreligious movement that would destroy Christianity and open the door to immorality,[13] but aspects of this republicanism became an influential part of our " Christian " culture.

Religious Experience as a Criterion for Truth

Both transcendentalists and early metaphysical leaders were convinced that the way to truth was through their intuitive religious experience. This led them to accept the validity of their own private revelations outside the context of evangelical Christianity.

If, as Perry Miller suggested, Jonathan Edwards was the link between Puritanism and transcendentalism [14] and, at least indirectly, the metaphysical movements, Puritan piety should never be confused with the experiential religion of the latter. Whereas Puritanism accepted the idea of universal law, thought of the cosmos in mystical and sometimes almost pantheistic terms, and emphasized the sense of the inner intuitive communication of the soul with God, still this awareness of God expressed itself in the doctrine of the individual's regeneration quite differently from that of the metaphysical movements. Moreover, the Puritan believed that God disciplined him into subjecting his intuitions to a code accepted by Puritan society.[15]

According to Miller the difference between Edwards and Emerson was not that Edwards was still a Calvinist, but that Emerson had rejected all systems of theology. It was rather that Edwards went to Nature to seek for impressions he could

13 Brauer, op. cit., p. 104.

14 Perry Miller, Errand Into the Wilderness (The Belknap Press of Harvard University Press, 1956), pp. 184–203.

15 Ibid., p. 192.

interpret, whereas Emerson went to Nature believing in a correlation between man and the impressions he received. Emerson was an Edwards " in whom the concept of original sin had evaporated," [16] a statement applying equally to the metaphysical movements.

Mysticism and Monism

Edwards prepared the way for the monism of the transcendentalists by his reliance upon Newtonian science, which drove him close to pantheism. He argued that God did not create the world from nothing but from himself. Edwards' Calvinism, however, prevented him from losing the distinction between God and his creation. Still, if one were to press the point, as Perry Miller does, and admit with Edwards that God created the world and man out of his own substance, it would not be hard to infer that "man is divine " and " nature is the garment of the Over-Soul." By such means Miller links Edwards again to the transcendentalism of Emerson,[17] and indirectly perhaps to the metaphysical philosophy, which rejected the orthodox Christian view that the world was created from nothing (ex nihilo).

When Puritanism became more rationalistic and abandoned its earlier enthusiasm, Emerson and others found a need for its absent mystical side. After casting away what seemed to them an outworn Calvinistic dogma that checked this inclination, they were again free to express a new kind of enthusiasm.

New philosophies appeared in the nineteenth century that were of little importance to the Protestant development of American culture. It was these, however, which furthered the distinctive qualities of transcendentalism and the metaphysical movements. To these their adherents would turn for expression of their mysticism. Indian monism and other Oriental philosophies were to vie with Swedenborgianism to capture their fancies.

Oriental philosophy first became important in the United States during the nineteenth century. Emerson, Thoreau, Al-

[16] Ibid., p. 185.   [17] Ibid., pp. 194–195.

cott, and other transcendentalists read such philosophical treatises as the Upanishads, the Bhagavad-Gita, and the Vishnu Purana from India; mystical studies of the Sufis from Persia; as well as Chinese works. All of these became Bibles of the world in which they might learn of God's revelations and seek to find them revealed in their own inner beings. They read these not so much for the purpose of following any system of philosophy as for what Emerson called the " lustres."

Emerson proclaimed the goal of religion to be the conscious union of man with God who could reveal himself through man's intuitions. Therefore, he thought that God had spoken to Socrates, Jesus Christ, the Buddha, Shakespeare, Swedenborg, and many others. All religions contained the truth, he said, since he could discern the true revelations of God in each. But more important for man was his own personal reception of God's truth. The metaphysical sects agreed upon all these points and moved toward eclecticism.

Emerson constructed a monistic philosophy in which God, the Divine, or Universal, Mind was all, and therefore, the essence of man was considered to be divine. If Emerson was influenced by Hindu monism in believing that God or Brahman was all and in-all, and was also man's real self or atman, it was not quite in the sense of the Vedanta philosophy according to which the individual was absorbed. Although this might be inferred in his poem " Brahma," the self was very important to him. As he said, " If speculation tends thus to be a terrific unity, in which all things are absorbed, action tends directly backwards to diversity." [18] His view might therefore be classified as a qualified monism, which has been also characteristic of the metaphysical sects. Since the philosophy of Swedenborg played such an important role in the development of Emersonian and metaphysical thought, some attention should now be given to it.

[18] Arthur Christy, *The Orient in American Transcendentalism: A Study of Emerson, Thoreau, and Alcott* (Columbia University Press, 1932), p. 268.

The Influence of Emanuel Swedenborg

Swedenborg's ideas entered transcendentalism largely through the works of Coleridge, Emerson, and Carlyle. Charles August Tulk, a leader in the formation of the Swedenborg Society in America, became acquainted with Coleridge in 1817. After becoming interested in Swedenborg, Coleridge even offered to write a " history of the mind of Swedenborg," but a failure in guaranteeing payment for this proposed work ended his intention.[19]

Emerson was first drawn to Swedenborgian philosophy after reading Sampson Reed's *Observations on the Growth of the Mind* while studying for the ministry at Harvard. The popularity of this Swedenborgian book among transcendentalists and others is attested by the nine editions printed in America from 1826 to 1910. From this treatise Emerson turned to Swedenborg's own works and to Swedenborgian periodicals, especially the *New Jerusalem Magazine*, from which many of his ideas were taken.

Although an admirer of Swedenborg's acumen, Emerson was still critical of his Biblical interpretation, which he felt to be incorrect, even though it gave spiritual truth.[20] The great importance of Swedenborg to him was expressed in a letter he wrote to Carlyle on November 20, 1834, in which he prophesied that the Swedenborgians would contribute more than any of the other sects to the " new faith which must arise out of all." [21] Little did Emerson foresee the development of the metaphysical movements in America, which would be allied partly through their indebtedness to both Emanuel Swedenborg and to himself.

Later in 1842 Emerson fell out with Reed over his interpretation of Swedenborg, and from 1845 to 1849 he was giving his critical lecture on Swedenborg, which was published in 1850. His objections increased against the Swedenborgians in general

---

[19] Clarence Paul Hotson, "Emerson and Swedenborg," Ph.D. thesis, Harvard University, 1929, p. 105.
[20] *Ibid.*, pp. 181–182.
[21] *Ibid.*, p. 187.

when they took a conservative attitude on the slavery question.[22]

Swedenborg's influence upon the metaphysical movements came partly through transcendentalists such as Emerson, and partly through his own works and those of his followers. Certainly the schools of New Thought, which confess their indebtedness to Quimby and Emerson, have received Swedenborgian thought through the latter's works. Moreover, the first to write about Quimby's ideas was Warren Felt Evans, a follower of Swedenborg. His first book on mental healing interpreted Quimby in a Swedenborgian framework.

Andrew Jackson Davis, the philosopher of Spiritualism, although not admitting he had read Swedenborg, explained the similarity of thought by alleging that Swedenborg had been his first mentor on the spiritual planes. Madame Blavatsky, the founder of Theosophy, also gave credit to Swedenborg in her writings.

Emanuel Swedenborg, the son of a Lutheran bishop, was born in Stockholm, Sweden, in 1688. Being well educated and interested in the natural sciences, he wrote numerous articles and learned treatises, many of whose ideas his countrymen were slow to accept. He also tried his hand at being a mining engineer and even became a member of the House of Nobles, one of the four Houses in the Swedish Parliament. Later his scientific and philosophical works won sufficient fame abroad for him to become one of the first elected members of the Royal Academy of Sciences and a corresponding member of the Academy of Sciences of St. Petersburg.

Swedenborg was searching for the mystery of life, and when physics and chemistry did not reveal it, he turned to anatomy and philosophy. His work on human anatomy, including the soul, the *Economy of the Animal Kingdom*, appeared in English between 1843 and 1846 and received praise from Dr. Spurgin, former President of the Royal College of Physicians, as well as the plaudits of Emerson and Coleridge.

Those rejecting his later theological writings, which resulted from his spiritual revelations, should note that they contained

<hr/>

[22] *Ibid.*, pp. 165, 170.

ideas foreshadowed in his earlier philosophical works. In the latter he had already come to the conclusion that one could only know God and the inner reality of things through intuitive knowledge,[23] a concept paralleling that of Kant. In a paper read before the Royal Swedish Academy of Sciences in 1760 he said: " Experience deprived of an insight into the nature of things is knowledge without learning, and a foundation without a building to rest upon it. The observations of the outward senses merely furnish data and give information about things which the understanding ought to investigate." [24]

In his work *The Worship and Love of God* is a statement of his doctrine of correspondences, upon which his later theology rests, and which became so important to followers of the metaphysical movements, as well as to Emerson and the transcendentalists. In his elucidation of it Swedenborg seemed to build upon Newton's discoveries that the quality of any object as seen by the senses would vary in accordance with the state of light by which it is seen, and from this he formed an analogue for the intellectual or spiritual sight.[25]

The year 1743 marked the beginning of his theological works, when he believed the Lord had begun to open his spiritual sight, and by 1745 he claimed he was able to speak with spirits and angels.[26]

Even if Swedenborg's thought has been influential, one must not infer that his theological works should be labeled metaphysical in the sense used here. For example, he had an orthodox Christian doctrine of guilt and sin that is generally lacking among the metaphysical sects. His diary, published in 1859, expresses his own feelings of guilt and unworthiness, which were as deep as any Calvinist's. " I found that I was more unworthy than others and the greatest sinner, for this reason that our Lord has granted me to penetrate by thought into certain things more deeply than many others."

And again he wrote: " I perceived in myself . . . that in

---

[23] George Trobridge, *Swedenborg: Life and Teaching* (Swedenborg Foundation, 1955), pp. 9–57.
[24] *Ibid.*, pp. 68–69.
[25] *Ibid.*, p. 77.
[26] *Ibid.*, p. 85.

every particular thought, and even in that which we consider pure, an infinite quantity of sin and impurity is contained, and likewise in every desire which enters from the body into the thoughts; these spring from deep roots. Although therefore, a thought may appear pure, it, nevertheless, is a fact that a person may think in a certain way from timidity, hypocrisy, and many other causes, as may also be traced out by an exploration of the thoughts; so that on this account man is so much the more unable to free himself from sin, and there is not a single thought which is not very much alloyed with uncleanness and impurity. . . . I have, indeed, observed that our whole will into which we are born, and which is ruled by the body and introduces thoughts, is opposed to the Spirit . . . and hence it is that we are dead to everything good, but to everything evil we are inclined from ourselves." [27] This should certainly satisfy the most orthodox Christian standard.

Quite different, however, was Swedenborg's Christology from that of the metaphysical sects and also from orthodox Christianity. Instead of being the second member of the Trinity, Jesus Christ himself was the triune God [28] who incarnated himself in the world and who, Swedenborg believed, was responsible for his revelations.

Swedenborg was closer to an orthodox view when he wrote: "That which is created in God by God is not continuous from Him; for God is *Esse* Being in Itself, and in created things there is not any *Esse* in Itself. If in created things there were any *Esse* in Itself, this would be continuous from God, and that which is continuous from God is God. . . ."[29] Every created thing by virtue of this origin is such in its nature that it may be a recipient of God, not by continuity, but by contiguity."[30]

Again in contrast with the orthodox view he opposed the doctrine of *Creatio ex Nihilo* and gave support to the metaphysical belief that the world was a creation out of God himself.

[27] *Ibid.*, pp. 87–89.
[28] *Ibid.*, p. 112.
[29] Emanuel Swedenborg, *Angelic Wisdom, Concerning the Divine Life and the Divine Wisdom* (The American Swedenborg Printing and Publishing Society, 1909), par. 55, p. 22.
[30] *Ibid.*, par. 56, p. 22.

He avoided a pantheism, however, by postulating his doctrine of correspondences and discrete degrees, through which Swedenborg paved the way for the metaphysical schools to regard their teachings as scientific. Let us examine this idea.

Swedenborg believed in a spiritual world and a natural world corresponding to one another as cause and effect, since the natural world had behind it a spiritual force producing and sustaining it.[31] The natural world was the image of the spiritual one, and both received an influx from the divine. Similarly, both natural and spiritual man were recipients of the divine by influx. Each stage, natural, spiritual, and divine, was separate from the other by what he called a discrete degree. Each was a correspondent of the higher, and the higher was the cause of the lower, its effect.

He also applied this law to the interpretation of the Bible. As a scientist, he had noted the discrepancies between science and a literal interpretation of the Bible. Theology, he said, was a " science, based upon revealed knowledge and the facts of human experience, confirmed by reason, and ministering to the practical needs of life." [32] The Bible was truly the " Word of God," if not outwardly appearing so. The literal interpretation corresponded to the natural characteristic of man. But in the historical narratives, the Gospels, and the prophetic books, he believed there was an interior spiritual sense revealed to him when his spiritual sight was opened. Therefore, he reinterpreted the books of Genesis, Exodus, and Revelation, and parts of others, giving to each a spiritual or inner meaning. In this way he comprehended the Bible as agreeing with science.[33]

Nearly all the metaphysical sects interpret the Bible in this assertedly intuitive way, so that the Bible may not be inconsistent with their particular " scientific " beliefs. In this manner the Bible is made to reveal the laws of a spiritual science that the particular group believes it has found.

When Mary Baker Eddy received her revelations contained in *Science and Health with Key to the Scriptures*, such a spir-

[31] Trobridge, *op. cit.*, pp. 128–129.
[32] *Ibid.*, p. 120.
[33] *Ibid.*, pp. 137–147.

itual interpretation was given. She prefaces her Glossary forming Chapter Seventeen as follows: " It contains the metaphysical interpretation of Bible terms, giving their spiritual sense, which is also their original meaning." We might at least note that a volume giving Emanuel Swedenborg's spiritual interpretations of Biblical words entitled *A Dictionary of Correspondences, Representatives, and Significances Derived from the Word of the Lord* was first printed in Boston in 1847, but there is no proof that Mrs. Eddy saw it.

After the Unity School of Christianity was established in the 1880's by Charles and Myrtle Fillmore, Mr. Fillmore wrote a complete dictionary of the Bible, giving the metaphysical or spiritual meaning for each word in an allegorical manner resembling Mrs. Eddy's.

The Theosophical Society has a similar method of Biblical interpretation, although adding a unique touch: " The distinguishing characteristic of this kind of writing is that, whilst its narratives have some historical basis, the language itself is largely, but not entirely, allegorical; it is constructed of symbols and allegories containing profound spiritual and occult truths. This language is also referred to as the Mystery Language, and it is said to have been invented by Initiates of the Ancient Mysteries in order both to reveal to those who could be helped, and to conceal from those who could not, spiritual knowledge and the power which its possession bestows." [34]

The " I Am " group, founded by Edna and Guy Ballard, the New Age Bible Center of Los Angeles, the Rosicrucians, the various autonomous New Thought organizations, and the Spiritualists all agree on this inner meaning of words which support their Biblical interpretations and their particular philosophy. At the seminary of the Universal Spiritualist Association, one of the courses is the Metaphysical Interpretation of the Bible, which requires each student to make his own metaphysical explanation of various passages.

Swedenborg believed God was neither impersonal nor arbitrary, but ruled entirely by law. Natural law was the reflection

[34] Geoffrey Hodson, *Man's Supersensory and Spiritual Powers* (London: The Theosophical Publishing House, 1957), pp. 119–120.

of its higher spiritual and divine correspondents, and man's salvation or regeneration partly depended on his living in harmony with God's laws.

All the metaphysical sects agree that their religion is scientific and stress the primacy of law and man's harmony with it as a means of salvation. Andrew Jackson Davis, the first of the American metaphysical philosophers, was consequently the first among them to teach these principles.

Davis most commonly referred to God as being all-in-all, as Infinite Principle, Infinite Mind, Positive Mind, or Divine Mind, terms in general use by the other metaphysical schools. According to him, God stood for the totality of reality which showed gradations, however, since Davis had an interpretation of Swedenborg's doctrine of correspondences. He believed in a finite representation of the reality of God " in a regular and harmonious succession of series, degrees, correspondences, and representations — all being limited, local, finite, and imperfect, when contrasted with him." These correspondences of lesser perfection were the consequence of the existence of an infinite and perfect Principle of God.[35] As God on the higher plane, he was love, will, and wisdom, the moving principle, and the great Positive or Divine Mind; as nature he became substance and the universe; as law, he was progression and development.[36] Elsewhere Davis declared nature to be the Positive Mind's sevenfold manifestation which existed in dependence upon God as his effect.[37] Human souls were " detached individual personifications of the Deific Nature and Essence . . ." [38] which would be realized eventually through progression.

The law of attraction, so important to Spiritualism and to other metaphysical groups, also had its basis in Swedenborg's doctrine of correspondences. This was the name which Davis gave to his theory that effects correspond to and represent the

[35] Andrew Jackson Davis, *The Great Harmonia: Being a Philosophical Revelation of the Natural, Spiritual, and Celestial Universe* (Benjamin B. Mussey & Co., 1851), Vol. 2, p. 288.

[36] *Ibid.*, pp. 138, 281, 285, 393.

[37] Andrew Jackson Davis, *The Penetralia: Being Harmonial Answers to Important Questions* (Bela Marsh, 1856), p. 75.

[38] *Ibid.*, p. 31.

essentials of their causes.[39] Like attracts like. In Davis' application it meant that after death a person would be attracted to the spirit plane corresponding to his development and progression in this world. Conversely, Davis maintained that thoughts of love and kindness would attract spirits of the higher planes to the séance. For such a reason many mediums begin a séance with one or two hymns, but others, having lost the original meaning, explain that singing gives the spirits greater power to manifest themselves. The metaphysical healing groups add a further interpretation to this law: each person's conditions, e.g., health, sickness, prosperity, poverty, etc., are attracted to him according to his thinking.

Davis also taught that the harmonial use of the laws could be the means of gaining one's aspirations. Those who wanted love would grow in love; those seeking knowledge would become rich in knowledge. " Therefore, is nature ever true to her children. Just in proportion as these departments of mind are opened . . . to the celestial atmosphere . . . will Love, and Knowledge, and Wisdom, increase the substance of the soul." [40]

This view, published by Davis in 1856, contains the seminal philosophy of Quimby who, unlike Davis, developed it into the mental science of healing. That Davis influenced Quimby indirectly or at least reinforced his view seems evident. Davis had already published several books before Quimby's earliest manuscripts were written; and even if Quimby never read Davis' works, his manuscripts reveal his acquaintance with Spiritualism, which depended on Davis for its philosophy. His criticism was never against the philosophy of Spiritualism, but against the validity of its phenomena. But even Davis, so revered by them, was critical of their spirit materializations in one of his works.

Emerson, like Davis, wrote that God was the Divine Mind and " Mind is the only reality of which men and all natures are better or worse reflectors." [41] By combining this idea with the

[39] Andrew Jackson Davis, *The Great Harmonia: Concerning Physiological Vices and Virtues, and the Seven Phases of Marriage* (Sanborn, Carter, & Bazin, 1856), Vol. 4, pp. 40–41.
[40] *Ibid.*, p. 55.
[41] Ralph Waldo Emerson, *Centenary Edition: The Complete Works* (Houghton Mifflin Company, 1903), Vol. 1, p. 333.

Swedenborgian concept that the spiritual is the cause of the natural, that spiritual laws are correspondents of natural laws, one has a basis for the New Thought and allied healing movements. As one of the New Thought writers expressed it: " As fast as you conform your life to the pure idea in your mind, that will unfold its great proportion. A correspondent revolution in things will attend the influx of spirit." This could just as well have been also written by Andrew Jackson Davis!

Theories Concerning Matter

In the monism of the metaphysical movements in which matter and spirit are generally distinguished as corresponding states of the one reality of God, the exact character of matter has received various interpretations. Due to the growing conviction that matter consists of vibrating atoms or forces, some metaphysical leaders have differentiated spirit from matter in terms of higher or lower vibrations. Therefore, some believe one may raise his material consciousness to higher spiritual vibrations through thought. At one time among New Thought students it was common to believe that affirmations of one's divine nature might raise one's vibrations to the higher consciousness of God. Even if this view is not so often expressed by them now, the vibratory hypothesis of matter and spirit is held by some metaphysical sects, e.g., the Spiritualists of the National Spiritualist Association and the Theosophists.

Although this theory was antecedent to the appearance of Swami Vivekananda in Chicago in 1893, he no doubt enhanced its popularity by lecturing often on the subject before Spiritualist, New Thought, and other audiences.[42] Vivekananda, who came to the United States to attend the Parliament of Religions of the World's Columbian Exposition in Chicago, stayed long enough to make an appreciable influence upon many metaphysical sects and to found the Vedanta Society.

The metaphysical sects also have views similar to Swedenborg's concerning matter. He said creation is an emanation from

[42] Swami Vivekananda, *Vedanta Philosophy: Lectures on the Raja-Yoga and Other Subjects* (Weed-Parsons Printing Co., 1897), pp. 34-45.

God; all life is spiritual and spirit is substance originating from God.[43] He likened the phenomenal world to one of appearances in which the things we see and touch are less real than things unseen.[44] Nature or matter exists by virtue of Being, without which, as the ground of its existence, it is nothing.[45]

In the *Economy of the Animal Kingdom*, Swedenborg also dealt with the problem of the lower or material mind, which he called the *animus*. To the degree that we might speak of the eyes and images as being material, he believed we might speak of a material mind. But to the extent to which material ideas communicated with the immaterial, he queried whether they were " any ideas at all before they partake of the life of the soul." Since the soul contains the essence of being and life which is not created, it is not proper to call it material according to him. " So for the same reason we cannot call the soul material in respect to its reception of this life; nor therefore the mind, nor therefore the *animus*, nor the sight, nor the hearing, nor even the body itself so far as it lives. For all these live the life of their soul, and the soul lives the life of the spirit of God, who is not matter, but essence; whose *esse* is life." [46]

According to his law of correspondences, there was then a lower and a higher mind, a lower and a higher truth. One might predicate the existence of matter, when speaking of the lower truth; and the nonexistence of matter, when talking in terms of the higher correspondent or the true reality as the ground of all being. Or as the Swedenborgian commentator, George Trobridge, explained, " If we judge by appearances, we may speak of the material world as real, but this is only a fallacy of the sense." [47]

Although Phineas P. Quimby, like Andrew Jackson Davis, was not supposed to have read Swedenborg, he was no doubt

[43] Trobridge, *op. cit.*, pp. 78–79.
[44] Swedenborg, *Angelic Wisdom, Concerning the Divine Life and the Divine Wisdom*, par. 40, p. 16.
[45] Emanuel Swedenborg, *The Apocalypse Explained According to the Spiritual Sense in Which the Arcana There Predicted but Heretofore Concealed Are Revealed* (The American Swedenborg Printing and Publishing Society, 1912), par. 1206, Vol. 6, p. 315.
[46] Trobridge, *op. cit.*, pp. 61–62.
[47] *Ibid.*, p. 123.

familiar with Swedenborgian ideas entering through Spiritualism. Moreover, Horatio W. Dresser, the historian of the New
Thought movement, said the Church of the New Jerusalem,
the Swedenborgian church, might be claimed as the forerunner
of New Thought. It opened the way for this movement as well
as for Spiritualism. Dresser also admitted Quimby's acquaintance with Swedenborg's views through a New Churchman living in Portland and cited the possible influence from Warren
Felt Evans,[48] his Swedenborgian friend and later interpreter.
Therefore, it is not surprising that his concept of matter agrees
with Swedenborg's. Quimby wrote: " There is no intelligence,
no power of action in matter itself. . . . The spiritual world to
which our eyes are closed by ignorance or unbelief is the real
world, . . . in it lie all the causes for every effect visible in the
natural world, and . . . if this spiritual life can be revealed to
us, in other words if we can understand ourselves, we shall then
have our happiness or misery in our own hands. . . ." [49]

He said that if the real world (i.e., the spiritual) is substantial,
this material world is like a shadow — a world of opinion.
Without denying existence to matter, he declared it to be the
source of false wisdom,[50] and, like Swedenborg, he could either
accept it in a provisional sense or deny it in respect to the greater
reality.

The later metaphysical healing groups have generally split at
this point. New Thought and allied organizations have accepted
the provisional reality of matter, but Christian Science has
denied its existence as the erroneous result of man's mortal
mind. One may query here whether the real difference between
the two views is not more semantic than real.

Another source for the theory of matter was Neoplatonism,
whose contribution, largely through Emerson, provided a foundation for the doctrine of evil.

[48] Horatio W. Dresser, *Handbook of the New Thought* (G. P. Putnam's Sons,
1917), pp. 192–193.
[49] Phineas Parkhurst Quimby, *The Quimby Manuscripts, Showing the Discovery of Spiritual Healing and the Origin of Christian Science*, ed. by Horatio W.
Dresser (Thomas Y. Crowell Company, 1921), p. 319.
[50] *Ibid.*, p. 327.

Doctrine of Evil

The metaphysical movements have been accused of stressing God's goodness and love at the expense of his wrath and judgment, but it has been pointed out by various authorities that revivalists in Edwards' time often made a similar emphasis which then became dominant in transcendentalism.

Most metaphysical sects believe in the totality of good as reality and equate apparent evil with unreality or ignorance. They reason that if God is all-in-all and is good, evil must be the absence of good and therefore unreal. This privative doctrine of evil was held by Emerson, who said in his Divinity School Address: " Good is positive. Evil is merely privative, not absolute: it is like cold, which is the privation of heat. All evil is so much death or nonentity. Benevolence is absolute and real." [51]

Emerson believed that the Divine Mind had a moral content and each man could know the right intuitively by listening to the divine self within. Since the laws of the natural and spiritual worlds were correspondents, he felt that when he heard a natural law, its higher correlative also resounded, because they were really one. This doctrine of evil seems to have developed from his interests in Neoplatonism.

Plotinus, the third-century founder of Neoplatonism, believed that God was One, a divine pleroma emanating into lower degrees of reality and goodness. Matter was the farthest extreme, the point at which his goodness and being had become extinguished. Therefore, matter was considered as nonbeing and evil. Since man's divine self was temporarily encased in matter, he participated in evil, the lack of goodness. Moral evil existed in proportion to his being influenced by his material side and not reflecting his real goodness of soul. Evil, therefore, was not a positive entity, but only the absence of good. [52]

Although the metaphysical movements retain the general moral precepts of the Hebrew-Christian tradition, they regard sin, an aspect of evil, as unreal. In fact, many metaphysical leaders avoid the use of the word. Some groups that show a strong

Hindu influence equate sin with ignorance. Others, influenced by Andrew Jackson Davis, prefer the word " progression."

Andrew Jackson Davis, while recognizing the law of correspondences, often placed his emphasis upon the unity of law. He tried to show that there was really no sin, because sin meant transgressing a law. Instead, he declared that man at times merely substituted another law for one less congenial to his nature. For example, if he burned his finger in the fire, he learned to use a law more harmonious to his being.[53] Therefore, progression became the keynote in the ethics of Spiritualism. Elsewhere Davis wrote: " Moreover, there can be but One infinite, One eternal, and One perfect principle in the constitution of things. There is not space sufficient to permit the existence of an infinite and eternal Evil Spirit. *God is positive, all else is negative.* If there exists an evil principle, would not that principle be an integral element in the constitution of the Divine Mind? . . . God is all-in-all; — would he not, therefore, be in the evil principle? . . . There is no principle, antagonistic to God; no empire at war with Heaven! " [54]

Emilie Cady, whose book *Lessons in Truth* has become one of the classics of New Thought, the Unity School of Christianity, etc., held a view reminiscent of Emerson and Davis. She wrote as one of her denials: " First: there is no evil. There is but one power in the universe, and that is God — Good. God is all good, and God is omnipresent. Apparent evils are not entities or things of themselves. They are simply an absence of the good, just as darkness is an absence of light. But God, or Good, is omnipresent, so the apparent absence of good (evil) is unreal. It is only an appearance of evil, just as the moving sun was an appearance." [55]

Influence of Occultism

If transcendentalism, with its prismatic facets of Neoplatonism, Oriental and Swedenborgian philosophy, contributed to the broad spectrum of the metaphysical movements, so also did

[53] Davis, *The Great Harmonia*, Vol. 4, pp. 11–15.
[54] *Ibid.*, Vol. 2, pp. 288–289.
[55] Emilie Cady, *Lessons in Truth* (Unity School of Christianity, 1928), p. 38.

the occult philosophy that flourished in eighteenth- and nine-teenth-century France. The occultism of this period was a de-velopment and mingling of many elements, among which were smatterings of Neoplatonic and quasi-gnostic ideas joined to Kabbalistic, astrological, and Hermetic philosophy. This mix-ture had earlier formed a basis for alchemy, whose followers searched in vain for the philosopher's stone to transmute baser metals into gold, and the magic elixer to ensure longevity and perhaps immortality.

During the Renaissance, portions of this occult philosophy had even influenced many Christians. They were faced with certain conditions analogous to those of today. Just as our pres-ent accelerated knowledge has spurred theologians to search for new hermeneutical principles and fresh ways to make the Bible relevant, even so the rediscovery of the Greek and Latin classics, the Hermetic texts, and the Hebrew Kabbala created a similar situation just prior to the Reformation. Various attempts were made to reconcile the Biblical interpretation to the newly discovered learning.

Some aspects of occult philosophy, however, had influ-enced churchmen and laity since at least the thirteenth century. Astrologers were often consulted by princes and popes alike, and many large families made out horoscopes for their children as soon as they were born,[56] even though there were men like Nicole Oresme, John Gerson, and Pierre d'Ailly who con-demned such practices.[57]

In the latter part of the fifteenth century and the early part of the sixteenth, the Kabbala and the Hermetic philosophy claimed the interest of such early humanists as Marsilio Ficino, Pico della Mirandola, Jacques Lefèvre, and others. Ficino re-vived the spirit of the Gnostics and tried to reconcile the wis-dom of the Greeks and the Bible according to methods that differed little from those practiced by the Gnostics, Basilides and Valentinus.[58]

[56] Augustin Renaudet, *Préréforme et Humanisme à Paris Pendant les Premières Guerres d'Italie (1494–1517)* (E. Champion, 1916), p. 149.

[57] G. W. Coopland, *Nicole Oresme and the Astrologers: A Study of His Livre de Divinacions* (Harvard University Press, 1952), *passim.*

[58] Renaudet, *op. cit.,* p. 139.

Pico della Mirandola led the way toward a Christian interpretation of the Kabbala, which had grown out of medieval Jewish esoteric speculation. He believed that Neoplatonism and Christianity could be reconciled through a hidden meaning of the Bible provided by the Kabbala. The Kabbala had interpreted the Scriptures of the Old Testament by a type of numerology employing the numerical value of the Hebrew letters. Its theory that different words having the same numerical value had the same meaning was applied to Greek, Latin, and other languages as well, so it was possible to derive interpretations believed hidden in the Scriptures.

The Kabbala postulated that the one God emanated in ten descending degrees, or *sephiroth*, forming the *Adam kadmon*, or archetypal man. According to its Christian interpreters, the three highest *sephiroth* became representations of the Trinity; the first emanation, the Father; the second, the Son or Logos; and the third, the Holy Spirit. They then went one step farther by identifying the incarnate Jesus with the sixth of the *sephiroth*, thereby separating Jesus from Logos.[59] Such separations of Jesus from the Christ have been characteristic of the later occult interpretations down to the present time.

The Kabbalists believed that man had a divine preexistent soul belonging to the sphere of the *sephiroth*, but encased in a body of lower emanation. Man's salvation lay in developing the seeds of perfection within his soul for the eventual return to the one God.[60]

Both Pico and one of his followers, Archangelus of Borgo Nuovo, saw in the Kabbala a distinction between natural and spiritual science, the latter of which included the science of alchemy.[61]

As the list of Kabbalistic interpreters grew, the more varied and subjective the interpretations tended to become. Some who have influenced our present-day occultism the most, such as Paracelsus and later Eliphas Lévi, added their own unique touches to the philosophy. Certainly much that passes for Kab-

[59] Joseph Blau, *The Christian Interpretation of the Cabala in the Renaissance* (Columbia University Press, 1944), pp. 1–16.
[60] *Ibid.*, p. 12.
[61] *Ibid.*, pp. 25–27.

balistic teachings among present-day occult groups bears faint resemblance to the Hebrew Kabbala.

As it was with the Kabbala, so has it been with the Hermetic writings. These texts which were probably composed in Egypt in the third century A.D. and ascribed to the mythical Hermes Trismegistus, show an inconsistent syncretism of Egyptian, Platonic, and other elements. While exhibiting at times a pantheism and at times almost a Gnostic dualism, they concern themselves primarily with the nature of God, man, and the world, and of man's return to the Godhead.

After the Hermetic texts were introduced to the European mind during the Renaissance, they were later often associated and mixed with Kabbalistic doctrines in the growing occult syncretism. Consequently, much that has been credited to Hermes Trismegistus in the development since the sixteenth century is a faint image of that which one finds in the Hermetic texts themselves.

Although the growth of science dispelled and exploded many of the ideas contained in alchemy, the church earlier rose against occultism. On February 19, 1493, it rendered a decision against astrology as being a superstition and an invention of the devil. Anyone practicing the art was in danger of mortal sin. Shortly before that in 1486, Pico della Mirandola was accused of heresy by the church for his reliance upon the Kabbala, and he escaped punishment only when his appeal to the pope gained him a pardon. During the Reformation, Luther and other Reformers struck out against occult practices, particularly astrology, which Luther condemned as destroying man's free will. Still the occult tradition was not extinguished but continued through the centuries as a quiet protest against Christian orthodoxy.

In the sixteenth century the figures of such men as Paracelsus, Van Helmont, and Agrippa von Nettesheim emerged with their own interpretations and accretions and were followed by Robert Fludd, Jakob Boehme, and a host of others, as beacons on the path of occultism for those of the later centuries. Partly scientists and physicians, partly alchemists and magicians, they were the predecessors of Eliphas Lévi, Anton Mesmer, and his

followers in France, who helped link the metaphysical movements in the United States to the magic of the past.

In Western occultism there is a belief in the correspondence
between the natural and spiritual worlds, expressed as the
" Hermetic principle " in the *dictum*, " As above, so below."
This concept is basic to a spiritual alchemy or spiritual science
through which it was believed a person might be transformed
spiritually. This principle of correspondences and representations of Hermetic philosophy became the foundation for a type
of white magic, influencing the Theosophical teachings of
Madame Helena Blavatsky. It blended together with the similar
doctrine of Swedenborg to become a cornerstone for most of
the metaphysical movements.

In eighteenth-century France, Mesmer made practical the
occult philosophy of many forebears. Like Paracelsus and
others, Mesmer believed that man attracted the influences from
planets like a magnet. The occultists taught that man was a min-
iature universe or microcosm, corresponding to the great universe or macrocosm, whose various celestial parts had an effect
upon man. Mesmer believed that this magnetic attraction, for
which he borrowed the name " animal magnetism," was manifested by a fluid emanating from the celestial bodies to and from
man. A concentration of the magnetic fluid transferred to another person through the will of the magnetizer could produce
cures of illnesses. Although Mesmer did not construct a scientific philosophy, he noted the therapeutic value of hypnotism
and he produced the trance state in his subjects.

When his followers introduced hypnotism to America in the
early part of the nineteenth century, the trance became important for both Davis' and Quimby's early healing experiments as
well as for the development of American Spiritualism, whose
story we next relate.

II

Spiritualism

Spiritualistic Precedents

ALTHOUGH AMERICAN SPIRITUALISTS trace the beginnings of organized Spiritualism to the rappings heard in Hydesville, New York, in 1848, the art of communicating with the dead has been witnessed in many cultures throughout the world since ancient times. In the Old Testament there are passages proscribing necromancy, the divination of the future, by conjuring up spirits to elicit prophetic words from them. Yet one may recall the incident of Saul's having the shade of Samuel called forth by the " witch " of Endor, which the Revised Standard Version now more correctly translates as " medium."

Trance-speaking by people who were thought bewitched was quite common to Western civilization believing in witchcraft, but these instances were cases of possession by demons rather than by spirits of the dead. Until our more enlightened era the threat of being condemned and burned as a witch kept these to a minimum. Of course, many people throughout the centuries have believed in haunted houses and poltergeists, i.e., mischievous spirits who are supposed to play irritating pranks on people.

Probably the first book on the spirits in English was the translation of *De Spectris*, by Ludwig Lavater, in 1572, from the 1570 French edition. This work was one upon which Shakespeare may have relied when he wrote *Hamlet*. Its author cautions the readers not to be easily deceived, but to be critical of the evidence.[1]

[1] Harry Price, *Fifty Years of Psychical Research* (Longmans, Green & Co., Inc., 1939), pp. 4–5.

The first séance, i.e., a "sitting" with a medium through whom the spirits manifest themselves in various ways, took place at least as early as 1762. In that year Oliver Goldsmith wrote a brochure on the Cock Lane Ghost to defend a man accused by his wife's ghost of murdering her. Goldsmith disclosed that the séance had been a device used when the husband had not succumbed to blackmail.

The immediate prototype of the modern séance was introduced by Mesmer. At his séances a number of people sat around a tub, or *baquet*, containing supposedly magnetized materials. Each held his neighbor's hand as well as a rod extending from the tub, while waiting expectantly to be magnetized, i.e., hypnotized and cured of his ailment.[2]

Even though the techniques and types of modern trance mediumship were expanded and popularized in America after 1848 and then gave new impetus to the Spiritualist movement in England and the Continent, the initial thrust of modern Spiritualism owes much to Mesmer and his followers in France. There from the eighteenth century on one hears of entranced persons who were cured of sicknesses; others who developed various clairvoyant powers, such as the ability to diagnose the ailments of others and to prescribe remedies, or to speak as though under the control of a spirit. While such forms of animal magnetism were becoming the topic of discussion on the Continent, the followers of Swedenborg quite naturally found interest in the subject. In 1788 the Swedenborgian Société Exégétique et Philanthropique of Stockholm issued a report concerning its own interpretation. It also gave an account of its experiments with a young woman through whom spirits had allegedly spoken during séances in 1787. Next, both Germany and England produced a number of magnetists who experimented with entranced subjects and wrote books on the phenomena of animal magnetism including spirit communication. Thus the works of such persons as H. M. Wesermann, Jung-Stilling, Justinus Kerner, Heinrich Werner, J. C. Colquhoun, Harriet Martineau, Chauncey H. Townshend, and Baron von Reichenbach added much to the literature of Spiritualism's phe-

2 *Ibid.*, pp. 9–15.

nomena in the first half of the nineteenth century. In 1848, Alphonse Cahagnet published in Paris the first volume of his *Arcanes de la Vie Future Devoilés,* giving the communications purportedly coming from thirty-six different spirits who described the various spheres of the spirit world.[3]

Whereas the first report on animal magnetism prepared by the Paris Royal Academy of Medicine in 1784 discredited Mesmer's work, the second by the Royal Academy's Medical Section in 1825 validated the trance state, the clairvoyant phenomena, and therapeutic value.[4] Even though the second report was inadequate and erroneous judged from our present knowledge and use of hypnotism, it indeed fostered the continued experiments in hypnotism and opened further the door to the development of Spiritualism, the metaphysical healing movements, and finally psychoanalysis.

At about the middle of the nineteenth century the central focus of Spiritualism moved to the United States, where its organized phase began, and where the influential philosophy of Andrew Jackson Davis was to have an abiding effect upon the interpretation of Spiritualism's phenomena.

Andrew Jackson Davis, Philosopher of American Spiritualism

Andrew Jackson Davis, heralded by most American Spiritualists as their first philosopher, professed to be a clairvoyant seer rather than a Spiritualist medium. Like Swedenborg, he claimed the power of seeing on the spiritual planes beyond the physical.

Davis was born in 1826 in Blooming Grove, New York, in humble surroundings. He had been dull in school, and in 1843, when he was already failing as an apprentice in the shoemaker's trade, he submitted to being hypnotized, an event that was to change his life. He had attended lectures on Mesmerism given by a traveling hypnotist, after which various members of his group began hypnotizing one another. Davis, along with others, sought out William Levingston, a local tailor, who had achieved

---

[3] Frank Podmore, *Modern Spiritualism: A History and a Criticism* (London: Methuen & Co., Ltd., 1902), Vol. 1, pp. 76–132.
[4] *Ibid.,* pp. 54–58, 72–75; also Price, *op. cit.,* p. 16.

some success at this art. According to his autobiography, Davis immediately exhibited clairvoyant powers when hypnotized. While blindfolded, he read the large print on the page of a newspaper, told the time by unseen watches, and diagnosed ailments afflicting some of those present. As he continued his experiments his powers allegedly grew. He claimed to be able to see people as transparent beings whose entire anatomies appeared visible to him in various glowing colors spreading beyond them to form auras. He attested that he could also see beyond the walls of the room he was in and even describe the interiors of houses that he had never seen.[5]

About the year 1844 he had a vision of a man whom he said was the spirit of Galen, the famous physician and medical writer of the second century A.D. He said that Galen gave him a magic staff by means of which he was able to learn about various diseases and their corresponding cures. Galen also allegedly divulged a synopsis of his thought, including the teaching that disease affected only the bodies of men and not their interior principle. The interior creative spirit, the healing essence in each person, determined his exterior condition. This spiritual principle was God. Immediately following this vision, he assertedly encountered Emanuel Swedenborg on the spiritual plane. Davis said the great Swedish seer had promised to be near and guide him, because Davis was to bring forth a new light to the world.[6]

It was after these visions that Davis' life began its next phase. For a time he determined to devote himself to diagnosing diseases and prescribing remedies while entranced. Although many people were cured in this way according to him, one might indeed wonder about the scientific value of some of the prescriptions. In order to cure deafness he directed the patient to apply the warm skins of freshly killed rats to his ear. For another, suffering from a felon on one of his fingers, he prescribed the application of a frog's skin. In both cases, however, Davis assured his readers that cures were accomplished by these methods.[7]

[5] Andrew Jackson Davis, *The Magic Staff: An Autobiography of Andrew Jackson Davis*, 10th ed. (William White & Co., 1869), pp. 9-216.
[6] *Ibid.*, pp. 234-248.
[7] *Ibid.*, pp. 255-256.

Although Davis developed a healing practice similar to Phineas P. Quimby's early experiments, healing was not to be his main concern. He wanted to record a revealed philosophy. His powers assertedly increased until he reached the "Superior Condition," which he believed to be a state beyond that of clairvoyance and one into which he soon could enter at will without anyone's aid. Then, instead of receiving information from spirits, he believed the truth came to him from the spiritual sun beyond the highest sixth concentric realm of the spiritual world. According to him, the Omnipotent Mind, called the Sensorium, had its residence at the center of the spiritual sun.[8] Although not the first to teach such a doctrine, Emanuel Swedenborg had earlier proclaimed that the spiritual sun, the higher correspondent of the physical sun, was the manifestation of God seen by angels of the spirit regions.

Davis' claim of increased powers finally included the abilities of visiting any part of the spirit realms at will and of seeing past and future events.

All his early visions were carefully copied down and appeared in his book, *The Principles of Nature, Her Divine Revelations, and a Voice to Mankind*, which was published in 1847. This was followed by a number of other works, including the five volumes of *The Great Harmonia*, his most important work, which appeared between the years of 1850 and 1855; *The Penetralia, Containing Harmonial Answers*, in 1856; his autobiography, *The Magic Staff*, in 1857; *The Harbinger of Health*, in 1861; and his *A Stellar Key to the Summer Land*, in 1867. Between 1847 and 1885 Davis compiled a total of thirty volumes, some of which went through many editions. His *Principles of Nature*, printed concurrently in London, had forty-five American editions,[9] and his autobiography, ten American editions.

It may seem ironical that Davis' philosophy is little read by modern Spiritualists. In spite of his voluminous works, one will search long before finding any volumes by Davis in a Spiritualist's library. Very few Spiritualists, in fact, know much in de-

[8] *Ibid.*, pp. 308–319.

[9] *The Harmonial Philosophy: A Compendium and Digest of the Works of Andrew Jackson Davis*, edited by "a Doctor of Hermetic Science" (London: William Rider & Son, 1917), pp. 421–424.

tail about his views, and probably no library has all his books except the Library of Congress. Many of his doctrines, however, are fundamental to modern Spiritualism, and though some of his " scientific " views of the world and man may now seem erroneous, he anticipated much of the mental-healing philosophy of the metaphysical sects. Some of his theories of the effect of the mind and emotions upon disease even sound strangely modern. The world, however, did not progress in the manner revealed to Davis, but these particular prophecies have been long forgotten. The Spiritualists are less concerned with knowledge of their pioneer now, because they believe in the continuing witness to their philosophy and science from the spirit world of the present day.

Davis never became a Christian, although he had acquired some knowledge of Christianity by attending various churches when young. Later he had become the close friend of the Reverend William Fishbough, a Universalist minister, who acted as amanuensis for his first books. His friendship was not lasting, however, because Davis became very critical of the Christian faith. In an exchange of letters between Davis and his erstwhile friend, he made it very clear he could not accept any scheme of salvation based upon Biblical teachings and contrary to his own philosophy,[10] which he believed was revealed by God. In this respect he partook of the spirit of the current transcendentalism and would have agreed with Emerson's statement that " Once leave your own knowledge of God, your own sentiment, and take secondary knowledge, as St. Paul's, or George Fox's, or Swedenborg's, and you get wide from God with every year this secondary form lasts." [11] Nevertheless, both Davis and Emerson still show the influence of Swedenborg's philosophy, if not his Biblical basis.

Davis' doctrine of eschatology is an adaptation of Swedenborg's. In the latter's scheme there are six planes beyond the natural or physical: three spheres of heaven and three of hell.[12]

[10] Davis, *The Magic Staff*, pp. 483–490.
[11] Emerson, *op. cit.*, Vol. 1, p. 145.
[12] Emanuel Swedenborg, *Heaven and Its Wonders, the World of Spirits, and Hell; from Things Heard and Seen*, tr. by the Rev. Samuel Noble (The American Swedenborg Printing and Publishing Society, 1872), par. 549.

The spirit after death gravitates to the place best fitted to the circumstances of his former life on earth. No spirit is ever sent to hell, but it may be attracted there because of its preference for evil. Even hell, however, is not necessarily a permanent state, because God is continually acting to make a change.[13] Like Swedenborg, Davis postulated six spiritual spheres, but to none of these could he give the name of hell. According to him, man gravitates to a level representing the extent his actions had been in harmony with God's laws. The way is never downward, but is only one of continual progression toward God. These higher spheres, called by Davis " the Summer Land," are long enduring but not everlasting. Eventually the world will become depopulated, at which time every spirit will be at least in the second sphere. When all have finally progressed to the sixth sphere, a new set of spheres will be created. They will be as much superior to the present as the second sphere is to the sixth. Therefore, the spirits will continue to progress through all eternity.[14]

Although Andrew Jackson Davis was not the first to offer a basis for modern Spiritualism, the early American Spiritualist organizations relied largely upon his views at their inception. His first work just preceded by one year the rappings heard by the Fox family.

The Birth of American Spiritualism

The birth of Spiritualism in America is generally credited to the events taking place on March 31, 1848, in a small house belonging to the John Fox family in Hydesville, New York. The house had a reputation of being haunted, perhaps because a former tenant had left it in 1847 on account of mysterious noises. Still the Fox family experienced no serious discomfort until March, 1848, when rapping sounds were heard. When the uncanny sounds continued, on March 31 it was suggested that loose sashes might be the cause of the disturbance. So Mr. Fox shook them. Then Kate, the youngest daughter (whose age has

---

[13] *Ibid.*, pars. 549–551.
[14] Davis, *The Great Harmonia*, Vol. 2, pp. 251–254.

been given variously as being from seven to twelve years), re-marked that the rappings coincided with the number of times her father shook the sash. Thereupon she said, " Mr. Splitfood, do as I do," while clapping her hands. Instantly there was a cor-responding response by the same number of raps. Then Mar-garetta, three years older than Kate, said in sport: " *No, do just as I do*. Count one, two, three, four," while clapping her hands. Immediately the raps responded as before. Thinking it might be a spirit making the noise, they gave the instruction to rap twice, if the answer was yes. There were two raps. Thus in this way a code was later devised with two raps for " yes," one for " no," and three, if the question could not be answered.[15]

Neighbors were then invited to witness the phenomenon, and the code revealed the spirit of a man who had been murdered in that very house. He rapped out the name of Charles B. Rosna, but his identity as one who had lived on earth was never estab-lished. According to his testimony, he had stayed in the house for one night and had been murdered for the little money he had. His body had been buried in the basement along with his tin box that held his wares. This memento is still to be seen at the Spiritualist Camp in Lily Dale, New York, where the house was later moved.

Needless to say, the rappings at Hydesville were a sound heard around the world. Much publicity was given to them in the press, and people came from far and near to witness them. Horace Greeley, the famous editor of the *New York Tribune*, investigated the girls and supported the veracity of their claims.

The rappings still continued when the family later moved to Rochester, but now various other spirits were involved. Wherever the two girls were, rappings could occur. In 1849 their older married sister, Mrs. Ann Leah Fox-Fish, discovered that she too had the same mediumistic power as her two younger sisters.[16]

In November of 1849, two different committees investigated the sisters at Corinthian Hall in Rochester without proving

[15] This is only one of several versions of the number of raps and their dele-gated meanings.

[16] Ralph G. Pressing, comp., *Rappings That Startled the World: Facts About the Fox Sisters* (Lily Dale News, Inc., n.d.), *passim*.

them fraudulent. In Buffalo, New York, in 1850, however, a group of professors at the University of Buffalo, after testing the sisters, came to the conclusion that the rappings could not take place when the toes of the Fox sisters were elevated and their heels were placed on cushions.[17]

From 1850 on, many other mediums began to appear, and rappings were heard in various cities over all the country. Many well-known people investigated the phenomena, and some became mediums. John W. Edmonds, a judge of the Supreme Court of New York, became famous as a medium and writer on Spiritualism. In England, Sir Arthur Conan Doyle and scientists such as Sir William Crookes and Sir Oliver Lodge became ardent investigators and believers in the validity of Spiritualistic phenomena.

As Spiritualism developed, many different kinds of mediums appeared. Some were rapping mediums, whose presence was necessary to get answers by this means. Others were tipping mediums who could lay their hands on furniture and cause it to behave contrary to the law of gravitation. Some were speaking mediums, who became unwitting vehicles of words inspired by spirits. Materializations, i.e., the embodiment of the spirits in material forms capable of being seen physically, became common. Spirit-slate writing appeared as a popular type of phenomenon in which a spirit allegedly writes messages on the inside surfaces of two slates bound together. Henry Slade, among others, became known for his spirit-slate writing, although he was exposed as a fraud a number of times. Daniel D. Home, who was never found guilty of deception, became one of the most famous early mediums for his great variety of phenomena including his act of levitation.

With the increase in the exhibition of the various types of physical phenomena, however, many mediums were caught in fraudulent practices. Some confessed their prestidigitation. Of all the confessions, certainly the most dramatic and important was the one made by Margaretta Fox Kane, followed by that of her younger sister. James Creelman published her confession in the *New York Herald* of September 24, 1888. Margaretta

17 Podmore, *op. cit.*, Vol. 1, p. 184.

Fox Kane, cofounder of modern American Spiritualism, blamed Leah, her older sister, for getting Kate and her to continue their deception for Leah's financial gain. Then on the stage of the Academy of Music in New York on October 21, 1888, she explained and demonstrated how she and Kate had made the raps with their toes. Her entire story appeared again in the *New York World* of October 21, 1888. She had admitted her guilt and again blamed her sister Leah for the continuation of a fraud that had begun when the two little girls had only started out to scare their mother.[18]

Although the confessions of the Fox sisters were a shock to many, they did not destroy Spiritualism, which by this time had become firmly established as a religion in America. This is not the end of the Fox sisters' story, however, because in an interview the following year Margaretta retracted her confession and was reaccepted as a medium into the ranks of Spiritualism.

Ralph G. Pressing, former editor of *The Psychic Observer*, a Spiritualistic tabloid, edited a group of articles giving the Spiritualists' view of the matter. It is alleged that a quarrel had broken out between Leah and her two younger sisters. Leah, who had achieved some social prominence through her marriage, had been embarrassed by the alcoholism and deterioration in character of her younger sisters. She had objected to the life Margaretta was living and blamed Kate, whose two children she also attempted to take from her.

Spiritualists have defended the two sisters on the grounds that mediumship amid a hostile public, commercial exploitation of their gifts, and their ignorance of the spiritual implications of Spiritualism had led them to alcoholism. Kate and Margaretta, however, having decided to seek vengeance for Leah's attitude, tried to ruin her by their confessions.[19]

In Margaretta's later unpublished retraction on November 20, 1889, it is said the reasons for the confession were her financial needs, the difficulty of maintaining her mental equilibrium because of excitement, and the psychological effect of

[18] Joseph F. Rinn, *Searchlight on Psychical Research: A Record of Sixty Years' Work, Interwoven with an Intimate Biographical Sketch of Houdini* (London: Rider & Co., 1954), pp. 54–64.
[19] Pressing, *op. cit.*

persons who were enemies of Spiritualism. The Spiritualists' stand is that their confessions only show the sisters to be fitting subjects for a psychiatric study, but should not influence the position of Spiritualism.[20]

Beginnings of Variant Revelations

Automatic writing, a popular phase of Spiritualism in the latter part of the nineteenth century, introduced new revelations that varied from those of Andrew Jackson Davis. The Spiritualists who claim this power believe some spirit or higher intelligence controls their hands. One of the earliest automatic writers, a Dr. Dexter, asserted that "Sweedenborg (*sic*) and Bacon" directed his pen.[21] The Theosophists believe that ascended masters were responsible for some of the writings of Madame Blavatsky. The Arcane School credits a Tibetan master for most of the works written by Alice Bailey.

In the early days of Spiritualism, Dr. John B. Newbrough became disgusted with the vacuity of ideas that mediums brought from the spirits. Believing in his own mediumistic powers, he was impressed to purify himself in order to attract a higher type of spirit intelligence. In 1881 after ten years of purification he felt guided by some power to purchase one of the newly invented typewriters. He then discovered that by sitting at the instrument an hour before dawn his hands would type without his conscious control, and one year later he published the manuscript entitled *OAHSPE: A New Bible*. This large work was allegedly written at the command of God, who declared himself to be the Chief Executive of the world rather than its Creator. *OAHSPE* gives instruction about not only all the great religions and cultures of the past, but also the changes that will take place in the new era since 1848.[22] An examination

---

[20] Pressing, *op. cit.*
[21] Podmore, *op. cit.*, Vol. 1, pp. 268–269.
[22] John B. Newbrough, *OAHSPE: A New Bible in the Words of Jehovih and His Angel Ambassadors. A Sacred History of the Dominions of the Higher and Lower Heavens on the Earth for the Twenty-four Thousand Years* . . . (Kosmon Press, 1942), pp. iv–v, "Preface to the Present Edition." A useful criticism of the work is to be found in Edgar J. Goodspeed's work, *Modern Apocrypha* (The Beacon Press, Inc., 1956), pp. 102–105.

of the work will quickly show, however, that much of the history of religions and culture may have to be rewritten, if this account is true. Nevertheless, a number of people have accepted the teachings of *OAHSPE* and have formed a sect known as the Faithists.

Still greater than *OAHSPE* in importance to the more esoteric groups of the metaphysical movements is the *Aquarian Gospel of Jesus Christ*, by Levi H. Dowling. Its author, who is known therein only by the name of Levi, did his writing early in the morning like Newbrough. Dowling felt that his information came from the *akashic* records, the imperishable impressions of all events, which Theosophists and other occult groups believe are retained forever in the ether or space. Various occult organizations teach that highly developed people may have the power to tune in on these impressions and bring them back to consciousness.

Dr. Edgar Goodspeed includes a discussion of Dowling's book in his *Modern Apocrypha*. He notes some of its historical mistakes and anachronisms. For example, Dowling has confused Herod Antipas with Herod the Great as the ruler of Jerusalem, when historical evidence shows that Antipas ruled in Galilee and never in Jerusalem.[23] Nevertheless, Dowling's book is supposed to supplement and augment the ancient manuscripts of the Bible. After appearing in at least twelve editions, it has been reprinted several times in recent years, and is still being well received by those interested in the occult.

Organized Spiritualistic Investigations

Spiritualism soon passed from the stage in which individual scientists tested the phenomena to that in which psychic research societies were formed by investigators. England led the way with the establishment of the Society for Psychical Research in 1882. In the early years the Society included mediums, such as Stainton Moses and Dawson Rogers, but also such notable figures as Sir William Crookes, Sir Arthur Conan Doyle, F. W. H. Myers, and Sir Oliver Lodge. Unhappily, however,

[23] Goodspeed, *op. cit.*, p. 17.

dissension largely over the validity of the phenomena has
marked the society's history. In 1885 both Stainton Moses and
Sir Arthur Conan Doyle resigned because they felt that Spiritualism was being unfairly judged. In 1885 the American Society
for Psychic Research was founded in Boston and has fared less
well than its British counterpart, although both are still continuing their investigations. Universities too have sometimes become involved in psychic research, e.g., Duke University and
the University of Pennsylvania.

Henry Seybert, an enthusiastic Spiritualist, gave money to
the University of Pennsylvania for investigating all systems of
philosophy and religion that assume to represent the Truth —
and, in particular, Spiritualism. Although a Commission composed of interested professors tested many notable mediums at
the university, it published a negative report in 1887.[24]

None should infer from what has seemed to be unfavorable
so far that all mediums are dishonest. The writer can testify that
many Spiritualist mediums feel they do have the power to communicate with discarnate spirits, and there are thousands of people who believe the messages received are evidential and proof
of both survival and communication. At the Spiritualist seminary of the Universal Spiritualist Association in Bradenton,
Florida, one may witness the enthusiasm and ostensible sincerity
of its students. Still one must admit that even apparently sincere
mediums may stoop to fraud occasionally. Arthur Ford, one of
the famous mediums of the twentieth century, has stated to the
writer that the power of attunement to the spirit world or even
of entrancement may vary greatly at times. He declared that
mediums, who may be otherwise honest but depend on their
psychic powers for a living, may be faced with a temptation
when the power is lacking but the money for the séance has
been paid. He said that on a number of occasions he has had to
send everyone home because the power to entrance himself was
not available. One of the students at the Spiritualist seminary
also joked about a *perceptible* lack of psychic power at the Spir-

   24 University of Pennsylvania, *Preliminary Report of the Commission Appointed by the University of Pennsylvania to Investigate Modern Spiritualism*
(J. B. Lippincott Company, 1887), *passim.*

itualist summer camps, when some mediums tried to call it forth each day. But the séances were still held.

The National Spiritualist Association of Churches

Due to the exposure of many mediums during the latter part of the last century, with the consequent loss of public attention and interest in Spiritualism, many sincere Spiritualists began forming organizations. This was for the purpose of protecting the honest mediums and discrediting the dishonest. The largest and most conservative group among these is the National Spiritualist Association of Churches of the United States of America, founded in 1893 [25] (hereafter referred to as the N.S.A.). It has a congregational type of government, with autonomous churches loosely held together by state associations. Its headquarters are in Milwaukee, Wisconsin, where its seminary, the Morris-Pratt Institute, is located.

The N.S.A. boasts of having the highest standards for mediums. Normally a medium must have been a member of a church for a year before going into training for two years to become a licentiate. A year of lecturing and a final examination by the National Board complete his requirements for ordination. Practically speaking, however, it may be noted that some of the best mediums in the organization have had no such formal training. Arthur Ford, for many years one of their leading mediums, and Billy Turner, the most highly regarded among their youngest, both denied they had the prerequisites. Turner added that he did not believe they were necessary. He said in an interview:

" When I first became aware of the strange power, I was impressed by the spirits that further education, which I had planned, might be detrimental to the power, and that I must make my choice. I believe that a medium either has the power or not, and education and development classes will not help him. After all, Spiritualism is based on the information we get from the spirits anyway, so why should special education be necessary? " [26]

[25] National Spiritualist Association of Churches of the United States of America (*Spiritualist Manual*, 1956), p. 15.
[26] Personal interview with William Turner.

Nevertheless, his statement needs to be qualified, because as part of his introduction before a psychic demonstration in Florida the medium mentioned that Mr. Turner had been a student in the Lyceum, or Spiritualist Sunday School, of that particular church.

The N.S.A. is the only national Spiritualist organization endeavoring to teach children the principles of Spiritualism. Spiritualism generally appeals only to adults, and especially to those in their middle ages and beyond. Children do not commonly share this interest for two reasons. In the first place, deep concern about death does not yet affect them because death seems so far away; secondly, children are less likely to have had very many close relatives or friends in a spirit world with whom to communicate. Consequently séances are not apt to hold their interest after the novelty has worn off.

The first Lyceum, or Sunday School, was organized in New York in 1863 from the inspiration of Andrew Jackson Davis. Davis fostered the idea because he wanted children to be taught " true Spiritualism," and he " saw the folly of inculcating orthodox theology into these impressionable minds for a few years, then trying to undo it all." [27]

Although the N.S.A. has promoted the idea of the Lyceum and has even provided special materials for teaching the youth, many of the churches have not availed themselves of the literature or even of the idea.

Although the details of belief may vary among the Spiritualists, most organizations have similar statements of principles, which some people might regard as creeds. According to Dr. Victoria Barnes, head of the N.S.A. Education Department, these tenets are not really beliefs but are the proclamation of scientific facts which Spiritualism can prove. Since the N.S.A. Declaration of Principles serves as a minimum basis for many Spiritualist associations, it is given here as a representative list:

" 1. We believe in Infinite Intelligence.

" 2. We believe that the phenomena of nature, both physical

---

[27] Dr. Victoria Barnes, *Advanced Course in the History, Science, Philosophy, and Religion of Modern Spiritualism* (National Spiritualist Association, n.d.), Lesson XI, pp. 5–6.

and spiritual, are the expression of Infinite Intelligence.

" 3. We affirm that a correct understanding of such expression and living in accordance therewith constitute true religion.

" 4. We affirm that the existence and personal identity of the individual continue after the change called death.

" 5. We affirm that communication with the so-called dead is a fact, scientifically proven by the phenomena of Spiritualism.

" 6. We believe that the highest morality is contained in the Golden Rule: ' Whatsoever ye would that others should do unto you, do ye also unto them.'

" 7. We affirm the moral responsibility of the individual, and that he makes his own happiness or unhappiness as he obeys or disobeys Nature's physical and spiritual laws.

" 8. We affirm that the doorway to reformation is never closed against any human soul here or hereafter.

" 9. We affirm that the Precepts of Prophecy contained in the Bible are a divine attribute proven through Mediumship." [28]

All modern Spiritualism would be in agreement with the N.S.A. that God is an immanent impersonal power manifesting Itself in life through all forms of organized matter. God, or Infinite Intelligence, the Spiritualists believe, is also Principle, and man's salvation depends upon his living in harmony with these laws which are a manifestation of God on the physical, mental, and spiritual planes of life. The *Spiritualist Manual* of the N.S.A. teaches that ultimately we may speak of these laws as one, and refer to them simply as " Natural Law."

In this life man is entirely responsible for the welfare of the world. If he wants heaven to be on earth, he must create it for himself and for others. If there is no vicarious atonement for wrong acts, but only remorse and suffering, there is also no eternal punishment in the life beyond, but only eternal progression.[29]

Although there is no end to progression, there is also no beginning. Man as uncreated spirit has always been in existence.[30] Victoria Barnes would say that he is spirit with a body, even

[28] N.S.A., *op. cit.*, p. 34; Barnes, *op. cit.*, XII, p. 2.
[29] N.S.A., *op. cit.*, pp. 35–36.
[30] Barnes, *op. cit.*, IV, p. 5.

though both spirit and matter are relative terms. " Matter is the least degree of Spirit and Spirit is the highest degree of Matter," she says. They are ultimately one. In another sense, spirit and matter are but higher and lower forms of vibration, since all life is vibration.[31]

Although all American Spiritualists accept Biblical teachings in their own interpretation, they do not accept Jesus Christ as the Savior. The N.S.A. follows the doctrine of Davis in considering Jesus as the greatest religious teacher, a great medium, a divine person in the sense that the inner being of all men is divine. He is the way-shower, who marks the path for man to follow.[32]

Although accepting the Bible in a limited way, the N.S.A. believes the spirit world is constantly revealing new truths to man through mediumship.[33] The agent for this communication is called a medium. Spiritualists believe all persons have some psychic powers, which most Spiritualists say may be developed by proper training. But only persons having abilities sufficient to effect communication with the spirit world can become mediums. Therefore, all Spiritualist churches have classes for the psychic development of their members. Those who become mediums develop one or more types of psychic gifts of mediumship, which are divided into mental and physical phases.

One way of communicating with the spirit world by mental mediumship is believed to occur when the medium goes into a state of trance. This resembles sleep, since the conscious mind does not function, but permits a controlling spirit to take over its role. Even though during this period the medium's spirit may leave its body and be in a higher or astral plane, it is still attached to the physical body by a slender cord, known as the pericord. The N.S.A., however, does not believe the foreign spirit occupies the medium's body. One spirit control allegedly expressed the relationship as follows:

" I am not inside the medium; I have not disturbed his etheric body; it is still in strict coincidence with his physical body. . . .

---

[31] *Ibid.*, XV, *passim;* also by interview with Dr. Victoria Barnes.
[32] *Ibid.*, IX, p. 104.
[33] N.S.A., *op. cit.*, p. 37.

The etheric or spiritual body resembles the physical in shape and function, but is more subtle and invisible, yet far more permanent. The physical body is surrounded by an aura. To take control I enter that aura and blend my own aura with it. With the auric conditions thus harmonized and their properties fused, my mind can exert its influence on his mind, brain and nervous system. . . . For sustained control over long periods of time there must be complete control of mind and brain. The brain determines the flow and the language which the control can use in giving his message." [34]

Another way of communication through mental mediumship is by billet reading, i.e., by answering questions written on small paper slips addressed to someone in the spirit world. Although this method is the most popular in most American Spiritualist churches, it is considered less accurate, because without being in trance the conscious mind of the medium may inadvertently color the message coming from the spirit. In this type of mental mediumship messages are received through clairsentience (clear-feeling), clairaudience (clear-hearing), or clairvoyance (clear-seeing). Clairsentience is the expression of certain feelings in the medium's body, which the spirits wish to impart. Clairaudience is hearing the words spoken by the spirits through the mind rather than through the ears. Clairvoyance is seeing the spirits, who indicate their messages by means of symbols interpreted by the medium.

Psychometry is another mental phase in which a medium upon contact with a physical object may learn its origin, its environment, and the characteristics of those who have touched it. The basis for this is the belief that a material object is a fragment of matter having certain vibrations. Each one who has touched the object has imparted to it his own unique vibrations which a trained medium may be able to interpret. As Dr. Barnes explains it:

" Everything in life has its particular aura, and when a medium finely sensitized to auric emanations comes in contact with this particular rate, type, and quality of vibration, she can interpret — or read — the result of this interblending of vibra-

[34] Barnes, op. cit., XIX, pp. 4–8.

tions through what she senses at the moment or through what is presented to her clairvoyantly. Anyone having touched or handled this object leaves the imprint of their (*sic*) auric emanation on it and this, too, can be read in the same way."

Another gift is prophecy, which may be either intuitional or mediumistic. The former method is one whereby certain vibrations strike a person's consciousness to give him feelings of impending danger. The latter is by means of a spirit who speaks through a medium. Spirits, who are familiar with the science of auric emanations, are believed capable of interpreting the aura surrounding each individual. According to the N.S.A., this emanation of varying colors carries one's life history from which predictions may be made as certain as those of a weatherman. It also teaches that everything ever existing in the universe still exists in vibratory form in the " Cosmic Conscious Ether." Spirits can see these vibratory forms and also " the events which begin to occur in another dimension before they materialize in this finite world of ours. . . ." [35]

Physical mediumship is that phase in which the spirit is said to manifest itself objectively. Among its many forms are rappings, table tipping, automatic writing, independent writing, materialization, independent voice, and apports.

Independent writing is a type of phenomenon in which the spirit draws from those at the séance the force necessary for it to write on paper.

The theory behind materialization is that a spirit must first lower its rate of vibration to conform to that of the medium's physical body. Then the astral, or inner, body of the entranced medium is projected from its physical encasement. Finally, the astral body is used as a frame upon which helping spirits mold ectoplasm into the likeness of the spirit to be materialized and made visible. Ectoplasm, which is described as a white or gray substance of fine material particles, flows forth generally from the nose and ears of the medium. At the end of the materialization it can be withdrawn and disappear into the medium's body in a fraction of a second.

Independent voice is the physical phenomenon witnessed

[35] *Ibid.*, XX, pp. 2–4.

during trumpet séances. In performing this type of mediumship Dr. Barnes says the " spirits simply convert thought waves into sound vibrations by changing physical vibratory force into a rate of psychoelectric pulsations. The subtle elements of sound waves are thus brought under control of the spirit operator and made the vehicle of expression of the medium's mentality." Then in order to magnify the spirit's voice, the spirits form a voice box from ectoplasm and place it in the small end of a long conical tube of lightweight material.[36] This is called a trumpet, which is standard equipment in most séance rooms.

Anyone treating popular forms of physical mediumship should include some discussion of apports. In its original French meaning applied to Spiritualism, an apport is an object dematerialized in one place and apported, or carried, to another where spirit chemists rematerialize it. This psychic exhibition has become increasingly fashionable in modern American séances. Like the demonstrations of independent voice and spirit materialization, apports usually require a dark or very dimly lit room. While the medium is in trance, the spirit control describes the various objects as they are materialized for each sitter. Such apports range from items of small monetary value such as feathers from an Indian chief's headdress or dime-store trinkets to some very fine pieces of furniture and ornaments. The expensive items are generally apported only for the mediums.

Occasionally some spirits seem to have lost the original meaning of the word. At one séance conducted by an N.S.A. medium, the spirit chemists were alleged to have created the apports from chemicals they themselves had mixed together on the spot. The spirit control said the ingredients were being taken from the sitters. Because of the predominance of red in their clothing that evening there would be a preponderance of that color in the apported jewelry.

As a medium progresses in development, he or she may have a number of different spirit guides, who act in various capacities. The controlling spirit is one who can attune himself or herself easily to the medium's vibrations, but is quite often the spirit of

[36] *Ibid.*, XXI, pp. 2–6.

a little girl. Her role is to protect the medium and to introduce spirits to the sitters, while generally providing a good bit of humor during the séance. Her levity amid eerie happenings in a darkened room seems calculated to calm any newcomer who might otherwise be uneasy.

The Gate Keeper is a guide who is the spirit of an American Indian. He protects the medium from unwanted spirits by admitting only those having some pertinent part in the séance. There is also the important Director, who " manipulates the forces governing interworld contact " and supervises the work of the other guides.[37]

One of the most valuable teachers for the medium is the Spirit Doctor. Because of his education he often gives brief lectures or bits of advice during the session. But not only mediums have Spirit Doctors. Anyone attending the Spiritualist meetings regularly receives eventually the names of his own Spirit Doctor and of his Indian Chief, who become his special guardians. Their advice is often given through the medium to their respective counselees, when they do not have the psychic ability to receive it.

Although most Spiritualists value their spirit guides very highly, they frequently differ in their stress upon having a great number. Some very important mediums speak only of their several guides, whereas others, often lesser known, are able to boast of a large retinue. But generally it seems that the types of phenomena mediums exhibit determine the size of their spirit bands. The belief in the necessity for spirit guides is that of the N.S.A. and kindred organizations, but, as we shall later see, there are some groups whose mediums make no use of any spirit guides.

One other phase of mediumship regarded as a special gift is healing. All Spiritualist churches have members claiming this power, even if no other. During their regular Sunday services there is a place for prayer and special treatment for the ill.

Spiritualists have a variety of views concerning the spiritual-healing process. Some believe a healing odic force flows from the healer's fingers. They say this is concentrated in the healer through the agency of the Spirit Doctor and spiritual helpers,

[37] *Ibid.,* XVIII, p. 8.

but at times the Spirit Doctor takes over directly. Others claim to discover the cause of illness by examining the patient's aura, which changes colors according to the particular disability. They often teach that a lack of proper " chemicalization " of an aura causes illness. The Spirit Doctors or Chemists effect a cure by supplying the necessary chemicals from the auras of others present.

These particular views are largely peculiar to the Spiritualists with the exception of the belief in an odic force. Even some Protestant ministers and laymen have accepted this idea as the basis for spiritual healing. The term " odic force " was made popular by Karl von Reichenbach, a scientist, whose work concerning it was first published in 1852. The name is derived from Odin, the ancient Norse god. Von Reichenbach, who was influenced by Mesmer, thought he had noted a magnetic force emanating from various crystals and from the fingers of " sensitives," i.e., persons believed to have paranormal, or psychic, powers.

In recent years new attempts have been made to photograph this force, which is still regarded by many as the healing power emanating from the healer's fingers, but the experiments are still inconclusive.

The Spiritualistic emphasis upon psychic healing has effected to an extent the renewed interest in healing among some Protestant churches. Probably the greatest influence has come from the Spiritual Frontiers Fellowship, an organization consisting largely of Protestant ministers and laymen who are pursuing the study of psychic research, healing, and prayer.

Not infrequently Protestant ministers and laymen interested in spiritual healing mention the ideas of the two sensitives, Olga and Ambrose Worrall. Ambrose diagnoses disease by clairsentience; Olga claims to see spirits clairvoyantly. Both have made their contributions to the published *Proceedings of the Spiritual Healing Seminars* sponsored by the Laymen's Movement for a Christian World at Wainwright House in Rye, New York, and have written for the *Gateway: Journal of the Spiritual Frontiers Fellowship*.

Until his retirement, Dr. Albert Day, a prominent Methodist

minister and author, worked with Olga Worrall in a spiritual
healing program. Together they established the New Life
Clinic in his Baltimore church. At the time I met her in 1958
she had a healing clinic in two Protestant churches, Methodist
and Presbyterian.

One should not omit the name of Harry Edwards, a Spiritualist healer in England, whose reputation is spreading around
the world. Although the British Medical Association has allegedly discredited his work, there are many Christians and
Spiritualists who attest to his healing powers. Dr. Leslie Weatherhead, a notable English minister, formerly of City Temple in
London, rejects Edwards' Spiritualistic hypothesis, but nevertheless credits his power to odic force.[38]

Some years ago the Reverend Alex Holmes, a Congregational
minister, visited Edwards, who inspired him to begin healing
services in his own church. The healing work Mr. Holmes did
at Cavendish Chapel was so publicized that Queen Elizabeth
made him her honorary chaplain before he moved to Canada.
Recently Mr. Holmes has been sought as a lecturer by various
Protestant ministerial groups in both the United States and
Canada.

Schisms in Spiritualism

Although the N.S.A., like the other American Spiritualist
organizations, regards the Fox sisters as the founders of modern
Spiritualism, it acknowledges Emanuel Swedenborg as " the
first to conceive the spirit world as a realm of law," [39] and Andrew Jackson Davis as its John the Baptist, who heralded the
advent of modern Spiritualism.[40] Since Davis did not believe in
the doctrine of reincarnation or accept other changes of view
represented by Allan Kardec of France and later by Madame
Blavatsky, these organizations which generally follow the tradition of Davis we may speak of as the orthodox Spiritualists

[38] Leslie Weatherhead, " Odic Force: A Rediscovered Healing Power," in the
Third Spiritual Healing Seminar, 1954, Laymen's Movement for a Christian
World (Wainwright House, 1954), Appendix, p. 4.
[39] N.S.A., *op. cit.*, p. 74.
[40] *Ibid.*, p. 97.

without impugning the claims of truth of the other groups.

Although Spiritualists have differences among themselves concerning the interpretation of their philosophies and phenomena, they generally show tolerance. Exceptions to this and reasons for schisms in the N.S.A. have been largely due to Spiritualists who advocated the doctrine of reincarnation and Theosophical principles, or who claimed to be Christian.

The belief in reincarnation, which has divided Spiritualism, entered its history in the nineteenth century. In France, M. Ravail, better known as Allan Kardec, became converted to Spiritualism in 1862. From communications he received through various clairvoyants he wrote a new Spiritualistic gospel advocating reincarnation.[41] His teachings were carried to South America, where Spiritualism has become one of the dominant religions of Brazil.[42] There one finds the Kardec brand of Spiritualism mixed with two earlier varieties of the Afro-Brazilian culture.[43] In 1957 the Brazilian government attested to its importance by issuing a stamp with the portrait of Allan Kardec commemorating the "First Centenary of Organized Spiritism." Although Kardec has had little direct influence in America, Madame Blavatsky has. Her Theosophical principles, including the doctrine of reincarnation, began sweeping through the ranks of Spiritualism before the turn of the century.

The first group to split from the N.S.A. over the doctrine of reincarnation became the National Spiritual Alliance in 1913. Then the New York Spiritualist Association, which was part of the N.S.A., withdrew in 1931 to become the General Assembly of Spiritualists of New York (G.A.S.). It opposed the N.S.A.'s threat to discipline those who taught this belief in rebirth. It also accused the N.S.A. of a sectarian attitude and of trying to get more power by eliminating the rights of the state associations.[44]

For some years the N.S.A. had watched with uneasiness the

[41] Podmore, *op. cit.*, Vol. 2, p. 161.

[42] Luis Rodriguez, "Brazil: African Heritage," *Tomorrow*, Vol. 8, No. 4 (Autumn, 1960), pp. 79–80.

[43] Wainright Evans, "Allan Kardec — Prophet of Reincarnation," *Tomorrow*, Vol. 8, No. 4, p. 85.

[44] George S. Lawton, *The Drama of Life After Death* (Henry Holt & Company, Inc., 1932), pp. 144–145, and note. Their letterhead gives the date of 1914, which is probably the date of the state association.

growth of this doctrine among its mediums. By 1930 it had become so influential among the Spiritualist churches that the N.S.A. had to pass a resolution against it at its National Convention. The statement declared that since the belief in reincarnation was not pure Spiritualism, and moreover was not proved through psychic research, any speaker, medium, or teacher guilty of teaching such a view should be subject to the discipline of the State and National Boards.[45]

The second main doctrinal reason for schisms in Spiritualist churches involves the question of whether Spiritualism shall be considered Christian or not. As seen before, Andrew Jackson Davis denied Christianity even in its most liberal form, preferring the authority of his own revelations to that of the Scriptures. The N.S.A. has taken a similar stand. Dr. Victoria Barnes, its spokesman, told me that she considers herself a Spiritualist rather than a Christian. This does not mean she rejects the Bible altogether. She credits it with teaching the Golden Rule, a principle of the N.S.A. also, and with illustrating all the various phases of Spiritualistic phenomena. For example, in her *Advanced Lessons* sponsored by the N.S.A., she classes as a Spiritualistic vision the Transfiguration scene, when Moses and Elijah appeared with Jesus to Peter, James, and John. She exemplifies as a materialization the appearance of Jesus to his disciples in the Upper Room. She interprets Ex., ch. 19, as the first record of a dark séance, because she said it was during a period of darkness that " Moses received the Ten Commandments *through a trumpet*." Their second reception on tablets of stone, she classifies as an exhibition of independent slate-writing. Thus she, like other Spiritualists, interprets many of the miracles as psychic events of Spiritualism.[46] Still, the official N.S.A. view is that there can be no Christian Spiritualist; nor can Spiritualism be classed as a division of Christianity.[47]

Although the organization may bind its members officially to its interpretation on these points, there are some of its mediums who consider themselves to be Christian and some who accept the theory of reincarnation and Theosophical principles.

45 *Ibid.*, pp. 153–154.
46 Barnes, *op. cit.*, XXV, pp. 2–4.
47 *Ibid.*, IX, p. 1.

Nevertheless, because of such rigidity in an individualistic religion like Spiritualism, other associations were bound to be established. As one might expect, these later organizations have had a tendency to feel closer to both Christianity and to Theosophy than the N.S.A. would allow.

Spiritual Science

The Spiritual Science Church was organized in 1923 by " Mother " Dr. Julia Forest, who had been a Christian Science Practitioner. According to the Reverend Glenn Argal, Spiritual Science at the present time has about forty ministers in various parts of the United States, although the association is stronger in New York State than elsewhere.

Spiritual Scientists consider their churches as a " religious denomination," which is both Protestant and Catholic, but not in the traditional meaning of these words. They have a governing body called the Ecclesiastical Council; a Spiritual Science Mother Church, which supervises the work of its member churches and issues charters; and a Spiritual Science Institute for training its ministers. Their avowed intention is to bring to mankind three principles of demonstration believed to have been manifested by Jesus Christ: Preaching, Communication, and Healing. The meaning ascribed to the first two seems to be unique. Preaching is defined as " giving out to each one, through messages, what God has for him to do," a connotation not found among traditional Christian churches. Their concept of Communication also differs from that of the N.S.A. and kindred churches. Spiritual Scientists have no special spirit controls or guides. They believe the messages come from the " Throne of Grace." Their transmission, so important to most Spiritualist groups, seems to be secondary in importance to the Spiritual Scientists. The Reverend Alice Tindall says they are more interested in man's relation to God, spiritually and scientifically. Therefore soul-development, soul-unfoldment, and the realization that they and the Father are one are their most important aims.

Spiritual Scientists also believe the Bible to be the inspired Word of God and the foundation of their belief in the demonstrative phases, e.g., healing, materialization, trumpet-speaking, spirit-writing, etc. According to their interpretation, God manifests himself triunely. He is the Father and Creator; the Son is Jesus Christ, born of a virgin, and the Word made flesh " to demonstrate . . . that God's Holy Law was possible when man desired to prove it to himself." Finally, the Holy Spirit is God who is ever-present as life in each soul and in all things.

Although man has a free will to choose either right or wrong, he is thought to know instinctively the proper action because of his conscience, which is God within him. Therefore, he is entirely responsible for his deeds and for his salvation.

Salvation, which is open to all, is considered to be a cleansing process through intelligent prayer. This seems to imply that it is obtained through works, because prayer is defined as following Jesus' teachings that heaven is at hand to be accepted by keeping God's law. Moreover, both heaven and hell are but states of the mind that man makes for himself now and hereafter. Even though he must pay for his mistakes, they teach that he has the innate desire to return to the right way, because man is created in God's image and therefore basically good. What else is there for him except to progress continually through the process of reincarnation!

Like other Spiritualist organizations, Spiritual Science devotes much time to the practice of healing. This is carried on by licensed practitioners who, however, cooperate with the medical profession. Since God is the healer, whatever the method, their healers are merely channels for God's healing power, illumining the soul and thereby healing the body.[48]

Spiritual Science has leaned more greatly toward the Theosophical principles of Madame Blavatsky than toward the philosophy of Andrew Jackson Davis. Like Theosophy, it accepts the belief in the ascended masters, those beings who have completed the course of their human evolution but assist in man's upward progress. The Reverend Glenn Argal said that, like many occult groups, Spiritual Science also offers the possibility of learning about one's past lives from the *akashic* records.

48 The Reverend Alice W. Tindall, " What Is Spiritual Science? " *The Washington Daily News*, March 3, 1955.

The Aquarian Brotherhood of Christ

The Aquarian Brotherhood of Christ has as its president the Reverend Caroline Duke, who had also been the first president of the Independent Associated Spiritualists, founded in 1925. The latter association had formerly included in its membership the Aquarian Brotherhood of Christ and Spiritual Science.

The Aquarian Brotherhood of Christ agrees with Spiritual Science in dispensing with spirit guides acting as controls. Mrs. Duke explained that during the séance " the call is made directly to God, who provides the message through one of his spiritual instruments." She also professed a belief in the ascended masters, who she said gave teachings anonymously through her mediumship. The anonymity of the masters marks one of the chief differences between the view of the Aquarian Brotherhood and Theosophy, since the general principles seem quite similar. When asked how she could distinguish between a master and a masquerading spirit, she replied: " You have to judge the truth of the message by the light the spirit brings. One always has the right to challenge the message, and you can also sense the vibratory rate of the lower spirits. You can demand then that they stand on the right hand in the name of the living healing Christ, whose servant I desire to be! If you make a sign of the cross, the advanced spirit will come. It is a call for help."

The Independent Spiritualist Association

The Independent Spiritualist Association was founded in 1924 by Amanda Flowers, who withdrew from the N.S.A. because of its restrictions on its members. She objected to the N.S.A. rule that allowed its mediums to work only in its own churches, and she wanted greater freedom of belief. Although the I.S.A. has educational standards and general beliefs that accord very closely with those of the N.S.A., it makes allowances for those who might hold faithfully to the doctrine of reincarnation and other Theosophical principles. Although it also recognizes the validity of physical phenomena, most of its mediums stress the mental phases of Spiritualism.

According to its president, the Reverend Carrol Ware, the Association has about seven hundred mediums, healers, and missionaries, and although the church had grown very rapidly in its early years, it was weakened when the Reverend John Bunker and the Reverend Clifford Bias, two of its finest and most notable mediums, left the organization.

The Spiritualist Episcopal Church

The Reverends Clifford Bias and John Bunker joined forces with Dr. Robert Chaney in establishing the Spiritualist Episcopal Church. These men were prominent mediums at Camp Chesterfield, the Spiritualist summer camp near Anderson, Indiana. Therefore, they had a good following immediately for their new venture.

If the Sunday morning services of the Reverend Dorothy Flexor's Spiritualist Episcopal Church are representative, it would appear that its pattern of worship formally resembles that found in many Christian churches. It includes devotional organ music, appropriate choir selections, a number of hymns, a call to worship, prayer, responsive readings, a sermon, and a benediction. Perhaps this form alone was sufficient for many former Protestants, because Mrs. Flexor explained that, unlike many members in other Spiritualist churches, all those belonging to her church had given up their earlier affiliations in favor of what they believed to be a Christian Spiritualism. Moreover, the resemblance of the architecture to that of a traditional New England Congregational church with its tall steeple probably helped additionally to create the traditional likeness.

Although the practice of healing is observed in this church, it does not form an integral part of the Sunday morning service. At that time those in need of treatment are separated from the main congregation for individual attention.

Mrs. Flexor said the Spiritualist Episcopal Church accepted the truths of all religions, but considered Jesus as the great example for mankind. Unfortunately, in the past, she explained, most teachers omitted both the mental and physical dimensions of "metaphysics." These her church included. Thus she exhibits mental mediumship by giving messages from the spirit world during the Sunday evening services, and displays its physical phases during séances held at other times.

Although Mrs. Flexor said the Spiritualist Episcopal Church did not accept the belief in reincarnation, at least two of the only living founders do. Both Robert Chaney and Clifford Bias, however, now belong to two different organizations. Chaney is a cofounder of the Astara Foundation, and Bias, one of the founding fathers of the Universal Spiritualist Association. The latter organization resulted from a schism in the Spiritualist Episcopal Church, which occurred in the following way.

In 1956 a morals charge was brought against one of its prominent mediums who was a candidate for church leadership the following year. During its national convention at Camp Chesterfield, Mrs. Flexor, the presiding officer, tried to dissuade the alleged offender from accepting the position if offered. In spite of her arguments, from the standpoint of public relations, many mediums there had already taken his part. Since she felt the church should be above such sectional influences as Camp Chesterfield, she moved the headquarters to Florida. Her adversaries interpreted this action as a usurpation of power. When Mabel Riffel, the secretary of Camp Chesterfield, received news of the change, she immediately forbade the church to hold its seminary classes there during the summer. Until then the summer school at the camp had been under the auspices of the S.E.C. On November 29, 1956, after Mabel Riffel ruled that none of its mediums could work at Camp Chesterfield, Mrs. Flexor's opponents formed the Universal Spiritualist Association, and the official seminary at the camp continued under its auspices.

The Universal Spiritualist Association

The Universal Spiritualist Association, founded in 1956, pulled twenty-six churches away from the Spiritualist Episcopal Church. These are distributed in the states of Michigan, Illinois, Ohio, West Virginia, Florida, California, Indiana, Minnesota, Colorado, and Virginia. Since the schism from the S.E.C. was on personal rather than on doctrinal grounds, one must expect a certain uniformity of belief.

According to the Reverend Lillian Dee Johnson, one of its leaders, her organization agrees with other Spiritualists that man was not conceived in sin; his conception was as immaculate as that of Jesus, who died not to save man from sin, but to prove personal immortality by his resurrection. Consequently, atonement should be interpreted as at-one-ment with God.

Man saves himself through the Christ Spirit within, which is realized by following the teachings of Jesus. Although most of the association's mediums seem to favor the doctrine of reincarnation, Mrs. Johnson said she believed man might be able to choose whether or not he returned to earth.

The Universal Spiritualist Association accepts the Bible, but prefers to interpret much of it metaphysically or allegorically. The Reverend Penninah Umback says that every great person in the Bible is a living allegory besides being historical. Because this method is used as a basis for one's own interpretation, it allows a greater freedom to accept many teachings of other occult and metaphysical groups. Therefore, the association's courses on Spiritualism, psychic healing, and the metaphysical interpretation of the Bible can fit into such subjects as astrology, numerology, esoteric psychology, comparative mysticism, etc., depending upon the penchants of the particular faculty at that time.

In this work no attempt is being made to include all the many Spiritualist organizations. The outline aims only to give examples of current proliferation with a sample of the philosophical variations and reasons for schism.

Spiritualist Camps

Although there are many Spiritualist summer camps in the United States, by far the most popular seem to be Camp Lily Dale in New York, Camp Chesterfield in Indiana, and Camp Silver Bell in Ephrata, Pennsylvania. Since the summer months would be less profitable for individual mediums, these camps, which attract devout Spiritualists as well as the curious, provide a place to pool their efforts. Many of the newcomers depart as devout Spiritualists.

Although Camp Lily Dale provides mediums who produce physical phenomena, it emphasizes mental mediumship. Camp Chesterfield, on the contrary, has been most famous for its large variety of physical phases. Fame, however, turned to notoriety in the summer of 1960, when *The Psychic Observer*, Spiritualism's leading paper, reported fraudulent materializations occurring there. Tom O'Neil, its Spiritualist editor, and Dr. Andrija Puharich, a psychic investigator, wanted some pictures of spirit materializations. Camp Chesterfield cooperated and permitted the use of infrared film capable of photographing material objects in darkness. Unfortunately, the photos of the materialized spirits seemed to reveal the likenesses of some well-known mediums as well as other alleged evidences of fraud. The story and pictures were printed in *The Psychic Observer* coupled with the demand that the organizations begin a housecleaning.[49]

Even though Mabel Riffel was until her recent death only the secretary of Camp Chesterfield, one had to be there but a short time to realize that she was the moving power behind the camp, and one whose word was law. She had been a trumpet medium and a loyal follower of the school of Andrew Jackson Davis. As a strict conformist to the ideas of progression without reincarnation, she would not allow such " Theosophical " doctrines to be taught at the camp. Therefore, during the summer the seminary teachers had to be mindful of their words, even though some might teach quite differently during the winter in Florida. A good case in point is Dr. Robert Chaney. Concerning him Mabel Riffel said:

"Robert Chaney was one of the best mediums here in the camp and a great teacher in the seminary. I just don't know what happened. He began to teach a lot of things like reincarnation and other ideas. He was one of my favorites here, but I just couldn't let him teach things like that in the camp."

Chaney, as a result, left, with his wife Earlyne, to found an influential occult group, whose story comprises another chapter.

[49] Hans Holzer, "Revolt in Spiritland," *Tomorrow*, Vol. 9, No. 1 (1961), pp. 19–23.

Reincarnation, a Point of Controversy

Since the doctrine of reincarnation has been such a disrupting force in Spiritualism, we must examine it. What are the arguments of Spiritualism for it, and on what basis are they made? *The Psychic Observer* published both sides of the question for about ten years during the recent heat of controversy. Unfortunately, most proofs for or against reincarnation rely solely upon the testimonies of alleged spirits. For example, W. T. Stead, a prominent Spiritualist before his death, spoke to one side of the question when he reappeared at a séance. He is reported to have said:

" People will have to rise above the idea of coming back to a body. When once started upon its individual career no spirit goes back to a mortal frame. . . . Of all the dogmas that retard the soul's development, that of reincarnation is worse in its effect upon the human race. It keeps down individual effort, which is everything.

" First of all, I must still further emphasize the fact that all that comes from the spirit world is not, therefore, true. It is a most mischievous and false idea. If you saw there the masses of spirits still Catholics, Presbyterians, Wesleyans, Reincarnation-ists, and others not yet progressed into the Absolute . . . you would understand how with other dogmatists, Reincarnationists cling to their belief, give messages to those on earth affirming its truth, and so perpetrate what is a misconception. . . . It is a dangerous error, for it weakens the will power and transfers the blame of wrongdoing on to another life or lives and keeps the soul in fetters. . . . The statement about spirits waiting to be again enfleshed is absolutely without foundation. . . . It is the spiritual development in earth life that is everything. Concentrate your thoughts upon that." [50]

On the other side of the question, Dr. Robert Chaney quotes an alleged spirit teacher who taught his class concerning reincarnation: " Men are anxious to know the length of time between incarnations. It will vary, naturally, with every individual. Perhaps for some it may be as short as fifty years. Of such

[50] *The Psychic Observer*, No. 365, Nov. 25, 1935, pp. 6, 10.

persons, however, we may say they have not risen to a high station of life, for they have remained in a savage state. . . . Others will remain a period of from fifteen hundred to two thousand years, as time is measured upon the earth, and some still longer.[51]

" It is important that you retain in your consciousness an ' essence ' of the accumulated experiences of your past lives. Not that you retain a memory of the incidents by which you acquired those experiences, but that you have assimilated and now make use of those past experiences of other lives." [52]

Nevertheless, Dr. Chaney would agree with opponents who say that some carry their belief in reincarnation to extremes. His spirit teacher has a word for psychic groups who believe they can learn the secrets of their past lives through the *akashic* records: " I earnestly beseech you, Beloved, save your money . . . and save yourself from the folly of indulging in a ridiculous belief as to who you might have been in some past life. Wear an understanding of this Truth with honor.

" For NO ONE can read the Akashic Records except he be a Master . . . and if he be a Master, he would never promiscuously reveal to persons their past lives." [53]

It does little good for Spiritualists who disbelieve in reincarnation to quote the Bible, because others like Robert Chaney will point to Matt. 17:12-13 as proof that Jesus taught this view, and that John the Baptist was the reincarnation of Elias.[54] In fact, this passage prompted a group of Spiritualists in Jacksonville, Florida, to organize a new church in 1953 called " The Baptist Movement of Divine Healing — Mediation." When asked why they chose the word "Baptist," they replied, " Because we are following the Spirit of John in our teaching." They believe the Bible gives them proof of reincarnation since Jesus said that Elias' spirit was in John.[55]

If extrasensory perception is ever proved beyond a doubt in the parapsychological laboratories, this would not necessarily

[51] *Ibid.*, No. 360, Sept. 10, 1935, pp. 1, 3.
[52] *Idem.*
[53] *Idem.*
[54] *Ibid.*, p. 4.
[55] *Ibid.*, No. 365, Nov. 25, 1935, p. 4.

prove the existence of a spirit world or its communication with ours. It would merely make psychic research a valid field for investigation. If one feels drawn to Spiritualism, however, what particular philosophy and science should he accept? Even though there is a common core of philosophy, there is great variation in details. If Spiritualism can be spoken of as a science, why is there such contradiction in its principles? Whether or not one reincarnates after death, or a spirit can read the *akashic* records, or would divulge their secrets; whether or not one needs spirit controls, or light is deleterious to ectoplasm, although some mediums have daylight materializations, these and other questions are subject to different explanations. In spite of all this variation, why do the spirits almost invariably agree with the particular medium through whom they express themselves?

What, then, is the future of Spiritualism? Certainly the great heyday of organized Spiritualism was in the last century. Moreover, if Spiritualism is declining, its fraudulent mediums must share the blame for its failure to prove its case, as even Spiritualists will admit. If the reality of the spirit world is ever proved, many mediums will be the most surprised.

When the question concerning the future of Spiritualism was asked of the medium, Billy Turner, his answer was: " I believe that organized Spiritualism is on its way out. Spiritualism is valid and true, but there are so many perverts and fraudulent mediums in Spiritualism that the public is getting wise to them."

When pressed further as to the outcome, he replied, " Because Spiritualism is true, its truths will gradually be taken up by the organized churches through such movements as the Spiritual Frontiers Fellowship started by Arthur Ford."

Arthur Ford and the Houdini Code

Arthur Ford had his initial psychic manifestations during the First World War, and even though he trained for the Christian ministry, serving a church in Kentucky, his earlier experiences aroused his interest in Spiritualism. He, therefore, soon relinquished his church to lecture on Spiritualism at the Chautauqua, and his lectures and clairvoyant readings to some of the most prominent people in this country and abroad brought him renown as a psychic.[56] His greatest bid for fame, however, was his claim of breaking the Houdini code — an assertion that made its repercussions felt among both Spiritualists and non-Spiritualists.

Harry Houdini, who died in 1926, had been one of the world's foremost magicians as well as a notable exposer of fraudulent mediums. Knowing that after his death many of these would pretend to have communicated with him, he arranged a secret code with his wife. His fears were confirmed, but all the messages were denied veracity until February 8, 1928, when Arthur Ford brought the first clue. During a private séance Fletcher, Ford's control, announced the presence of a spirit who said she was the mother of Houdini. She desired to reveal the one word Houdini himself had waited to receive as proof of her continued existence. This word was " Forgive."

After being informed, Mrs. Houdini acknowledged its correctness in the newspapers.

The first word of the second message came through Ford in November, 1928, but it took eight separate sittings during a period of two and a half months before the full message was revealed. Finally, on January 5 of the following year, the ten words of the code were given in the following sequence: ROSABELLE — ANSWER — TELL — PRAY — ANSWER — LOOK — TELL — ANSWER — ANSWER — TELL!

Mrs. Houdini received a copy along with an invitation to attend a séance at which the solution would be given. Upon receiving the coded words, she exclaimed: " It is right! Did he say ROSABELLE? "

After an affirmative reply and a few more details concerning the message, she agreed to carry out her husband's prearranged plan. At the séance, which included a representative from the United Press, Mrs. Houdini said that the code was one that she and her husband had used in a mind-reading act. Then, in an intricate manner, Ford gave the solution, which she confirmed.

[56] Arthur Ford, *Nothing So Strange: An Autobiography of Arthur Ford in Collaboration with Margueritte Harmon Bro* (Harper & Brothers, 1958), pp. 1–27.

" ROSABELLE, BELIEVE! " was the message to prove that he, Harry Houdini, still lived.

The newspapers publicized the story, but jubilation appeared premature because the reporter later said she knew the complete message twenty-four hours before its reception.

Ford defended himself by declaring that she had threatened to expose the message as a hoax unless he interceded for her to get some personal letters from Beatrice Houdini. He said that his refusal to enter into the affairs of Mrs. Houdini resulted in her attempt to discredit him.

Ford's troubles continued when three members of the United Spiritualist League of New York City had a " spurious " meeting to annul his membership. The League's charges were then carried to Ford's own church, the First Spiritualist Church of New York. His Trustees and the governing body of the League met conjointly to study the case, but none of the three accusers appeared at the inquiry. When the testimony appeared contradictory, Ford was exonerated of all charges. His three indictors resigned from the United Spiritualist League before their dismissal could be acted upon.[57] After his retirement in recent years, Ford became the key figure in the formation of the Spiritual Frontiers Fellowship.

The Spiritual Frontiers Fellowship

This organization was founded in March of 1956 after Albin Bro, missionary and educator, Paul Higgins, former minister of the Hyde Park Methodist Church in Chicago, and Arthur Ford called a conference of Christians interested in the study of psychic research. The purpose of the association has been " to encourage the study within the Church of psychic phenomena as related to personal survival, spiritual healing, and prayer." It is a nondenominational group with a membership of over a thousand including a number of well-known Christian leaders, authors, and ministers. Although the majority of its members are drawn from the larger Christian denominations, it has at-

[57] *Ibid.*, pp. 60–74; Francis R. Fast, *The Houdini Messages: The Mediumship of Arthur Ford* (1929), pp. 3–17.

tracted a few Spiritualists, Christian Scientists, Theosophists, etc. Besides its annual meeting the association meets sectionally in various parts of the United States to present papers and hold discussions on many phases of its objectives.

Perhaps it is the combination of Ford's reputation as a psychic and his erstwhile connection with the Christian ministry that makes him the dominant figure in the Spiritual Frontiers Fellowship. Since its inception he has been devoting most of his time to its promotion by lecturing at Christian churches throughout the country.

He asserts that properly instructed small groups working together for psychic development will eventually produce results, since everyone is psychic to a certain extent. Therefore, one does not need to attend a Spiritualist church to prove personal immortality, because those in the Christian churches can discover this for themselves.

Gradually these study groups are spreading within the churches throughout the country. Every sectional meeting of the Spiritual Frontiers Fellowship may result in new study groups. The lectures by Ford have inspired both ministers and laymen to experiment with the possibilities of mediumship. Although one hears of one such group having a modicum of success in developing mediumistic gifts, the association's official journal does not yet bear witness to it. At its annual meeting in Chicago in 1958, however, there was at least one member who felt he was developing psychic powers. He was a Methodist minister from the Middle West, who told me he had been able to entrance himself and believed he soon would develop the gift of independent trumpet. When asked concerning its relevancy to his ministry, he replied:

" I used to have difficulty preaching a funeral sermon, because I felt I was not really quite sincere in what I often said, but now that I know that the dead are *really* living, I can put my whole heart into the sermon and give much greater comfort."

Not all members, however, are interested in psychic phenomena. Some are primarily concerned with spiritual healing, the study of prayer, and the deepening of the spiritual life. Although perhaps most of the active members would support the possibility of spirit communication, one may occasionally hear some criticism of the stress put on this phase. For others, however, the psychic and spiritual are one and the same. Such an identification and absolute correlation would certainly not accord with the interpretation of most Christians.

What is the philosophy behind the S.F.F.? On the basis of Ford's lectures there will emerge a system in close agreement with the Spiritualistic interpretation of Dr. Victoria Barnes. As we have already seen, she herself has accepted the moral teachings of Jesus and has alluded to the miracles in the Bible as examples of psychic phenomena. But she declared herself to be a Spiritualist rather than a Christian and did not believe Spiritualism and Christianity were the same, as indeed they are not. Perhaps the central difference is that the resurrection of Jesus Christ has no meaning in Spiritualism except as an example of psychic phenomena.

Does this mean that a person who accepts the possibility of a spirit world cannot be considered a Christian? Although the Bible proscribes attempting to communicate with spirits, still the Christian tradition contains interpretations permitting a belief in immediate personal immortality. But if one accepts the purported spirit revelations, he must decide which spirits to believe. Because of the many doctrinal differences among various "authoritative" spirits, how does one know which authority to accept?

Regardless of Spiritualistic influences, the purpose of the S.F.F. is not to advocate any specific philosophy but to examine all things that may bear truth. Since its membership represents so many different traditions, this necessitates as many philosophies. Probably the best single expression of its mood would be the statement of the Reverend Archie Matson, a member of its Executive Council:

" The men and women who founded Spiritual Frontiers Fellowship are convinced we are indeed standing on a new frontier, a spiritual frontier, a frontier which offers as much, yes more, for the men and women of the last half of the twentieth century, as did the voyages of Columbus for those in the fifteenth and sixteenth centuries. This exploration is not a matter of long and dangerous voyages but of self-discipline, usually in small groups, and of exploring what happens when we really trust the little we know of God's presence and power.

" My theory is that, just as light, the X-ray, and radio waves are all manifestations of one great system of physical phenomena, so also effective prayer, telepathy, clairvoyance, spiritual healing, and many forms of psychic phenomena are all aspects of a sixth sense, a spiritual communication system which uses the same nonphysical mechanism. . . .

" The place where most of us have had experience with this sixth sense is in prayer, so it is our conviction that we should begin with prayer, and allow it to grow in depth and power; and that by gathering in small groups we can better cultivate our spiritual capacities, and so learn to be sensitive to the still, small voice on various levels. We feel that as we work together, following the discipline of a prayer fellowship, most members will discover that they have some spiritual gifts along the lines suggested in the twelfth chapter of First Corinthians. Sometimes even mediumship may appear, and a gift for healing far more often, but always there will be a heightened spiritual awareness in those who are faithful in spirit and in practice." [58]

For those who want to begin an S.F.F. prayer group a special study kit is provided. The titles included in it show the range of religious traditions: *Prayer Group Guide*, published by the National Association of Camps Farthest Out; *Prayer Groups*, by H. W. Freer, published by The Methodist Church; *Prayer Groups for Lay People*, by Austin Pardue, published by the Forward Movement Publications (Episcopal); *Prayer Groups*, by Norman K. Elliott, published by the United Prayer Tower; *A Drill in the Silence*, published by the Unity School of Christianity; *Study Group Suggestions*, by Arthur Ford, an S.F.F. reprint.

Even though the S.F.F. membership in 1962 had slowed to an annual increase of less than one hundred new members,[59] its influence may be far greater than its official size. Arthur Ford has

[58] *Spiritual Frontiers: Journal of the Spiritual Frontiers Fellowship*, Vol. 4, No. 4 (July-Aug., 1959), p. 4.
[59] *Ibid.*, Vol. 7, No. 5 (May, 1962), p. 5.

lectured not only in Christian churches but even at theological seminaries, which may receive the S.F.F. periodical free. The two-day seminars meet not only in lesser known churches but also in those as well known as the Riverside Church in New York. A seminar there in November, 1962, attracted nearly five hundred registrants.[60]

The S.F.F. is also beginning to make its program known by articles in other than its own publications. Several national magazines have carried stories concerning the organization. One is not surprised to read in its own magazine about the psychic experiences of its members, e.g., how the retired Congregational minister, the Reverend Owen R. Washburn, has demonstrated his use of spirits in counseling his laymen.[61] But one *is* surprised to read similar testimonies by S.F.F. members in official denominational publications, e.g., recent articles in the *United Church Herald* of the United Church of Christ and the *United Church Observer* of the United Church of Canada.

The S.F.F. is not a unique organization. Its predecessor is the Churches' Fellowship for Psychical Study, founded by Reginald M. Lester of the Church of England. Although narrower in scope than the S.F.F., it is an interdenominational group intending " to afford an opportunity for Clergy, Ministers, and Laymen to study today's psychical phenomena, to see what relation, if any, they bear to the psychical phenomena in Holy Scripture." It includes in its membership the Bishop of London, some ten other bishops, the Dean of St. Paul's, Dr. Leslie Weatherhead, former minister of City Temple, the Very Reverend Dr. W. R. Matthews, and formerly the late Reverend G. Maurice Elliott. Thus for the first time in history, as T. Rowland Powell has said, men of the cloth have become interested in psychic research.[62]

The quest of man to peer behind the veil of death through the eyes of Spiritualist mediums will raise questions in many people's minds. Some will query whether the Christian church has

---

[60] *Gateway: Journal of the Spiritual Frontiers Fellowship*, Vol. 8 (Jan., 1963), pp. 8–9.
[61] *Spiritual Frontiers*, Vol. 4, No. 6 (Nov.-Dec., 1959), p. 9.
[62] T. Rowland Powell, " The Church and Psychic Science," *Hibbert Journal*, Vol. 58, p. 126.

any business investigating the validity of psychic phenomena, or whether such matters should be left to others until psychic research is validated. To be sure, the mind and spirit of man have many unexplored channels. The beginning of the departments of parapsychology in some universities here and abroad has kept alive the hope of proving survival after death as well as of showing the validity of telepathy, clairvoyance, and other extrasensory gifts. The existence of fraud in Spiritualism does not in itself preclude the possibility of personal immortality of the soul, but the inconsistency of the Spiritualistic views must certainly raise problems concerning the proof. Still, the door is open to all seekers; so let us pass through it to examine the views of Theosophy, which has been so influential upon the views of many Spiritualists.

III

Theosophy and Its Allies

The Early History of Theosophy

THE PRINCIPAL FOUNDER OF THEOSOPHY and its guiding spirit
was Helena Petrovna Blavatsky, née Hahn, who was born in
Russia in 1831 of a well-to-do, aristocratic family. If her account is true, her psychic development began during her early
life, because even as a child she had invisible playmates and believed in superhuman and subhuman spirits. As she grew older,
Theosophists claim, her psychic powers increased. She developed astral clairvoyance, i.e., she could see beings in the spirit
world on the plane just beyond the physical. They also credit
her with the power to materialize various articles at will and
with the ability to move objects through the force of her mind,
i.e., telekinesis.

After an unfortunate marriage with General Blavatsky when
she was seventeen, she soon ran away to become a wanderer
through many foreign lands. From 1867 to 1870 she was allegedly in India, where she studied occult knowledge before
founding an uneventful Société Spirite in Cairo, Egypt. Then,
after a short stay in France she came to the United States in
1874 to defend the validity of Spiritualistic phenomena. Here
she met Colonel Henry Steel Olcott, who became a cofounder
of the Theosophical Society.[1]

Colonel Olcott, who had obtained his title in the Civil War,
was a well-known lawyer, besides being the agricultural editor
of the *New York Tribune*. For many years he had been inter-

[1] G. Baseden Butt, *Madame Blavatsky* (London: Rider & Co., 1925), pp. 2–54.

ested in Spiritualism, and in 1874 he had written a series of articles for the *New York Sun* concerning the materialization séances of the Eddy brothers in Chittenden, Vermont. Attracted by these reports, Madame Blavatsky herself visited the séances where she first became an acquaintance and then a close friend of Olcott. They attended and defended together the séances of a Mr. and Mrs. Holmes of Philadelphia, who had been accused of fraud by skeptical investigators. Upon their return Madame Blavatsky began to write articles in defense of the Holmeses and of Spiritualistic phenomena. Her bold statements and apparent range of knowledge soon attracted the attention of Spiritualists, investigators, and the general public, while Olcott's praise made her apartment in New York the center of attraction for Spiritualists and students of the curious and marvelous.

On October 20, 1875, the Theosophical Society was organized with Olcott, President; Madame Blavatsky, Secretary; and William Q. Judge as Counsel. The original Society had the following three objectives:

" 1. To form the nucleus of a Universal Brotherhood of Humanity, without distinction of race, creed, sex, caste, or color;

" 2. The study of ancient and modern religions, philosophies, and sciences, and the demonstration of the importance of such study; and

" 3. The investigation of the unexplained laws of Nature and the psychical powers latent in man."

From the standpoint of her published works and those of Olcott, Madame Blavatsky's philosophy appears to have had a three-staged development. During the first period until 1875 she defended Spiritualism. From 1875 to 1879 she began her attack upon Spiritualism, but still rejected the doctrine of reincarnation. Not until 1879, after her return to India, does the fully developed Theosophy appear.

When the Society was first established in 1875, most of the members were Spiritualists. They had been attracted to Madame Blavatsky by her writings and by the expectation of seeing the phenomena they believed she could produce. She herself, however, seemed to be suddenly disinterested in phenomena and turned her attention to writing her first book, *Isis Unveiled*, which appeared in 1877. If many Spiritualists had already left the organization, after she failed to satisfy their desire for phenomena, they became greatly indignant when *Isis Unveiled* presented a heretical view. Many of her erstwhile supporters regarded her as a foe of " true Spiritualism."

Whereas she defended the reality of Spiritualism's phenomena, she now attacked the Spiritualistic theory concerning the reality of the spirits seen at the séance. She claimed that instead of the occult philosophy she could give them, the Spiritualists were accepting teachings of " intelligences " with less wisdom than a child. She prophesied that without her kind of help Spiritualism would vegetate and be rejected by both scientists and theologians. In its modern aspect it was neither a science, a religion, nor a philosophy.[2]

She confided once to Olcott that what had appeared to them at a séance as the pirate-spirit of Henry Morgan was only a " humbugging elemental."

" Understand me," she said, " the phenomena were real, but they were done by no discarnate *human* spirit." [3] Theosophists explain an elemental as an astral spirit evolving separately and remaining subhuman.

At another time Olcott reported that the entities seen at the Eddy séances were nothing but the medium's etheric double which had escaped from his body and clothed itself in another appearance.[4]

Nevertheless, Olcott's testimony seems to show Mrs. Blavatsky's ambivalence. On the basis of unpublished manuscripts discovered after her death, he argues that she was sorry she had to identify herself with the Spiritualists. She had been sent to America in order to prove the validity of the Spiritualistic phenomena as well as to show the fallacy of the Spiritualistic theory.[5] But Olcott himself recorded her words that the famous

[2] *The Theosophical Movement, 1875–1925: A History and a Survey* (E. P. Dutton & Co., Inc., 1925), pp. 13–39.
[3] Henry Steel Olcott, *Old Diary Leaves: The True Story of the Theosophical Society* (G. P. Putnam's Sons, 1895), p. 11.
[4] *Ibid.*, p. 9.
[5] *Ibid.*, p. 13.

medium, Daniel Home, whom she met in Paris in 1858, " converted " her to Spiritualism. There is also the testimony of her articles defending Spiritualism, in which she could call it " our belief " and " the whole belief of *us* Spiritualists." Even in the *Spiritualist Scientist* of March 8, 1875, she could still write about the " divine truth of our faith (Spiritualism) and the teachings of our invisible guardians (the spirits of the circles)." [6]

The doctrine of reincarnation, so important in later Theosophy, does not seem to have been held by Madame Blavatsky when she wrote *Isis Unveiled*. In that work she defended the theory that human souls went to other and more spiritualized planets after death. She even wrote:

" Reincarnation, i.e., the appearance of the same individual or rather of his astral monad, twice on the same planet, is not a rule in nature; it is an exception, like the teratological phenomenon of a two-headed infant." [7]

She said such exceptions occurred when the design of nature had been interfered with, e.g., in cases of abortion, or the death of infants before a certain age, etc.

Olcott recalls she had not taught the doctrine of reincarnation until 1879 during their visit to India. He also referred to an article he had written for *The Spiritualist* concerning the Theosophical beliefs. He said that man's soul would join its divine spirit after death and live forever; or if debased sufficiently to lose its spirit, it would become an *elementary* and obsess mediums until its life burned out. When British Spiritualists attacked his article, Madame Blavatsky herself defended it in the same magazine but again maintained that human reincarnation was the exception.[8]

---

[6] *Ibid.*, pp. 70–72. Olcott's statements are in part confirmed by other sources, e.g., an article printed in the *Daily Graphic*, New York, Vol. 6, November 13, 1874, according to which she confesses not only to being a Spiritualist at that time but also that she was converted to Spiritualism by Daniel Home in Paris. The article has been reprinted and appears in *The Complete Works of H. P. Blavatsky*, edited by A. Trevor Barker (London: Rider & Co., 1933), Vol. 1, p. 17. See also pp. 27–38 for her defense of Spiritualism and her identification as a Spiritualist.

[7] Helen Petrovna Blavatsky, *Isis Unveiled: A Master-Key to the Mysteries of Ancient and Modern Science and Theology* (J. W. Bouton, 1877), p. 351.

[8] Olcott, *op. cit.*, pp. 278–283. Olcott's testimony is confirmed by a reprint of the article "Views of the Theosophists," by Madame Blavatsky, in her *Complete Works*, Vol. 1, p. 183. The article had appeared in *The Spiritualist*, Feb. 8, 1878.

Olcott was indeed perplexed by her later view, because she had supposedly written *Isis Unveiled* largely under the guidance of an ascended master who occupied her body or inspired her from the psychic realms. He even asserted that he himself had received confirming letters from a mahatma. He finally concluded that either due to " imperfect cerebropsychic training " the truth was garbled, or since there were possibly sixty-three stages of adeptship, perhaps the master might not then have known the truth.[9] Part of the Theosophical defense has been that she later corrected in other writings the mistakes that had crept into her earlier work.[10]

The Theosophical basis was partly an occultism such as was current in France. Particularly the works of Eliphas Lévi, *Histoire de la Magie*, 1861; *La Clef des Grands Mystères*, 1861; and *Dogme et Rituel de la Haute Magie*, 1861, became popular among many people interested in occultism.

The Rosicrucians also made their contribution. Although the dates and identity of their founder, as well as the authenticity of some of their literature, are still debatable, the early seventeenth century probably marks their beginning. An anonymous tract entitled *Fama Fraternitatis* was published in Germany in 1614. It tells of a human and divine Reformation that is to usher in a New Age, and for which the Brotherhood is to prepare. C. R. C., supposedly Christian Rosenkreuz, the founder of the order of the Rosy Cross, or Rosicrucians, had ostensibly traveled to the East and learned the secret of all wisdom. After accepting some disciples he was credited with starting what later became the Rosicrucian Brotherhood. This work was followed by the *Confessio fraternitatis* and *Die chymische Hochzeit*, ascribed to the same man, and then by a host of other works to

---

[9] Olcott, *op. cit.*, p. 278.

[10] Charles J. Ryan, *H. P. Blavatsky and the Theosophical Movement: A Brief Historical Sketch* (Theosophical University Press, 1937), pp. 6–72. Ryan, besides speaking of the problem as due to mistakes creeping into the manuscript, further defends Madame Blavatsky by citing passages in *Isis Unveiled* that he feels had shown her belief in reincarnation. A careful examination of these in context will reveal that she taught a doctrine of the transmigration of the spirit from here to higher planes or spheres, upward and onward in evolution toward God. She at one point referred to this belief as being similar to that of the Kabbalists. Nowhere among these passages was there an indication that she believed that reincarnation on this earth was to be normally expected.

the present time.[11] Taking the Rosicrucian literature as a whole, one sees an attempt to establish a Christian fraternity, whose philosophy would include Kabbalistic, alchemical, and Hermetic theories. It is therefore a type of spiritual alchemy in which man's material nature may be spiritualized.

That the adepts from which Christian Rosenkreuz supposedly received his divine knowledge of ancient wisdom have been identified with the Theosophical masters of the Great White Brotherhood I can affirm from Theosophical lectures I have heard. That Madame Blavatsky believed she was also presenting such a spiritual alchemy is seen in her first book, *Isis Unveiled*. The belief, however, that these masters of the Great White Brotherhood have passed the need to reincarnate, that they have the duty to help others toward their salvation, and even some of their names, all show the influence of Mahayana Buddhism.

Although Olcott praised Madame Blavatsky's breadth of knowledge displayed in *Isis Unveiled*, he admitted she made great use of the following: King's *Gnostics*; Jennings' *Rosicrucians*; Moor's *Hindu Pantheon*; Lévi's various works, and others of this kind.[12] These, however, only prepared her for greater philosophical development revealed in *The Secret Doctrine*, which was written and published after she and Olcott sailed to India in 1879.

Their move to India promised success for the Theosophical Society. After a short stay in Bombay, the permanent headquarters were established in Adyar, whence the organization branched out with small centers in various parts of India. The Indians welcomed both leaders because they made no distinction between race, creed, or color; did not keep themselves aloof from the natives as so many of the English had done; and they proclaimed a philosophy favoring Hinduism. Their work and the publication of *The Theosophist*, which began in 1879, increased interest in the study of Sanskrit and Indian philosophy. For this reason even Max Müller, the celebrated Orientalist,

[11] Arthur Edward Waite, *The Brotherhood of the Rosy Cross, Being Records of the House of the Holy Spirit in Its Inward and Outward History* (London: William Rider & Son, 1924), pp. 113–214.

[12] Olcott, *op. cit.*, p. 207.

was attracted to them, although he was also one of their critics. While praising them for helping to revive the love of Sanskrit, Müller complained bitterly that they were supporting Hindu superstitions by giving esoteric meanings to the Hindu scriptures.[13]

If Theosophy owes much to Madame Blavatsky for its doctrinal development, it must also give credit to Olcott for its organization and extension in the Asiatic countries, and to William Q. Judge for its later growth in America. Nevertheless, that which augured great success initially soon presaged setbacks and decline.

Before their arrival in India, an alliance was made with the Arya Samaj, an Indian reform movement dedicated to the preservation and purification of Hindu religion. For a short time the Theosophical Society even bore the name of the Theosophical Society of the Arya Samaj, but this wedding was not lasting because dissension soon arose between the two groups. Swami Dayanand Saraswati, founder of the Arya Samaj, protested against the friendly relations the Theosophists were developing with the members of other faiths, e.g., the Buddhists and the Parsis. The Theosophists, however, felt their Hindu allies were too sectarian, whereas Theosophy had to be entirely neutral and nondogmatic, if it was going to establish a Universal Brotherhood among mankind. Therefore, their association with the Arya Samaj was severed in 1882 by mutual agreement.[14]

In England, meanwhile, trouble also broke out in the London Lodge, which had been established when the founders had visited there before going to India. The contestants were A. P. Sinnet, author of *Esoteric Buddhism*, and Dr. Anna B. Kingsford. Dr. Kingsford had considered herself a Christo-Theosophical and Hermetic mystic and seer. She was the author of *The Perfect Way*, in which she pictured Christian doctrine to be the same as in other religious systems. Consequently, she opposed the Theosophical accent upon the Eastern interpretation as being less fitting than the Christo-Theosophical view.[15] She also took occasion to criticize Sinnet's book, *Esoteric Buddhism*, in a pamphlet issued to members of the London Lodge

[13] Ryan, *op. cit.*, pp. 101–102.   [14] *Ibid.*, pp. 82–83.   [15] *Ibid.*, pp. 168–171.

in 1883.[16] The majority of the London Lodge agreed with Mr. Sinnet, and Dr. Kingsford left with her own coterie to form a " Hermetic Society." [17]

Trouble still mounted. In 1884, while Olcott and Blavatsky were pouring oil on troubled waters in England, serious difficulties occurred at their Indian headquarters. Mrs. Coulomb and her husband, who were in charge of their household, were involved in strife with the Theosophical Council. Letters supposedly from Madame Blavatsky to Mrs. Coulomb had been given by the latter to Christian missionaries, who published them as an exposure of fraudulent phenomena produced there.

The Society for Psychical Research sent Richard Hodson to investigate. His adverse report proclaimed the validity of the letters and accused Madame Blavatsky of deception. This was a severe blow to Theosophy, but the leaders pointed to the conflict between the Coulombs and others at the headquarters. Madame Blavatsky declared the letters were some of her notes that had been interpolated with forged sentences.[18]

The whole vexing case, the vacillation of even her close followers concerning her defense, and the growing realization that her aim of Universal Brotherhood had failed, caused a break in the founder's health. She resigned her position as the Society's Corresponding Secretary and went to Europe to convalesce.[19]

If there were such wise adepts or masters, one wonders why they did not protect their Messenger more ably. The Theosophist replies that rarely do masters interfere with an individual's course of life but allow the law of karma, or compensation, freely to operate. The effects of our bad deeds must be suffered before the soul reaches salvation. Earthly life is regarded as a school in which lessons must be learned.

This type of notoriety did not help the fortunes of Theosophy, but failed to eclipse the career of Madame Blavatsky. She continued her work, writing among other books, *The Secret Doctrine*, which became the final authority for many Theosophists.

[16] *The Theosophical Movement, 1875–1925*, p. 54.
[17] Ryan, *op. cit.*, p. 171.
[18] *Ibid.*, pp. 177–186; also *The Theosophical Movement, 1875–1925*, pp. 59–91.
[19] Ryan, *op. cit.*, pp. 204–210.

The American development of the work was also important. In 1882 a Theosophical Society was established in Rochester, New York. Its founder Josephene W. Cables, who had been a "Christian Spiritualist" medium, soon wearied of trying to contact the masters and renamed the Society "the Rochester Brotherhood." [20] Therefore, the organization of the Theosophical Society in America really fell to William Q. Judge, a charter member of the original group. After ten years the Society's work was under the leadership of Madame Blavatsky in Europe, Olcott in India, and Judge in America.

By 1885 Judge had begun the rejuvenation of the original Aryan Lodge in New York. He edited a practical and devotional periodical, *The Path*, whose popularity tripled the number of branches within a year, and led to the formation of the American Section of the Theosophical Society in 1889. This was a federation of Lodges with internal autonomy, but external recognition of the General Council's supremacy in India. [21]

About this time the development of the Esoteric Section became a second important phase of Theosophy. This was a key to later manifold troubles, for whoever could dominate the Esoteric Section controlled policies and ruled with a divine right. Leadership of the Esoteric Section, while giving authority, sowed the seeds of distrust and dissension through curtailment of freedom.

Although in 1880 the Council at Benares decided to divide the Society into three sections — the masters, the more advanced fellows (the Esoteric Section), and the probationers — little was done to organize the advanced group until Madame Blavatsky promoted it during her last years in London. Since William Q. Judge was also making strong demands for such a section, in 1888 he was invited to collaborate with her on the rules. It was recognized that although the Society had done much on the esoteric and utilitarian plane, it had not moved toward Universal Brotherhood. So to save the endangered Society, the Esoteric Section was called upon to foster this aim at least among a choice minority. Each one would receive enlightenment in

[20] *The Theosophical Movement, 1875–1925*, pp. 120–126.
[21] *Ibid.*, pp. 106–108.

proportion to his contribution toward this end. The Esoteric Section would be separate from the official Theosophical Society, but it would draw its membership from that body. Therefore, the section was renamed " The Eastern School of Theosophy."

This brought new difficulties. Olcott did not favor the move, but finally gave it his reluctant support. While he was in Europe, Richard Harte, the temporary editor of *The Theosophist*, not only opposed the establishment of the Esoteric Section, but even accused Madame Blavatsky of conspiring against the authority of Adyar. These further disruptions in the Society led Olcott to offer his resignation in favor of Judge, the vice-president, but it was refused.[22] It was now evident that power was passing from Olcott and the ailing Blavatsky to Judge in America, who, after the death of Madame Blavatsky in 1891, opposed her successor, Annie Besant. When this occurred, one of the immediate problems related to the Esoteric Section. The two most likely candidates for leadership were Judge and Besant. It was decided at the General Convention that the two should be coleaders.[23] This was evidently a mistake, and harmony did not reign for long.

In 1894 Colonel Olcott wrote to Mr. Judge that he was being charged by some with misusing names and handwritings of the masters, and should therefore immediately retire from his offices in the Society. A return cable by Judge declared the accusations to be false. At the annual American Convention in the same year, sixty-one active Lodges declared their confidence in the integrity of their leader. It was claimed by the American Theosophists that these charges had originated with Annie Besant, growing out of friction between her and Judge over policies in the Society. In her published statement, however, she denied this responsibility and suggested that the accusations were greatly exaggerated. Mr. Judge accused Mrs. Besant of becoming so enamored of Hindu thought as to depart from the original nonsectarian idea of Theosophy. Annie Besant reproached Judge for trying to make the Society into a Blavatsky sect. Finally, the American Section split from the parent organization

22 Ryan, *op. cit.*, pp. 259–266. 23 *Ibid.*, pp. 301–304.

in 1895 and formed the Theosophical Society in America under the presidency of William Q. Judge. Similar schisms then
occurred in England, the European countries, and Australia,
and the Society was hopelessly and irrevocably divided. In
America only a few Lodges remained with the original Adyar
group; the majority of the European, Australian, and all the
Indian section remained faithful to Adyar.[24]

The Indian parent group still had its troubles. In about 1906
one of the prominent English members, Charles W. Leadbeater,
then living in Adyar, was accused of " infamous conduct and
teaching to boys confided to his care." Leadbeater was said to
have admitted the charges and resigned from the Society. He
was later reinstated after the death of President Olcott, when
Annie Besant became President. Another cause of disorder in
the Society was the President's endorsement of the Liberal
Catholic Church founded by Leadbeater. Many members
thought this was a departure from the original purpose of the
Society.[25]

In 1910 Mrs. Besant organized the Order of the Star in the
East to prepare for the coming of a great new World Teacher,
a new Christ. Jiddu Krishnamurti, a young Hindu boy, had
been chosen as its Head. It was believed he would provide the
physical vehicle for the incarnation of this very high adept; but
trouble reoccurred when the boy's father complained to Mrs.
Besant about Mr. Leadbeater's influence upon his son. When
Krishnamurti came of age, however, he dissolved the order and
left the Theosophical Society to lecture and write as an independent teacher.[26]

Theosophical Teachings

Before finishing the final phases of the history of Theosophy
with the accent on the American scene, let us turn to the Theosophical teachings. Theosophy teaches that man evolved from
animal, vegetable, mineral, and elemental life, as part of a group-

---

[24] *Ibid.*, pp. 325–333.
[25] *The Theosophical Movement, 1875–1925*, pp. 685–687.
[26] Ryan, *op. cit.*, pp. 337–339; also *The Theosophical Movement, 1875–1925*,
p. 686.

soul, before attaining manhood and his individual soul. Since the constituents of matter remain the same, though subject to rearrangement through evolution, even in the lowest stages the Theosophists may speak of the potentiality of a Shakespeare or a Beethoven residing in each small germ of life. From mineral life they believe there are two parallel streams of evolution: one is the human, and the other, entirely separate, leads from nature-spirits or fairies to angels or devas.[27]

According to Annie Besant, man is a spark of God, "a fragment of the life of God," which at one stage of its evolution individualized as a human ego. As a "Son of God, made in his image," he progresses through many reincarnations toward the realization of his true nature.

During any incarnation man consists of seven different bodies through which he either functions or has the potentiality to function. The three lowest ones making up his personality are discarded one by one after death, to be renewed in the next incarnation.

Besides his physical body man has an astral body. The word "astral," which is derived from the Greek word astēr, or star, is a term used by early occultists and alchemists such as Paracelsus. Paracelsus held that since man was a microcosm corresponding to the macrocosm, he therefore contained astral matter. This belief, predating Paracelsus, becomes basic to the idea that the heavenly bodies may affect mankind, and that their relative positions at the moment of each man's birth exert an influence upon the course of his life.

The idea of astral material in man was probably also the origin of Mesmer's belief in a magnetic fluid that could be transmitted from the planets through the mesmerizer to the subject. As before noted, this magnetic fluid was later considered by some as the force coming from the hands of the magnetizer. It gave rise to the "odic" force theory of the healing power emanating from the hands of the magnetizer. In Theosophy and other forms of occultism this astral substance becomes the basis for the astral plane and the astral body of man.

[27] C. Jinarajadasa, *First Principles of Theosophy* (The Theosophical Publishing House, 1947), pp. 20–25.

According to Annie Besant and other Theosophists, the astral body consists of matter with higher vibrations than the physical, and emits various colors, visible to a clairvoyant, in accord with one's emotions. The astral body is the vehicle of feelings and desires through which man has consciousness on the astral plane during sleep. Also if one has had strong desires while living, he will suffer intensely for a time when dead, because he will not have a physical body to gratify himself. Finally, the soul sheds its astral body and dwells temporarily on the mental plane, because the astral plane, though like a purgatory, is not a permanent place for the soul to inhabit.

The mental sphere has two divisions: the lower, which is divided into four subplanes; and the higher, consisting of three. Thus Theosophy postulates a lower mind and a higher one, known also as the causal body. These planes or bodies interpenetrate the lower ones in a way corresponding to the influx of Swedenborg's spiritual into the natural.

A part of the lower mental plane is a kind of heaven-world called devachan, where discarnate spirits enjoy the fruits of their good thoughts during life. After a time the lower mental body is cast off, leaving only the causal body, which becomes a higher-heaven world.

The causal body contains the true personality of the individual, his karma, representing the results of his earthly deeds, as well as the permanent atoms or seeds of his lower mental, astral, and physical bodies in his next incarnation.

The intuitional plane, where the Christ-nature manifests itself, is not very highly evolved in most people. Theosophists believe that when this matures, one will be able to discern the nature of reality and realize that there is only one unseparated Self in everything.

On the still higher spiritual plane, the last to unfold in human beings, the will becomes united with that of God. The two highest planes, the monadic and the divine, are only latent in man,[28] but presumedly develop during the superhuman state as progression continues.

[28] *Ibid.*, p. 159; also Annie Besant, *Theosophy* (T. C. and E. C. Jack, n.d.), pp. 23–40.

Theosophy teaches that once the soul has become individualized as a human being, it never returns to the animal stage, but only progresses. It need not reincarnate necessarily in the same ethnic race or stay in the same locality, however. One time it may have lived as a person on even Atlantis, Lemuria, or Mu, which Theosophists accept as ancient sunken continents.

A person may reincarnate either as a man or as a woman, but during any incarnation he usually associates with many known previously in a different relationship. The karma which has accrued through such contacts must be worked out in either the present life or in some future one.[29]

This process continues until one's karma permits him to attain the superhuman state when he may direct his own destiny by choosing whether or not he wants to accept Nirvana. Jinarajadasa explains the state of Nirvana as a higher spiritual activity incomprehensible to our consciousness, and does not entail extinction as sometimes interpreted. As an alternative to accepting Nirvana one may choose to remain close to this world and help mankind. He then becomes an official member of the Great White Brotherhood of Masters.[30] Theosophy shows a similarity to Buddhism at this point. Forgoing the acceptance of Nirvana to help man on earth is an ideal in Mahayana Buddhism.

The soul's awakening begins when a person becomes altruistic rather than self-seeking, at which time a master will appear and take him as his disciple. Then a period of probation begins with purification and adjustments of karma, so the pupil will have opportunities for wider knowledge and self-expression through service. During this time he gradually becomes more closely related to the master and his work until he is proposed for Initiation into the Great White Brotherhood. Upon becoming a master, he transcends his causal body, which disappears. He now functions on the intuitional plane, and his will is united with the will of the Logos that the majority of mankind shall fit into His plan.[31] As His agent he becomes a supervisor of a particular

[29] Jinarajadasa, *op cit.*, pp. 61–89.
[30] *Ibid.*, pp. 226–228.
[31] *Ibid.*, pp. 328–340.

department in life's evolution and a directing power behind the world's government.[32]

The Theosophists believe these masters have been historical persons who have finished their earthly evolution and have acquired power over space, time, mind, and matter. Among these are founders of religions, such as Confucius, the Buddha, and Jesus; Old Testament figures, e.g., Abraham, Moses, and Solomon; and even many from India and Tibet, who are unknown to most of the West. In order to bring new truths to mankind, they have often worked through messengers, e.g., St. Germain, Jakob Boehme, Paracelsus, Mesmer, and Madame Blavatsky.[33]

The masters of this world's inner government form a graded hierarchy with ten initiations. Among those at the top is the Lord of the World, transmitter of energies from the Logos; the World Teacher or Bodhisattva, bestower of divine Wisdom; and the Maha-Chohan, who reveals " activities which are typical of the Third Logos, the ' Holy Ghost '." Also important are the Silent Watcher, the former Lord of the World in the last round of development; and the Buddha, who was previously the World Teacher.[34]

According to the Theosophical lectures of Thomas Yerex, the World Teacher or Bodhisattva is also known as the Lord Maitreya, the future Buddha of the Buddhists. In order to reveal new truths, he has incarnated many times, using as his vehicle, Krishna in India, Mithra in Persia, Lao-tzu and Confucius in China, and Jesus of Galilee, who was not crucified but only disappeared. In fact, it is taught that he is still living today as a master among the Druses of the Lebanon mountains. Thus Jesus, who became a master, is to be distinguished from Maitreya, who is believed to have occupied Jesus' body. This same Maitreya or Christ-consciousness was to have used the body of Krishnamurti, who was being trained for this role as a new World Teacher until his disconnection from the Theosophical Society.

[32] *Ibid.*, pp. 1–3.

[33] William Q. Judge, *The Ocean of Theosophy*, 15th ed. (The Theosophy Co., 1943), pp. 1–10.

[34] Jinarajadasa, *op. cit.*, pp. 318–323.

Gottfried de Purucker, former president of the American Society at Point Loma, believed there was a connection, unrecognized by Christians, between ideas about Jesus and those in the ancient mystery religions. He interpreted the Christian Scriptures allegorically as referring to the cycle of Jesus' initiations into the mysteries. The Christ-Spirit, the Logos or the Word, was the spiritual sun. This did not mean Christians were sun worshipers any more than were the Persian worshipers of Mithra, but rather that the physical sun was a manifestation of the inner spiritual and intellectual powers which flowed from it. He wrote:

" Behind the physical sun is the Cosmic Solar Spirit, which works outwards through the physical sun, even as man's spirit and his intellect and his intuition, his sympathies, his love, his pity, his compassion . . . work through him and give light not only unto himself but unto others. It is this divine sun that is the source of the individual Christ spirit that is in all men." [35]

These latter ideas stem from an occultism dating in its rudiments from the early centuries of our Christian era, as before noted. Occultists have depicted the universe as a macrocosm or cosmic man to which man, the microcosm, corresponds. Rather close to this was Swedenborg's conception that the planes of the heavens and hells had the form of a cosmic man, in one part of which each spirit resides according to its classification. The physical sun was the embodiment of a spiritual sun seen in the spirit world as a manifestation of the Lord. Andrew Jackson Davis and Madame Blavatsky held similar solar views. Also Davis' physical and heavenly planes, like Theosophy's seven planes of man's nature, lead to the divine sun and form parts of a whole. Davis stops here in his cosmology, but Theosophy has higher celestial ramifications, as we shall presently see.

Theosophy's cosmology is essentially a theogony of emanations from the Divine One, and since Theosophy teaches that all religious philosophies have similar truth, it does not seem strange to the followers that its expression is made in both Neoplatonic and Hindu terms. Annie Besant, in her *Esoteric Chris-*

[35] Gottfried de Purucker, *The Esoteric Tradition* (Theosophical University Press, 1935), Vol. 2, pp. 1079–1101; also Blavatsky, *op. cit.*, Vol. 1, pp. 29, 255.

tianity, *or the Lesser Mysteries,* chose essentially the former, but equated this truth with that found in the mystery religions of Egypt, Persia, Greece, as well as the Gnostics.[36] Closer to a typically Theosophical expression, however, is the view of Jinarajadasa, a former president of the Theosophical Society.

First, there is the One without a second, known as God, Allah, etc., but particularly by Theosophists as the Cosmic Logos. He energizes the universe in three modes of expression as Brahma, the Creator; Vishnu, the Preserver; and Shiva, the Destroyer.[37] As the Cosmic Logos in action, he has seven embodiments of his nature, the seven Cosmic Planetary Logoi, to one of which every star is associated and finds expression in its life. One such star is the Solar Logos, the Lord of our solar system, and God for mankind on earth. Though he mirrors the Cosmic Logos and his seven expressions, he also energizes his own system as a Trinity of the Father, Son, and Holy Ghost; and manifests himself in the seven Planetary Logoi, corresponding to the Seven Prajāpati in Hinduism; the seven Amesha Spentas in Zoroastrianism; and the seven spirits before the throne of God in the Hebrew-Christian tradition. Again each of these is the Head of hierarchies of creative entities that build and sustain the solar system, the Devas or Angelic Hosts, etc.[38] We have now arrived at the point where the masters help execute the plan of the Logos and constitute the world's inner government. The Lord of the World, the Bodhisattva, and the Maha-Chohan form the lowest of these superhuman divine Trinities at the head of our world's hierarchy of masters.

Theosophy, like the other metaphysical groups, claims to be a philosophy, a religion, and a science. As a science, it tries to discover hidden spiritual laws, while believing that ultimately both spiritual and natural laws will be discovered to be one.

As a religion, Theosophy aims to be nonsectarian, nondogmatic, and the ground of every religion. It therefore views all religions as essentially the same, but separated from one another

36 Annie Besant, *Esoteric Christianity, or the Lesser Mysteries* (Theosophical Publishing House, 1901), pp. 22–26.

37 These three are the Hindu expression of the three ways in which the Absolute Brahman or God manifests itself.

38 Jinarajadasa, *op. cit.,* pp. 188–194.

only by the dogmas and encrusted superstitions, when the pure truths have been lost. To learn and to accept the hidden esoteric meaning in the sacred texts would be, according to Theosophists, to discover the unity of these great primordial truths in all religions. Consequently, for the outside critic to point at Theosophy's obvious eclecticism would be quite agreeable to most Theosophists. They would only pity him who could not see the oneness of truth.

If critics point to differences between Theosophy and Christianity, Theosophists will answer that they are not against the teachings of Jesus, but against the dogmas developed by the church. Perhaps the fact that Theosophists have placed the Buddha one initiation higher than the Christ, whose traditional significance as been obliterated, has helped make Theosophy less palatable to most Christians. If others mention the strong Buddhist influence, due perhaps in part to Olcott's interests, Theosophists will reply that their views, though not Buddhist, contain the same truths.

In the beginning of the movement few Christians were interested in Theosophy. Its members were those concerned with the occult, and included many Spiritualists, even though as a whole they were numbered among its strongest critics.

Whether correctly or not, Theosophists have claimed among their adherents some scientists such as Thomas Edison, Sir William Crookes in his later years, and Luther Burbank. The writer himself remembers that a distinguished Dean of the Engineering Department of the University of Washington was once the head of one of the Lodges, and more recently a president of a Christian college was numbered among its ranks. Indeed, besides a few Christian laymen, even a small number of ministers have become interested in Theosophical teachings, although the greatest influence is still upon other sects of the metaphysical movement.

The Point Loma Experiment and Later History of Theosophy

The story of Theosophy would not be complete without some mention of Katherine Tingley's very interesting Point

Loma experiment, which adds an important part to Theosophy's American development. For this account one can utilize the objective treatment of the movement written by E. A. Greenwalt, to whom the writer is greatly indebted.[39]

Katherine Tingley, who was born in 1847 of Puritan stock, had much in common with her older contemporary, Madame Blavatsky. Like her, she seemed unsuited for happy matrimony, rebelled against religious conservatism, spent many years in travel, became interested in Spiritualism, and was mediumistic. It has been hinted that she was also a member of a traveling stock company for a time, and her later dramatic productions seem to bear out the truth of this surmise.

Mrs. Tingley combined an interest in the occult with a real flair for social work. Perhaps the latter reflected the growing Protestant emphasis of the times, because in the 1890's Protestant pulpits had already begun a crescendo, proclaiming society's salvation through social reform. It would seem that after her first two unhappy marriages Mrs. Tingley was ready to give up her interest in family life for a short time and plunged herself into social work. She organized the Society of Mercy to visit prisons and hospitals, supporting the work by dramatic recitals and spiritualistic readings.

Finally, after venturing into a third marriage to Philip B. Tingley in 1888 and opening the Do-Good Mission on the East Side of New York in the '90s, she became acquainted with William Q. Judge. He taught her about Theosophy, which she felt to be more substantial than Spiritualism. From then on through the trying times when he was accused of forgery and fraud until his death in 1896, she was his staunch supporter. And afterward, it was she who called together the Theosophical leaders in a series of history-making conferences.

In 1896 at the convention of the Theosophical Society in America, Ernest Hargrove was confirmed as president, and Katherine Tingley brought news from Judge through her mediumship. She also proposed a " School for the Revival of the Lost Mysteries of Antiquity," which was in line with Madame

[39] Emmett A. Greenwalt, *The Point Loma Community in California, 1897–1942: A Theosophical Experiment* (University of California Press, 1955).

Blavatsky's idea that modern science, philosophy, and religion should utilize the "Ancient Wisdom."

The name of the person who was to be the Outer Head of the important Esoteric Section, the one with real power as spokesman for the masters, was not disclosed at the convention. But later at a wedding President Hargrove revealed that Katherine Tingley was to occupy this office.

Moreover, he reported that Mrs. Tingley had planned a Theosophical crusade throughout the world, which would culminate in founding a school in the West. It would seem that hers was not to be an ordinary school, however, but a utopian community where, besides the basic courses, all might learn and put to use the "Ancient Wisdom."

As Greenwalt reminds us, this was a period when many were interested in utopias, because between 1884 and 1900 there were at least forty-eight utopian romances published, such as Ignatius Donnelly's *Caesar's Column*, his *Atlantis: The Antediluvian World*, and Edward Bellamy's *Looking Backward*. Utopian communities had been founded earlier, such as Robert Owen's New Harmony, the Brook Farm experiment, the Amana villages, and the Oneida community; and economic stresses in the '90s helped foster, among others, an unsuccessful utopia at Altruria, California.

In 1896 the crusade of Theosophists headed by Tingley and Hargrove invaded the major countries of the world. Their mission in England, despite opposition from the Besant Lodges, received favorable response from the newspapers, because the Theosophists did not limit themselves to the higher classes, but gave Brotherhood suppers to which even the destitute were invited.

Ireland also was responsive, and delegates from many countries swarmed to the Dublin convention where the Theosophical Society of Europe was organized. Hargrove was elected President and Katherine Tingley became Corresponding Secretary, the post formerly held by Madame Blavatsky in the parent organization.

After establishing footholds in other European countries, Asia, and Africa, they made their way to India. If they had had only skirmishes with the Besant forces so far, they were to have their first real battle in India, because there they were confronted by Olcott and Besant, who had already suffered the loss of the American Lodges to Judge.

The latter were not ready to surrender to the invasion of their own territory. Concomitant with the crusaders' arrival in Bombay, a notice appeared in the *Times of India* over the signatures of Olcott, Besant, and other Adyar leaders repudiating " certain persons who are at present masquerading in India under the name of the Theosophical Society." The crusaders counterattacked in the *Bombay Gazette*, claiming that the real Headquarters were founded in New York and that the American Society constituted about three fourths of the Theosophical membership. Katherine Tingley, however, was no match there for Annie Besant. Contrary to Mrs. Tingley, Annie Besant had not only praised India's culture instead of criticizing it, but also had done so much for education and social amelioration that she was honored by becoming the first female president of the Indian National Congress.

Still Katherine Tingley was able to capitalize on the Indian venture in a different way. Knowing that the Outer Head presupposed the Inner Head of Masters, she was determined to meet one of these adepts, as Madame Blavatsky had allegedly done. Having learned from the latter's description the approximate location of one of their retreats, she began her search with Hargrove, who was reluctant to let her travel alone. At Darjeeling, however, during the night she quietly stole away from her all too suspicious companion. Upon returning two days later, she spoke in enraptured tones of her meeting with a master in the shadow of the Himalayas — a master clothed in Tibetan garb and " whittling on a yoke peg, while one of his chelas plowed a nearby field."

From India the crusade moved its sphere of operations to Ceylon, and then to Australia in time for its annual Theosophical convention. The Australian branch, which had only recently broken with Adyar, allied itself with the Tingleys and promptly elected Americans as its principal officers.

In 1897, just before the triumphal return home, the place for the new community and school had been purchased at Point Loma in San Diego, where two years later lavishly built edifices would begin to rise above the wind-swept heights. About the time the first cornerstone was laid, however, the papers in New York and elsewhere took pleasure in announcing the reinvasion by Annie Besant, who scored a sweeping victory. Katherine Tingley, battle-weary from her crusade, did not contest her rival. Therefore, when Mrs. Besant returned to India in 1897, she was able to claim about fifty Lodges, approximately one third formerly credited to the American association.

Meanwhile, Katherine Tingley, in the vanguard of her organization, plunged herself into social work. A home for " unfortunate women " was established in Buffalo. In California, Theosophical meetings were being held in prisons. She then founded the International Brotherhood League with herself as life president. It aimed to teach Universal Brotherhood to children of all nations, to give aid to " unfortunate women," to rehabilitate those who had been in prisons, and to help all suffering people, including those who had been visited by such calamities as flood, famine, and war.

This was no dummy organization, and the war with Spain in 1898 offered new opportunities for Mrs. Tingley. When twenty-two thousand sick men were sent back from the fever-ridden Cuban swamps to Camp Wickoff on Long Island, the United States was not prepared to provide enough ambulances. Katherine Tingley, however, quickly organized the Sisters of Compassion and the Relief Committee of the International Brotherhood League, known also as the War Relief Corps. It quickly pitched tents near the docks and gave help to the thousands who poured from the ships to be stranded on the shore. The newspapers praised her work, President McKinley commended her, and the War Department addressed a notice to the Commanding Generals in Cuba, Puerto Rico, and the Philippines authorizing cooperation with the Brotherhood League. When peace was declared in 1898, Katherine Tingley and her assistants moved into Santiago de Cuba and gave emergency relief to sixteen hundred Cubans.

Meanwhile, many Theosophists cared little for this social emphasis and preferred their old Lodge meetings and lectures on the " Ancient Wisdom." President Hargrove shared this disaffection, but doubtless felt like a puppet dancing to the tune of Mrs. Tingley. Shorn of his power but suspicious after the Darjeeling incident, he decided to resign the presidency, seek out allies, and regain his position at the next convention. With sufficient backing he could displace Mrs. Tingley and redesign the pattern.

If Katherine Tingley's crown was heavy, she was still not to be easily dethroned. Word of Hargrove's intentions reached her, and she quietly planned her own *coup d'état*. Before the convention she drew up a new constitution under the name of Universal Brotherhood and Theosophical Society, according to which she would be " Leader and Official Head " for life, with the sole right of appointing and removing officers. A two-thirds vote of any congress, which only she could call, would be necessary for any amendment, which she still had to endorse.

Having gained approval of the constitution from several of her closest supporters, at the 1898 convention she turned it over to a committee on resolutions composed largely of her henchmen. The committee then presented it to the convention and quickly moved its adoption without debate. The Hargrove faction was taken completely by surprise and failed to keep it from passing by 290 against 24. Protests were to no avail, and even the courts turned down their appeal. Soon the dissident Lodges, which existed briefly as a separate group, dwindled and dissolved. The London group also received the constitution and approved it.

With autocracy secure by divine and civil right, and the war with Spain now over, Madame Tingley rushed to Point Loma to make real her dream castles. Through aid from wealthy Theosophists the settlement became a tourist attraction by 1900, and the following year it provided tourist guides and collected admission fees from more than one hundred daily visitors. Inside its Roman and Egyptian gates rose massive buildings, whose great round domes with leaded glass were strange and bizarre like illustrations for a fairy tale. But this was not to be just an exotic Disneyland, but a community of American Theosophists and others who would study and develop under the Tingley plan.

The school, which provided for all ages through college, charged tuition in accord with its students' means at first, but later raised it to a residence fee of five hundred dollars, in order to keep out promiscuous entries.

The Tingley educational theory approached the Platonic idea of controlled environment. Children were separated into groups of six to twelve members with one teacher in charge of each both day and night. They lived together in boys' and girls' dormitories and were only allowed to see their parents on Sunday afternoons.

The basic philosophy stressed the physical and spiritual duality of man. Although the physical had its weaknesses, its passions, and its imperfections, it was not evil but undeveloped good. The spiritual soul, the real knower and inspirer through its vehicle, the mind, could open up infinite human possibilities. To attain the spiritual apogee and let the flood tide of inspiration flow into one's daily life, Mrs. Tingley believed that self-control had to be taught at an early age. By curbing the lower nature the higher self would have a chance to express itself in the individual. It is said that observers had noticed a seriousness in work among even the very young that was not apparent among those in public schools.

Of the twenty-five hundred students who were graduated from the school, the results varied, although not perhaps because of the courses taught. Besides the " Ancient Wisdom " there were basic educational subjects and many practical courses such as domestic science for girls. Some, however, had revolted because of the strict discipline; others were described as being like " babes in the wood " when they were forced to depend on themselves in the world. Still others did very well outside Point Loma's confines, particularly those in music and arts. Drama critics praised the school's productions of plays, and Walter Damrosch, director of the New York Symphony, lauded its orchestra when he at one time became its guest conductor.

Besides its cultural achievements, Point Loma developed extensive gardens and orchards, which became world-renowned for their yield and for agricultural experimentation that attracted the attention of the U.S. Department of Agriculture and various universities at home and abroad. It was a pioneer in raising avocados, and this thriving California industry as well as others owes much to Point Loma experimentation.

Notwithstanding the outward appearances of success, the expenditures had been greater than the income, and a crisis became imminent in the twenties. Mrs. Tingley's former wealthy backers had passed away one by one. There were by this time no Lodges from which support could be drawn. Mrs. Tingley had disbanded the Lodges after weakening them by drawing most of the Theosophical leaders to Point Loma. Many dissatisfied Theosophists had formed separate autonomous Lodges in the United Lodge of Theosophists, which was organized in 1909 by Robert Crosbie after his ejection from Point Loma for insubordination. The situation at Point Loma became critical in 1928, when much of the property had to be sold to meet the demands of creditors. And to make matters still worse, Katherine Tingley died in Europe following an automobile accident.

Gottfried de Purucker, a prominent Theosophical writer and teacher at Point Loma, became the new head who tried in vain to help the situation. He changed the name of the organization to the old title of Theosophical Society, reduced the staff, and cut down the program, but still they were plagued by debts. While seeking strength by trying to revive the Lodges, he even approached Annie Besant concerning reunification on the hundredth anniversary of Madame Blavatsky's birth, August 11, 1931. He claimed the masters Morya and Koot Hoomi had talked with him about starting this fraternization.

Annie Besant accepted his proposal, replying that one of the masters, the Chohan, had approved. Unfortunately, however, she made the mistake of announcing that Bishop Leadbeater would accompany her to the centennial meeting. Because of Leadbeater's unpopularity with so many of the Theosophists, de Purucker sent his refusal to allow a Liberal Catholic at a meeting for only Theosophists. Consequently, the conference never took place, even though Leadbeater was later invited to come.

As Point Loma continued to decline, its buildings and grounds insufficiently maintained and student body diminishing, a move became necessary. Therefore, in 1942 the community bought the property of the former California Preparatory School for Boys at Covina near Los Angeles, and Point Loma became the site for California Western University. The Covina estate also could not be maintained, and after surrendering it to the California Baptist Theological Seminary in 1950–1951, the organization selected three separate sites in Pasadena and a Headquarters in Altadena near Pasadena.[40]

After de Purucker's sudden death in 1942, an attempt was made to change the constitution to a more democratic form, and finally Colonel A. L. Conger was anounced as President in 1945. With his passing in 1951 the Society again experienced trouble, because the Cabinet opposed the appointment of William Hartley, whom Conger had chosen as his successor. J. A. Long secured the Cabinet's agreement to reject Hartley on the grounds that he had presented a photostat of the appointment instead of the original copy. Long then immediately announced that the " Leader " had *taken possession of the office,* when he, Long, rejected Hartley's claim. This again split the now very small Society. Since Hartley's death in 1956, no new successor has been named to his branch, while Long still claims his organization to be the only " formal organization through which the White Lodge works." [41]

Thus through continual fragmentation and lack of growth this one branch of the Theosophical Society has almost lost its existence, but the parent Society too has suffered from schisms. Dr. Rudolf Steiner, an outstanding Goethe authority and leader in the German section of the Society, rebelled against the formation of the Order of the Star of the East to promote Krishnamurti as a new messiah. When Steiner subsequently expelled members from the German section for belonging to the Order, Annie Besant retaliated by canceling his Charter. She offered reinstatement to Lodges that would abide by the Society's Constitution, which prohibited expulsion of any person on account

40 *Ibid., passim.*
41 Pierce Spinks, *Theosophists: Reunite!* (Christopher Publishing House, 1958), pp. 72–73.

of his belief. In 1912 Dr. Steiner founded the Anthroposophical Society, which has become quite influential in Germany and in other parts of Europe, and now has centers in the major cities of the United States.

Conflict over the Liberal Catholic Church, founded by Charles Leadbeater with Annie Besant's endorsement, has caused many Theosophists to leave the Society or be removed from its rolls. Among the latter was T. H. Martyn, formerly General Secretary of the Australian Section of the Theosophical Society, who in 1923 founded the Independent Theosophical Society.[42]

In America further splits have also occurred. Max Heindel, a former lecturer for the Adyar Theosophists, broke away to found the Rosicrucian Fellowship of Oceanside, California. A splinter from that took root in San Francisco under the name of the Rosicrucian Anthroposophic League. In Los Angeles the Gnostic Society, emphasizing the study of Madame Blavatsky's works, was organized.[43] Probably the most important American schism has been Alice Bailey's Arcane School, whose interesting story will be told later.

F. Pierce Spinks, a Theosophist who received his education at Point Loma, believes Theosophists would like to be united, since their chief differences have been less over beliefs than over leadership, but Universal Brotherhood, the first and primary aim of all the Societies, has not been practiced. To be sure, there have been difficulties over what the Society should emphasize, but the greatest problem has concerned its final authority — Madame Blavatsky, Annie Besant, William Q. Judge, or someone else.[44]

According to their Constitutions, it would be possible for a person to be a Theosophist and carry out to the letter the objectives without ever believing in the masters' infallibility, although that person might be hard to find. On the contrary, Theosophists have relied too greatly on the alleged masters' statements, which was not even Madame Blavatsky's intention. As Spinks reminds us, Madame Blavatsky herself opposed anything approaching a dogmatic fanaticism based on anyone's infallibil-

[42] *Ibid.*, pp. 74–75.   [43] *Ibid.*, p. 82.   [44] *Ibid., passim.*

ity.[45] Certainly there is apt to be trouble within an organization when two or more persons claim an authoritative special revelation. But if Theosophy's multiple divisions and loss of strength are due primarily to personal differences rather than to belief, one might finally ask what is the meaning of "Universal Brotherhood," if it does not connote understanding, self-sacrifice, forgiveness, and repentance for one's own shortcomings.

THE ARCANE SCHOOL

The Story of Alice Bailey

If Theosophy, like a once bright flame, seems to be dwindling to a flicker, the Arcane School is rising like a phoenix from its embers. Although Alice Bailey's movement is not yet well known, her books, which are being read in many languages, are beginning to become influential among members of the organized Christian churches.

The founder, who was born as Alice La Trobe Bateman in Manchester, England, in 1880, was of a well-to-do family, proudly tracing its lineage back to Hollingshead, "The Chronicler." Both she and her sister received their early education from private tutors, and this secluded life was not to Alice's liking.[1] Her misery was at times so intense that she tried to commit suicide on three occasions before she was fifteen years old.[2]

Although, as a member of the Church of England, she says she had an interest in religion and became a Sunday school teacher, an important event in her life allegedly preceded when she was only fifteen.

One Sunday morning while she was at home reading, the door suddenly opened and a tall stranger clad in European clothes and a turban walked in and sat down beside her. She was terrified at first until he began to speak. He told her of the important work planned for her in the world, but to do it, she

---

[45] *Ibid.*, p. 231.

[1] Alice Bailey, *The Unfinished Autobiography* (Lucis Trust Publishing Co., 1951), pp. 12–25.

[2] *Ibid.*, p. 21.

would have to change her disposition considerably and start to exercise some self-control. Then, after promising to keep in touch with her at several years' intervals, he departed.

His visit had been brief, and although she had not known his identity, she supposed that he was Jesus. She said that it was not until 1915 that she learned his name, after seeing his picture on the wall at the Theosophical Society. Only then did she realize that he had actually been Koot Hoomi, whom she believed close to Christ, and one who had collaborated with Madame Blavatsky.

On another occasion she told of her very strange vision of being somewhere in the Himalaya Mountains, where she was attending the Wesak festival celebrating the birth of the Buddha. There she saw the Christ standing with two other figures, when suddenly they stretched out their arms toward the heavens where still another person descended. Subjectively she recognized the last one to be the Buddha. Still it did not seem to her that the Christ was " belittled," but only that all existence was moving in unison toward the demonstration of God's glory.

During her adolescence Alice was emotionally torn by two conflicting presentiments of her religion. On the one hand, she described herself as a fundamentalist believing in a transcendent, often cruel God, who loved only those who recognized him, and who had slain his only Son so that people might be saved. On the other hand, she had an innate tendency toward mysticism expressing itself in her continued search for the immanent presence of God in nature, whether on the Scottish moors, or on a green hillside near Lake Geneva. This was a God behind all forms, who loved all beings good and bad, and who could be really known. Her conflict was not resolved until she left the church for a newfound faith. In the meantime, the first presentiment ruled her heart and drove her relentlessly to the task of saving souls from hell.

Before she was of age, she became interested in Y.W.C.A. work. This led to a position connected with the British army when she was twenty-two. She was employed by various associated soldiers' homes stretching from Ireland to India and was now able to pursue her evangelism more freely.

One Sunday afternoon in Quetta, Baluchistan, she preached on the fire and brimstone of hell, and succeeded in losing most of her audience.[3] Afterward, when rebuked by one of the soldiers for not preaching the truth, she again became so disturbed that the event helped to contribute to a nervous breakdown.

After the failure of her mental and physical health, she returned to England where she married Walter Evans, whom she had met in India. Their union was brief. Upon coming to America, where her husband studied to become an Episcopal priest, they soon separated and were divorced.[4]

A good deal of mental suffering occurred before she was introduced to Theosophy through friends at Pacific Grove, California. In a short time, however, she felt her understanding of it was clearer than that of most Theosophists, because she had the advantage of learning from two former students of Madame Blavatsky.

Three Theosophical beliefs gave her immediate mental satisfaction, she said: first, the idea of a divine plan, according to which humanity was slowly returning to God, made sense to her; secondly, the view that a hierarchy of masters, led by Christ, was working to fulfill the plan replaced the concept of Christ and his church; and thirdly, the doctrines of karma and reincarnation offered her a solution more acceptable to her individual and personal problems.[5]

One might wish to note, however, that in trying to reconcile her former beliefs with Theosophy she not only departed from her fundamentalist position, but also, due to her added emphasis upon the Christ, she invited criticism by Theosophists.

After her increasing interest in Theosophy brought her to the American Headquarters of the Theosophical Society, then at Krotona, California,[6] she met and later married Foster Bailey, the present head of the Arcane School. He became National Secretary of the Theosophical Society, and she, editor of the sectional magazine, *The Messenger*.

Just two years later, in 1919, Alice Bailey claimed that she first contacted the master known as the Tibetan, hearing his

---

[3] *Ibid.*, pp. 31–84.
[4] *Ibid.*, pp. 86–104, 124–125, 156.

[5] *Ibid.*, pp. 138–140.
[6] *Ibid.*, p. 144.

voice while alone on a hillside. He asked whether she would be his amanuensis for some books he would write. After first refusing, she said she later accepted when her own master, K. H., gave his approval. *The Theosophist* published a few chapters of the first work entitled *Initiation, Human and Solar* and then stopped, for reasons that Alice Bailey referred to as " theosophical jealousy and reactionary attitude."

After joining the Esoteric Section of the Society and finding disharmony among its members, she herself became quite critical of its policies. She objected that to be a " good member " one had to sever conections with other groups and pledge loyalty to the Outer Head; or to be a disciple of the masters one had to be notified by Annie Besant, who had apparently overlooked her. Finally, she found fault with the demand to accept the authority of the Esoteric Section. The severity of the controversy, which developed within the group, caused Foster Bailey to complain to Mrs. Besant. She sent B. P. Wadia from India to arbitrate, but to no avail.

The troubles increased to a climax at the annual convention at Chicago in 1920. Alice and others felt that the autonomy of the American Lodges was threatened because only members of the Esoteric Section controlled by Mrs. Besant were put into office. After much argument the Esoteric Section prevailed. The American president resigned in favor of Louis Rogers, who dismissed both Foster Bailey and Alice from their positions, thus ending their services in the Society. After their marriage in New York their work led to the founding of the Arcane School.

Founding the Arcane School

In New York, Alice Bailey at first divided her time between teaching classes on the Secret Doctrine and publishing works by the alleged Tibetan master. Then due to increased correspondence resulting from the sale of her books, she and her husband organized the Arcane School in April, 1923.

The inspiration for the school is credited to Madame Blavatsky. Through a friend of William Q. Judge, the Baileys had received a copy of Madame Blavatsky's instructions for organizing the Esoteric Section. They also discovered in one of Judge's papers the assertion that she had desired it to be called the Arcane School, whose name they decided to use for their own organization.

The Arcane School offers graded courses in its occult philosophy. Their popularity has been sufficient to require the services of 140 secretaries, who are senior students, besides the staff at Headquarters. More than 30,000 students representing nearly every country of the world have allegedly taken its courses, and in addition to the New York offices the Arcane School has others in England, Holland, Italy, and Switzerland.

It considers itself as nonsectarian, and its students are not required to separate from any organization to which they belong. Moreover, although its teachings differ certainly from those of Christianity, many of its members are listed on the rolls of Christian churches. This influence may be due to the Arcane School's claim of bringing men closer to God independently of theology. It affirms that if it can succeed in deepening their spiritual life, they should continue to perform in the church and society in whatever groups they are in. The principal requirement is to " remember that all paths lead to God and that the welfare of the one humanity governs all their thinking."

The spiritual life, which the organization strives to develop in its students, is not supposed to be a *selfish* self-development, however. Alice Bailey called it a true occult obedience. Although this is the obedience to the dictates of one's soul, it allegedly orients the student toward a life of service as the way to approach the masters.[7] This twofold emphasis of self-development and service to others is purported to have been given by Djwhal Khul, the Tibetan master, through the instrumentality of Alice Bailey. Therefore, the Arcane School represents itself as a mystery school in which the individual through meditation strives to " build the new man in Christ." It seeks workers, a part of whom may qualify to act directly under the masters.

Alice Bailey felt that present so-called esoteric schools were only preparatory to the real one which is yet to be established.

[7] *Ibid.*, pp. 155–197.

In her opinion the masters had been inadequately represented. The different organizations had built closed corporations of adherents who follow the commands of masters. But this, she said, violated " the occult law that no Master ever gives a command or expects obedience." While not willing to indict others for trying to establish such esoteric mystery schools, she conjectured that humanity was still not ready for them. Nevertheless, she was confident there were now enough intelligent men and women to warrant forming advanced preparatory training schools, which during the next seventy years would make possible the real esoteric one. By that time teachers would understand the spiritual nature of authority, so they would merely tread the way for others to follow, and students would contact the masters directly.[8]

The Arcane School does not demand obedience to any master, but emphasizes following the master in one's heart, considered as the true spriritual man. Consequently, no person is obliged to believe any teaching, whether it be the existence of the masters, the hierarchy, or reincarnation. Nor is loyalty to the Arcane School demanded. The keynote of the school is " *service*, based on *love of humanity*." [9] And since service is such an important concept for the Arcane School, let us explore its meaning and expression.

New Group of World Servers

In 1932 the Arcane School issued a pamphlet entitled the *New Group of World Servers*, describing the formation of a group that would become the " nucleus of the coming world civilization." Each member should have such qualities as " a potent desire selflessly to serve one's fellow men plus a definite sense of spiritual guidance, emanating from the inner side of life." Of its two divisions, one consists of those aspiring to be disciples of the masters, and who will act as intermediaries between the hierarchy and the mass of humanity. The masters,

---

[8] Alice Bailey, *What Is an Esoteric School?* (Lucis Trust Publishing Co., n.d.), pp. 2–3.
[9] *My Work*, by the Tibetan (Lucis Trust Publishing Co., n.d.), p. 6.

working under the Christ, will develop plans for the salvation of the world through it, so that during the next two thousand years the barriers between men and nations will slowly disappear. The disciples and spiritual aspirants, who will treat all men alike regardless of race, creed, or color, will work for " the promotion of international understanding, economic sharing, and religious unity."

The second group of servers is composed of men of good will, who want justice and kindness to prevail throughout the world. They may know nothing about the hierarchy of masters, but they will be trained in practical ways of expressing goodwill under the direction of the masters' disciples.[10]

The Arcane School has a number of subsidiary organizations, such as its publishing company, the Lucis Trust, the World Goodwill Information and Research Service, and the Triangles. Among its periodicals is *The Beacon*, which aims to present " deeper meanings behind surface events " and " to stimulate an understanding of the spiritual realities which can influence and control human attitudes and behavior." This institution is accredited by the United Nations in New York and in Geneva as a nongovernmental organization, whose work is being financed by voluntary donations from interested people throughout the world.

The Triangles, which began in 1937, represent still another activity, whose purpose is " to unite like-minded men and women of goodwill in a spiritual service to humanity." Here the Lucis Trust promotes units of three people sharing the same purposes and similar thoughts to unite with other similar groups in " using the power of thought and of prayer to set creative energies in motion and to release light and goodwill into the subjective atmosphere of human consciousness." From its founding year to 1958 there have been about seven thousand workers registered as members.[11] These ways in which the Arcane School endeavors to promote spiritual and social welfare are to help prepare mankind for the New Age.

The Arcane School, like all others stressing occult doctrines

[10] Alice Bailey, *The Unfinished Autobiography*, pp. 230–234.
[11] *Lucis Trust*, 1958, *passim* (brochure with unnumbered pages).

kindred to Astrology, believes we are now about to enter a New Age, the Aquarian Age, as distinguished from the former, the Piscean. Astrologers have divided the heavens, through which the planets and sun pass, into twelve zones or signs of the zodiac, whose names represent twelve constellations. The occultists teach that the sun has appeared to move through the constellation of Pisces, the fish, for a period coterminous with the Christian era. But soon it will seem to pass through the constellation of Aquarius, the water carrier, marking a New Age and a new religious dispensation, which many occultists believe will terminate the Christian period. The Arcane School takes a mediating position that portrays Jesus Christ as recognizing this coming era at the time of the Last Supper. According to Alice Bailey, the New Age will witness the real meeting between East and West, the fusion of Christianity and Buddhism, and the advent of the Messiah.

The Second Coming of Christ

The Arcane School discloses that the Messiah of the New Age is the Christ, who, with his disciples, the masters, will approach closer to humanity and appear on the physical plane. At this point one might logically ask concerning the original unmentioned disciples, whose places seem to have been taken mostly by those of Hindu or Tibetan origin.

The Reappearance of the Christ, apparently written by Mrs. Bailey just after World War II, predicts that due to the great human distress, the divine will-to-good will be transformed into human goodwill, which will result in peace on earth. The return of the Christ, she said, necessitated three conditions that have already come to pass: " First: a general planetary condition which has unfortunately (owing to man's selfishness) proved to be so catastrophic in nature that humanity has been forced to recognize the cause and source of the disaster; secondly: a spiritual awakening which would have its impulse in the deepest depths of man's consciousness and such is the case today as a result of the World War (1941–1945); thirdly: a steadily mounting invocative cry, prayer, or demand, directed toward high spiritual sources, no matter by what name such sources may be called." [12]

The activities of the New Group of World Servers, forming the general staff of the Christ, are accepted as signs of Christ's coming. Mrs. Bailey said that through their work and the effect of a special Great Invocation the message had gone to Christ's dwelling place and higher to the Father, so that he will direct his attention to humanity and accomplish his purposes more quickly.

The Great Invocation

The Arcane School's men of goodwill have been responsible for spreading the use of the Great Invocation, as one of their activities since 1935. Most persons listening to their radios or television sets late at night will perhaps have heard it at some time. It is used regularly by many stations as the closing prayer when signing off. It reads:

> From the point of Light within the Mind of God
> Let Light stream forth into the minds of men.
> Let Light descend on Earth.
>
> From the point of Love within the Heart of God
> Let Love stream forth into the hearts of men.
> May Christ return to Earth.
>
> From the center where the Will of God is known
> Let purpose guide the little wills of men —
> The purpose which the Masters know and serve.
>
> From the center which we call the race of men
> Let the Plan of Love and Light work out
> And may it seal the door where evil dwells.
>
> Let Light and Love and Power restore the Plan on Earth.

[12] Alice Bailey, *The Reappearance of the Christ* (World Goodwill, n.d.), pp. 4–5.

The Arcane School regards this invocation as having almost magic and divine potencies. Mrs. Bailey called it "the intelligent organization of spiritual energy and of the forces of love." And she said that its recitation could evoke the response of high "spiritual beings," enabling them to work openly and to link the Great White Brotherhood with mankind.[13] Therefore, the Arcane School's disciples use the Great Invocation in their own meditation and promote its use in the various media of communication, e.g., radio, television, and newspapers, in order to speed the reappearance of the Christ and his disciples, the masters.

The Christ himself has allegedly introduced the Great Invocation to the world. It is said his first coming was to bring us the fundamental law of love and the Lord's Prayer, but in 1945 he decided to return to humanity in physical form because of its terrible postwar condition. Since his appearance, however, would presuppose the initial stages of establishing right human relations, he purportedly gave to the world the Great Invocation at the time of the first full moon in June, 1945. This was allegedly the translation of an ancient prayer which hitherto only the most exalted spiritual beings had permission to use.[14]

Through its promotion the Great Invocation has circled the world, and its use has spread far beyond the Arcane School. Foster Bailey has recorded over two million copies distributed from the New York office alone since 1945, and within ten recent years over eight hundred thousand Invocation letters, leaflets, and pamphlets have poured from New York. This still represents only a part of its dissemination, since it does not include that from the various centers in foreign countries, but its distribution by volunteer unpaid workers still continues.[15]

Although the Great Invocation may have guided many to the books of Alice Bailey and to her correspondence courses, one should not infer, however, that the Arcane School employs it as just an advertising device. In many cases one hears it or sees

[13] *The Great Invocation: A Manual on Its Use and Significance* (World Goodwill, n.d.), p. 10.
[14] *Ibid.*, pp. 11–13.
[15] *World Goodwill: A Report on the World-wide Distribution and Use of the Invocation* (Arcane School, n.d.), pp. 1–3.

it printed with no reference at all to the organization or to its beliefs.

Principles and Beliefs

The Arcane School, which aims to reveal the divinity in man, has the following seven principles:

" 1. The Arcane School is a training school for disciples. It is not a school for probationary disciples or for devotional aspirants.

" 2. The Arcane School trains *adult* men and women so that they may take their next step upon the path of evolution.

" 3. The Arcane School recognizes the *fact* of the Spiritual Hierarchy of the planet and gives instruction in the mode whereby that Hierarchy may be approached and entered.

" 4. The Arcane School teaches the practical belief that the ' souls of men are one.'

" 5. The Arcane School emphasizes the necessity *to live* the spiritual life and rejects all claims to spiritual status.

" 6. The Arcane School is nonsectarian, nonpolitical, and international in scope.

" 7. The Arcane School emphasizes no theological dogmas, but simply teaches the Ageless Wisdom, as recognized in all lands down through the ages." [16]

Besides its seven principles there are eight main statements of belief representing its interpretation of " Ageless Wisdom." It instructs that:

1. The Kingdom of God, which is interpreted as the hierarchy of masters for this planet, will be materialized here on earth.

2. The transcendent God expresses his knowledge, love, and will immanently through mankind, his sons.

3. God has revealed himself to man continuously throughout the ages.

4. Because the divine life expressing itself through multiformed existence is one, individual human beings are necessarily one.

[16] Alice Bailey, *The Unfinished Autobiography*, pp. 281-282.

5. Within each person is a divine spark or soul, which Paul referred to as the " Christ in you." To demonstrate this " divine livingness " is man's aim toward which his discipleship will take him.

6. The individual aspirant may achieve perfection eventually through the evolutionary process. The Arcane School seeks to study this development from its lowest stages on through to the high plane where the Lord of the World, i.e., the Buddha, is working out the divine plan.

7. Unchangeable laws, which are God's will expressing itself, are continually being revealed to man as he progresses.

8. God manifests himself as love, which is the fundamental law of our universe.[17]

Since nothing in the statement of beliefs or principles concerns the specific question of sin or evil, something should be said about it. While accepting the general moral precepts given in the Bible, the Arcane School, like many metaphysical sects, prefers to speak of ignorance rather than of sin. This is in keeping with the popular Hindu Vedanta philosophy, in which *avidya*, or ignorance, of one's true nature as being one with the Absolute God, Brahman, is regarded as the cause preventing man from salvation, and also the true meaning of sin. In one of the editorials in its periodical, *The Beacon*, entitled " Sin — What Is It? " the Tibetan master is recorded as saying he preferred the word " ignorance " to sin. The Arcane School feels that " sin has been applied mostly to the weaknesses of the flesh, and that the body is made the scapegoat of all our derelictions." Sins, it says on the contrary, are of the spirit, which include " our separativeness from our fellow men, our own souls, and the one final reality of spirit." Therefore, our existential estrangement from God is through ignorance of our essential identity with Being or God, which gives rise to the lesser errors, resulting also in our wrong sense of values. The Arcane School rejects the idea of original sin, because " God is the Being of all beings, and we are as Gods to him, through whom he revealeth himself," as quoted from the seventeenth-century mystic, Jakob Boehme. Its adherents feel they have escaped from a

17 *Ibid.*, pp. 294–295.

medieval theology believed to be still current in the traditional churches. According to the Tibetan, our remaining in an outworn form of thought is a grave error, which is impeding evolution and delaying precipitation of the hierarchy's plan on earth.[18]

The Arcane School, like Theosophy, accepts the doctrines of reincarnation, karma, the masters of wisdom, etc., but its social emphasis sets it apart from most of the Theosophical organizations except the Tingley group. Although the Theosophical Society at Adyar has done much toward social reform in India, it has had no social program elsewhere. Nevertheless, while the Arcane School is interested in sponsoring groups whose activities include social amelioration, its approach, which is only through the power of thought and prayer, distinguishes it from socially minded Christian churches.

It differs again from Theosophy in stressing the importance of the master Maitreya, not just as the World Teacher, who incarnates himself at times as the revealer of new religions, but as the Christ, who will soon return in physical form. While emphasizing this belief, it agrees with Theosophy that all religions are really one in their basic truths.

Alice Bailey was also critical of the Theosophical doctrine concerning the masters of wisdom, preferring to believe that the Tibetan master had given a corrected interpretation of the hierarchy and its office. According to him, the Theosophical view made the masters exclusive rather than inclusive, and precluded their operations from movements other than Theosophy. He was also critical of some movements claiming to have contact with the masters, e.g., the " I Am " movement, founded by Edna and Guy Ballard, which he regarded as a " travesty of the reality." [19]

The Arcane School does not teach the development of psychic powers, but offers courses by means of which the student may gain " personality integration," in order to develop his mind so that it may control his emotional nature. Having at-

---

[18] "Sin — What Is It? " Editorial in *The Beacon*, Vol. 34, No. 10 (Jan., 1956), p. 285.

[19] Alice Bailey, *The Unfinished Autobiography*, pp. 255–256.

tained his goal, he may work at a higher synthesis, that of the soul with the personality, known as a " soul-infused personality." This is the integration of the higher Self with the lower Self. For its accomplishment the Arcane School sets up no standards of moral living; nor does it require the student to be a vegetarian or to give up the use of tobacco or alcohol. Although these problems remain with the student, it is believed that the soul will eventually sets its own standards.

The Arcane School is not interested ostensibly in founding a new movement. Even if it allows groups to form for study of its teachings, it claims no responsibility for them or for what they teach. That there are such in various parts of the country the writer can confirm, but there is no way of knowing exactly how many there are. Notwithstanding this position, the organization still desires to make its teachings known to all people so that eventually there will be only one spiritual group, the " great heresy of separateness " will be countered, and the foundation laid for the new civilization based on the belief that the " souls of men *are* One." [20]

Recent Developments

Since the death of Alice Bailey in 1949, the movement has been led by her husband. From offices near the United Nations, Foster Bailey and his staff issue correspondence courses to their followers working toward various numbered degrees. The lessons are based on the books written allegedly by the Tibetan through the instrumentality of Alice Bailey. Here are also some of the secretaries who communicate regularly with students in answer to their questions.

The Lucis Trust is the publisher of Alice Bailey's works, the correspondence courses, various pamphlets, and periodicals. Although publishing books by other authors outside its own organization, it retains all copyrights and money accruing from royalties. In addition to this income it benefits from many donations coming from all over the world. In 1956 the contributions amounted to $116,490, out of which $70,350 came from Amer-

20 *Ibid.*, pp. 282–290.

ican pockets. From 1923 to 1956 the total was $1,527,380, of which American benefactors accounted for $1,201,700. A graph depicting their receipts from contributions during these years would show an increase from 1941 to a peak in 1946 after World War II. Although there have been fluctuations since that date, the level is still high.[21] Perhaps the rise in donations during the war years and the continued development afterward reflect the insecurities of people, who then seek safety in views such as the Arcane School represents.

In recent years there has been a split in the organization. Those who had worked with Alice Bailey on the preparation of the correspondence lessons resigned to form a similar institution called the School of Esoteric Studies, but there are neither doctrinal differences nor criticism, one against the other. Foster Bailey told the writer that everyone had the right to make his own choice, and the split meant nothing at all. The more groups there were teaching the true meaning of mankind, the better it was. " They are all doing the same good work," he concluded.

If the Arcane School by itself is not of impressive size, its influence upon religious culture probably greatly exceeds its own membership. Certainly in many cities in the United States it is not uncommon to find members of Protestant churches who are well acquainted with and sympathetic toward the works of Alice Bailey.

THE ASTARA FOUNDATION

The Astara Foundation, which was established in October, 1951, by Robert and Earlyne Chaney, aims to combine features of Spiritualism with those of Theosophy, the Arcane School, and Christianity. The Chaneys regard it as being Christian because they consider Jesus as the leading master of the hierarchy, and among his disciples are some who, they assert, have particular functions in the work of Astara. There are three, they say, who aided in the founding of the organization:

[21] *Lucis Trust, op. cit., passim.*

the masters Rama and Zoser, neither of whom is recognized by Theosophy, and Kut-Hu-Mi, an important master also to both Theosophy and the Arcane School. Astara considers itself to be a modern mystery school, teaching the " Ancient Wisdom," and it proposes to work toward the union of all such organizations.

Robert Chaney, who was born in La Porte, Indiana, in 1913, later attended Miami University for a year and a half until the depression of 1929 terminated his study. He then tried his hand at many types of occupations, including office work and salesmanship, until becoming a Spiritualistic medium.

Although Chaney had attended several different Sunday schools of the Methodist, Episcopal, and Lutheran churches, he admitted to a perfunctory acquaintance with their teachings.

His first encounter with Spiritualism was made through his parents, who in the latter part of their lives became interested in the psychic world. They visited Chesterfield, the well-known Spiritualist summer camp, and here Robert, after becoming aware of his own psychic abilities, studied to be a medium under the Reverend John Bunker. Before starting the Astara Foundation with his wife, Earlyne, he worked at his new profession at Camp Chesterfield and in Spiritualist churches for thirteen years, during which time he also became a cofounder of the Spiritualist Episcopal Church.

Earlyne Cantrell Chaney, who was born in a little town north of Dallas, Texas, describes her early life as being " hectic." When she was quite young, her father deserted the family, and although she learned to love her stepfather very much, she still felt like a foreigner wandering in a strange land. Consequently, she often withdrew from her family to spend considerable time by herself, and during these solitary periods she began developing a companionship with " one of the invisibles," whom at first she did not know — but who seemed to be like a father to her. Then at about thirteen years of age she used to awaken at night, feeling someone had called her. She said she would often get up and go out of the house to a big woodpile, where she would sit and talk with this someone she called " Father." The strange companionship grew until on one occasion she saw him, either physically or clairvoyantly. While he stood visibly beside her, she asked his name, and he replied, " Kut-Hu-Mi." Of course, at her age his name meant nothing to her, because she had not yet heard of Theosophy, nor did she know about this master's association with it until she studied the subject as an adult.

At this same meeting he told her the time would come when she would lose someone very dear to her. This would change her entire life and send her on her true mission — the quest for the answer concerning death and immortality. Although subsequently her contacts with the master were rare, she could reach him through meditation and prayer, and at times of need she could feel his presence as a source of strength and confidence.

When she was about nineteen she came to California to study and train to be an actress, while supporting herself as a secretary. Small parts soon led to better roles. She was in *Kiss and Tell*, starring Shirley Temple, and a number of comedies for Columbia; *Women's Army* for MGM; and pictures for RKO and Warner Brothers. She was well on her way to stardom when she fell in love with a captain in the Air Force. She went home to tell her parents of her forthcoming marriage. Then it happened. She received news of his death in an airplane crash. With her intense grief came the realization that this was the person she had to lose before her life would be changed. While still distraught with sorrow, she prayed and fasted for three days until her master appeared. He told her about the Yoga practices she was to pursue, and allegedly gave her a " formula " to use for the unfoldment of her psychic powers. He also directed her to study " communication " (Spiritualism) as well as every facet of every religion she could learn that would be applicable to the New Age. Thus began her quest in deep earnestness for the true meaning of life and immortality — a search that would lead her to Theosophy, the Self-Realization Fellowship, and on through the whole gamut of metaphysical philosophies including Spiritualism.

Her pilgrimage finally brought her to Camp Chesterfield where she met and married Robert Chaney. She had discovered in him a kindred spirit, because he had developed a philosophy similar to hers. Both wanted to teach more than Spiritualism, but for the time being they felt under obligation to Mabel Riffel, the Camp secretary, not to teach what she regarded as " that crazy stuff " — reincarnation, etc. They therefore supplemented their studies with correspondence courses from such institutions as the College of Universal Truth in Chicago and the College of Divine Metaphysics in Indianapolis, and thereby received their Doctor of Divinity degrees. Finally, as Earlyne Chaney said: " We decided to open the place that could combine communication, the master teaching, reincarnation, and all the Ancient Wisdom — Yoga, and whatever it takes for an individual soul to find God in his way. We hope that we have not left out anything." [1]

And indeed, one must admit that Astara is all inclusive.

The Founding of Astara

Besides their two masters, Rama and Kut-Hu-Mi, the Chaneys give credit to Robert's spirit-doctor-teacher, Dr. George Anthony Zeller, for the inspiration to found Astara.

Astara's purpose and its relationship to the master Jesus is embodied in an interesting story allegedly told by Rama. During a séance at the beginning of Astara in Santa Monica, he said that millions of years ago great beings called the Lords of the Flame came to this planet from Venus to help mankind in its evolution. One of these dedicated beings, known also as the twelve Kumaras, was Jesus. Led by the Ruler of the Earth, the Sanat Kumara, they took up residence on an island called Shamballa in what was then the Gobi Sea. Jesus, we are told, was only one of four Kumaras who sacrificed themselves for the sins of the earth and the instruction of the ignorant. He gained his Christhood during his last earthly incarnation and still dwells in the Kingdom of the Gobi. Jesus then took Rama as his disciple, who in turn selected Robert Chaney to be his. Jesus had allegedly requested that Rama seek a disciple in order to expedite plans of the White Brotherhood for further enlightening man-

---

[1] The foregoing was taken from a tape recording of an interview that the writer had with the Chaneys in 1957.

kind. This is assertedly the purpose for founding Astara. Therefore, the Chaneys teach that although the work of Astara is directly under the authority of Kut-Hu-Mi and Rama, both are
under the guidance of the master Jesus, who gives much attention to this new mystery school.

They believe all other mystery schools, both past and present, have been founded by masters, but the time has finally arrived for these different schools to be combined, since there are
those living who would now be able to grasp the full truth of
the mysteries and not just some portion of it.

Astara's Ministry of Healing

Astara, like other metaphysical groups, has an active interest
in healing. The master Zoser, who was historically a former
pharaoh of Egypt and builder of the Step Pyramid at Sakkâra,
is their principal healer, and they maintain that he had become
famous for his curative powers while living on earth. Now,
however, he dwells in the astral Astara, a counterpart of the
physical Astara on the astral plane, where he directs the healing
work.

Astarians are invited to send their requests to " The Circle of
the Sacred Seven " for help in solving problems no matter what
they may be. The Circle consists of three highly developed
Astarians and four spirit teachers, who form a triangle and a
square respectively on the physical and spiritual planes, and
who through prayer and spiritual attunement endeavor to activate cosmic laws that will manifest the things desired. Upon receiving a request for help, the triangle group immediately
begins to work with affirmations, prayers, and mental visualiza-
tions, while the four on the spiritual plane start to influence
cosmic forces in the person's behalf.[2]

Those who attend the services of Astara at Santa Monica
may, of course, take part personally in the healing program conducted by Earlyne Chaney. There at that time in a darkened
room a spotlight illumines her slender figure clad in a long

[2] Robert Chaney, *You and Astara: A New Age Mystery School, Bringing
Light to the Minds of Men* (Astara Foundation, n.d.), pp. 4–9.

white formal, while with a well-modulated voice supported by soft background music she recites devotional poetry and prayers for the sick.

Without confirming or denying the efficacy of various healing practices, one cannot help observing comparisons and contrasts between many Evangelistic healers and the Chaneys. Both make use of testimonies by those believing themselves to have been healed. Perhaps the unconscious motive they have in common is the reassurance of health among those alleged to be cured, which not only strengthens the faith of the healed but that of others desiring to be healed. During the Chaneys' service, however, such words of witness are not recited by those who believe themselves to have been made whole, as is the case among many Evangelistic healers. The Chaneys get a wider coverage for these testimonials by often publishing one or more in their leaflet, *The Voice*, which is sent free to every Astarian.

Without contrasting obvious theological and philosophical differences as well as methods, one should note the pattern of ostensible clairvoyance which differentiates occult types of spiritual healing from others. A fair percentage of Astarians who may never have seen Earlyne Chaney except in pictures mention seeing her at the time of their healing. Others speak of the white healing light enveloping them, the feeling of the healer's presence, or other occult phenomena. By these printed testimonies the Chaneys bring faraway Astarians into closer fellowship with the organization, instill greater confidence in their methods, and help bolster the faith of other members in their teachings.

Initiations of the Chaneys

Both Earlyne and Robert Chaney testify that the masters have given them several initiations, the following one of which assertedly took place inside Mount Shasta. (Those familiar with the teachings of the " I Am " group will recall a similar incident described by Guy Ballard, one of the founders of that movement.)

During a materialization séance shortly after Astara was

founded, the master Rama allegedly instructed them to prepare for this event by journeying to Mount Shasta. Earlyne Chaney said that subsequently on its slopes they met a mysterious person who guided them through a small opening to a grotto inside the mountain. Here they stopped briefly, and while meditating with their companion, who recited an ancient chant, they suddenly realized they had left their physical bodies and were " in the Spirit." Then they were conducted on the astral plane to a temple where they saw many doctor teachers, Indians, and master teachers, most of whom they had previously seen clairvoyantly at their church services. Zoser next became their guide and led them to a magnificent astral cathedral at the peak of the mountain. There they met Rama and Kut-Hu-Mi, as part of a gathering of twelve great masters who conducted their very impressive initiation ceremony. Among other things they received an astral staff, which they were told could help them with their healing work. (One will recall the magic staff allegedly given to Andrew Jackson Davis for a similar purpose.)

Having received congratulations on their initiation, they soon realized another treat was in store for them. Although there had been twelve seated masters, there was an empty thirteenth chair. Suddenly in the dim light the lid of a great chest on the altar opened, revealing a huge mirror. This they were told was soon to catch the light from a distant star and be reflected through a large magnifying glass in the dome of the ceiling. At the propitious moment a cloud appeared on the mirror, taking the form of Jesus. Thus, they said, through " some cosmic ' hookup ' " they were able to see and hear him on his higher plane.

He then allegedly told them of the grave conditions on the earth, and of the chaos and the holocaust that we perchance face. The planet was entering a new field of expression with higher vibrations that many would not be able to stand. Therefore, they would have to leave this planet and wait for another to enter this field before continuing their evolution.

Since there was so much bad karma, the cosmic debt would have to be paid, and as a consequence, we could expect great destruction. America, isolated from the rest, would not be destroyed because there were already many advanced souls incarnated here — souls belonging to Aquarius, the new field of expression, which would form the nucleus of the coming race. Little by little people would then learn to live together in peace and in accordance with the law of love.

At this point the Chaneys allegedly realized their task was to do whatever GOOD they could, so as to erase as much bad karma as possible and lessen the destruction.[3]

Teachings of Astara

Astara teaches a philosophy resembling that of Theosophy and the Arcane School, but also upholds the validity of Spiritualism. It maintains that the " Teachers do not err in their teachings," but it is possible for those who receive their words to make errors in their understanding and interpretation.[4]

The Chaneys, besides recognizing Jesus as a master and the head of the hierarchy, have the following to say concerning his nature:

" Jesus was man — and he was also God. He was not God as a Being compressed in physical form. He was God as an individual manifesting the God nature which resided with him . . . the highest spiritual aspect of his own nature, and of yours." [5]

Robert Chaney disagrees with the traditional Christian interpretation that "the Word " in the prologue to the Gospel of John refers to Jesus Christ. He teaches, on the contrary, that "the Word " has reference to the " Ancient Wisdom " doctrine concerning sound. It means "the Divine Sound incarnate." [6] This interpretation of "the Word " as the "Holy Shabda " — the word *shabda* means " sound " in Sanskrit — is part of the philosophy of Astara's secret Yoga, and is similar to the meaning given to it by the Self-Realization Fellowship and the Ruhani Satsanga, two Hindu implantations in America.

---

[3] Earlyne Chaney, *Secrets of Mount Shasta* (Astara Foundation, 1953), *passim.*
[4] Earlyne Chaney, *The Long Journey of Becoming*, the First Degree Lesson, No. 1 (Astara Foundation, 1955), p. iv.
[5] Robert Chaney, *Jesus — Man or God?* Lessons in Everyday Living, Series No. 1 (Astara Foundation, 1958), p. 5.
[6] *Ibid.*, p. 2.

Lama Yoga, the secret teaching given only to Astarians who become Brothers of the first degree, is taught by Earlyne Chaney, who says: " Lama Yoga can carry the Disciple into attunement with the Life Stream through the Holy Shabda . . . the Divine Call which issues forth from God in the Dawn of each planetary Creation," and " can only be heard by the Inner Ear." Through this Yoga the student will be led gradually into a new birth and contact with his higher self.

A Church Through Correspondence Courses

Astarians not only consider their movement to be a mystery school and a brotherhood, but a church. At their headquarters in Santa Monica, classes are conducted every week partly by the Reverend Robert Chaney, partly by alleged teachers and masters from the spirit side of life, and partly by others who " still dwell in their physical bodies and live in remote locations upon the earthly plane." While Chaney is entranced during his classes, these adepts allegedly transmit the lessons by direct voice. Since the Chaneys believe the average disciple is not able to assimilate mentally the complete lesson at a single hearing, it is seldom given entirely at one sitting. Earlyne Chaney assertedly receives the remaining portion by what she calls " Telephonic Inspiration." [7]

These lessons, when multilithed, are offered as pamphlets to Astarians unable to hear them in person. Similarly, there are others containing secret teachings for students working toward various Astarian degrees. Through these many are drawn to Astara, who have never seen nor may never see the Chaneys in person.

When one joins Astara, he usually enrolls for the twenty-two lessons comprising the first degree, and upon their completion he may continue with those for the second degree, etc. And as one progresses upward, Astara offers him the possibility of being initiated into the Great White Brotherhood and becoming a master, but this of course is said to be only at the discretion of the masters who would have to decide. On the other hand,

[7] Robert Chaney, *You and Astara*, p. 2.

no one is asked to believe all the teachings, since the Chaneys do not want a person to accept anything that seems incongruous to his mind.

The Santa Monica Church

Because the main church of Astara suffers from property limitations, its sanctuary holds only 125 persons, but a closed circuit television pipes Astara's message into an overflow auditorium. Therefore, one must arrive early to see and hear the Chaneys in person during their Sunday services at two thirty and seven thirty P.M. The afternoon hour was chosen ostensibly so that many members might first attend their own denominational church services. Although such dual memberships are evidently not uncommon, most Astarians have already left their traditional churches for their newfound faith. When the writer visited Astara, one elderly lady introduced herself as the mother of a Congregational minister and explained that after many long years of searching she had really found what she wanted at Astara.

As added attractions Astara often features in its services many well-known personalities, who are not necessarily its members. They may speak on occult subjects or an extrasensory perception, and their works of this nature are sometimes published and distributed by Astara. Among those who have lectured there are such persons as Dr. Hornell Hart, formerly professor of Sociology at Duke University; Elaine Rogers St. Johns, author and lecturer; and Jesse Lasky of motion picture fame. Dr. Gustaf Stromberg, a scientist, after retiring from the Mount Wilson Observatory, wrote a number of works published by Astara on " scientific " aspects of religion.

In 1957 the Sunday services featured a lecture and blindfold billet-reading by Robert Chaney and concluded with a healing service conducted by his wife, Earlyne. In the same year, while claiming about six thousand members, Astara was adding about three hundred a month, with approximately eighty-four percent renewals in membership. If the figures are reliable, they would represent an annual increase of forty-four percent.

Methods and Reasons for Expansion

New members are obtained in a number of ways. Sometimes it is through the referral of a friend who is a member. At other times it may be due to the Chaneys' public lectures in various cities. But it is even more through the method so successfully used by Frank B. Robinson, of Psychiana fame, viz., circularizing large numbers of people whose names appear on various subscription lists. The Chaneys said that persons interested in any kind of metaphysical study seem to be good possibilities for their teachings. Their own radio program, which began in 1959 and was broadcast on Saturday and Sunday evenings, undoubtedly helped. Although it has now been discontinued, it was called " Quest Eternal " and featured interviews with authorities on many different religions and metaphysical movements.

Whence comes the growing popularity of Astara? Certainly one might mention its widely eclectic character and extreme tolerance of all religions. It also combines healing methods advocated by both Spiritualists and New Thought adherents, and its philosophy and exhibitions of psychic phenomena draw many from the Spiritualist and Theosophical sects. Its claim that Jesus is the leading master in its pantheon is apparently attractive to persons who have not found satisfaction in Christian churches, but want to be identified as followers of Jesus. Astara offers them a philosophy and an assurance of personal immortality, demonstrated to their satisfaction in ways unacceptable to Christian churches. Anxiety and doubt can strengthen the desire and the will to believe anything that assuages grief over the loss of a loved one and mitigates the essential anxiety of one's own death and loss of selfhood.

Among factors contributing to the organization's sustainment are the warm and congenial personalities of both the Chaneys and the ability to make all members feel part of the Astara family. Through its publication, *The Voice*, one becomes closely acquainted with details of past and forthcoming events. One also learns by words and pictures the everyday happenings in the Chaney family, which are focused on Sita, their beautiful little daughter. And in the course of time many become intimately associated with the joys and cares of the Chaneys and share empathetically in their lives.

Astara's New Age Dispensation

Astara is a herald of the New Age messiah, whose revelation proclaims the truth of all religions embodied in the " Ancient Wisdom," and the passing of " orthodox " Christianity. Thus Astara, like most metaphysical sects, represents a new form of dispensationalism with Swedenborgian overtones. Swedenborg believed his Biblical interpretation marked a new dispensation. Emerson and other transcendentalists went a step farther. As before noted, Emerson believed Swedenborg's thought would play a major role in the new religion to supersede Christianity.

Astara points to the New Age of Aquarius and the violent demise of the Piscean era. The Chaneys believe that if a world catastrophe comes, Astarians are to be among the elect who will survive to form the nucleus of the new civilization, when the master Jesus will reign supremely on earth. Such views are held in slightly differing forms by Theosophy, the Arcane School, Christian Science, the Unity School of Christianity, and other New Thought derivatives.

Messianic and millennial beliefs also prevail among many Christians. The expectation of this age's immanent end and the consequent need to experience salvation has been one of the drawing cards for Billy Graham and other evangelists. Likewise, the baptism of the Spirit through speaking in tongues was noted recently as a terminal sign at the interdenominational meeting of the Christian Life Advance. This organization consists of ministers and laymen of a number of Protestant churches, e.g., Presbyterian, Disciples of Christ, United Church of Christ, Methodist, Episcopal, Baptist, etc., who are united in the belief of speaking in tongues. Thus Astara and other metaphysical groups are in their own way participating in the messianic and apocalyptic tendencies of the growing Pentecostalism. Their voices are subconscious testimonies to the insecurities and rapid cultural changes that have eroded so many people's religious foundations.

We now end our sojourn with the " charismatic " leaders of occult metaphysical sects and move to another area of metaphysical religions, whose philosophies show similar cultural origins.

IV

Phineas P. Quimby and Warren Felt Evans

ACCOMPANYING THE WEEKLY LISTINGS of church services appearing in the metropolitan newspapers, one may also notice the names of other groups, whose backgrounds and philosophies may not be apparent to the ordinary reader. The latter are advertised as Mental Science, Divine Science, Truth Center, Metaphysical Science, etc. In many cases their addresses will lead one to a public hall or an auditorium, the use of which has been reserved for the eleven o'clock hour on Sunday morning.

These are the autonomous organizations of New Thought, whose size is often proportional to the personality and appeal of the leader, whose philosophy of self-realization promises health, happiness, prosperity, and all the good things of the American way of life, and whose roots spread out from the thought of Phineas P. Quimby and Warren Felt Evans. During the development, however, the movement has at times received additional graftings from Christian Science, Gnosticism, Indian philosophy, Emersonian transcendentalism, Spiritualism, Theosophy, Neoplatonism, modern psychology, and psychoanalysis in various proportions according to the predilection of the individual leader. On the other hand, since the philosophy of Quimby has much in common with that of Spiritualism, it is appropriate to note in this chapter more of the basic points of agreement and possible influence.

While the individual New Thought groups are independent and held together by their respective leaders, there are also organizations of these having a similar philosophy, but which may or may not wish to be classed as a form of New Thought, e.g., the Church of Divine Science, the Church of Religious Science, and the Unity School of Christianity. Still, all began with the purpose of mental healing and owe some debt, even though indirectly, to Phineas P. Quimby and Warren Felt Evans.

The shift of emphasis from the psychic world to the practice of healing begins with Quimby, although the latter interest in healing has never been absent from the other wing of the movement.

Both Quimby and Spiritualism's philosopher, Andrew Jackson Davis, began experimenting on similar lines about the same time and within a few hundred miles of each other. Although the streams of thought from Quimby and his followers gradually flowed into different channels from those of Davis and the Spiritualists, not only was there a common pool of ideas in this cultural milieu, but also the possible unconscious borrowing from Davis, whose works were known to others besides Spiritualists.

Phineas Parkhurst Quimby was born in Lebanon, New Hampshire, in 1802, but most of his later life with which we are concerned was spent in Portland, Maine. We need to say little about his early life except that in spite of his meager education he apparently had scientific proclivities which some inventive ability seemed to show, and although never a member of a Christian church, he regarded Jesus as a reformer and later thought of his own work as the " Science of Christ." [1]

Quimby's Early Experiments in Hypnosis

Shortly after Charles Poyen, a Frenchman, introduced hypnotism into the United States, Quimby attended a lecture and demonstration of it in 1838 at Belfast, Maine, and by 1840 he himself was practicing the art.

He formed a partnership with one of his subjects, a young man named Lucius Burkmar, who was said to have exhibited

[1] Phineas Parkhurst Quimby, *The Quimby Manuscripts, Showing the Discovery of Spiritual Healing and the Origin of Christian Science*, ed. by Horatio W. Dresser (The Thomas Y. Crowell Company, 1921), pp. 8–11. Hereafter cited as " Quimby."

clairvoyant abilities [2] similar to those of Davis, and they traveled
through the neighboring area giving demonstrations for several
years.[3] Later Quimby began using the entranced Burkmar for
diagnosing diseases and prescribing remedies as Davis had done.
Though affirming that cures resulted from this method,
Quimby gradually developed his own theory about the reason,
which resulted from noticing that Burkmar would sometimes
prescribe a remedy so absurd that there could be no scientific
correlation between it and the cure. This led him to the conclusion that disease was a " deranged state of mind," and its cause
lay in the patient's belief, which Burkmar recognized clairvoyantly. Through the change of belief the person was cured.

He claimed to have proved his theory first in his own case.
Having been in poor health himself, he had been told that the
pains in his back were caused by his ulcerated lungs and " partly
consumed " kidneys. Then on one occasion Burkmar, while entranced, described Quimby's condition and the next day told
him that an almost-severed piece of kidney had grown back
and that he was cured. Although the pain had left, Quimby reasoned that Burkmar had only read his thoughts about himself
and had given an absurd remedy. This event, however, made
him conclude that he had only been deceived into a belief of
illness, and that it was through faith in Burkmar that his mind
had been changed and his cure effected.

During the period from 1843 to 1847 Quimby used Burkmar
in many ways through hypnotism. Witnesses testified that
Burkmar, like Davis, had the power " to discern the internal
structure of an animal body," and according to an excerpt from
the *Bangor Democrat*, April, 1843, he was able to describe in
detail places unknown to him. Moreover, if given a slip of paper on which the name of a deceased person was written, he
could describe the one mentioned and state his family relationship. Once when Burkmar supplied such detail as a hair lip,
Quimby attributed this particular to his question concerning
any peculiarity the deceased might have had. He felt that if

    [2] Horatio W. Dresser, *A History of the New Thought Movement*
(The Thomas Y. Crowell Company, 1919), pp. 29–30.
    [3] Quimby, p. 31.

such had existed, those in the audience who knew him would create it by thought, but had there been any Spiritualists present, they would have maintained that Burkmar had actually seen the spirit. Therefore, Quimby rejected the Spiritualist hypothesis in favor of telepathy.[4] Finally, Burkmar was also reported to have described accurately passengers on a ship at sea, and at various sittings he noted the ship's progress until it arrived in port.[5]

The discussion is, of course, largely academic, since the participants are no longer living and the validity of Burkmar's alleged powers cannot now be tested. Of still further interest, however, is the fact that Quimby in 1861 claimed that he himself became clairvoyant without hypnosis and utilized the power to cultivate the spiritual sense and to aid the sick.

Horatio Dresser, explaining Quimby's early thought, said, " Whatever enlists the attention long enough to produce a distinct impression, has power to affect the body, and an idea accepted as truth is as good as reality in its influence upon the person believing it." [6] This seems to be partly true and may help explain some types of healings.

Quimby Compared with Swedenborg and Davis

Quimby denounced magnetic healing and the Spiritualist hypothesis that spirits can diagnose and prescribe for the patient.[7] Therefore, he developed in his later years a philosophy to fit his own practice of healing, which was undoubtedly influenced by his Swedenborgian friends. He made similar distinctions between natural man and spiritual man, and analogously he separated natural man's " mind of opinions," which was subject to suggestions and error, from the " mind of Science " or " mind of Christ " possessed in one's higher self.[8]

As already noted, Swedenborg believed that only the spiritual self of man could know the Bible's spiritual sense, and Quimby's manuscripts at the Library of Congress express this in Swedenborg's terms:

[4] Ibid., pp. 31–52. [6] Ibid., p. 56. [8] Ibid., p. 59.
[5] Ibid., p. 54. [7] Ibid., p. 58.

" Spiritual wisdom is always shadowed forth by some earthly or literal figure; thus the Bible is spiritual truth illustrated by literal things, but the people receive the shadow of literal explanation and know nothing of the true spiritual meaning." [9]

We may say that Swedenborg tried to resolve the antithesis of religion and science by resorting to his law of correspondences. A similar attempt by Quimby attributed less efficacy to natural science, which he relegated to the mind of opinion or error. He favored what he believed to be the higher or real science, the science of health. This he equated with God, Wisdom, and the real nature of man according to his spiritual interpretation of the Bible. The Old Testament, which he regarded literally as a heathen superstition, became a " Science of health " from his allegorical viewpoint. [10]

Quimby believed he possessed a higher " wisdom " to which his senses were attached through the power of clairvoyance. [11] This view he shared with Davis and Swedenborg but exceeded the latter in the belief that by means of clairvoyance he could sense his patient's illness through what Swedenborg and he called " mental atmospheres." [12]

Davis had used the term " atmosphere " in a slightly different sense. He identified it with the " magnetic power " emanating from each individual, a force that the hypnotist used to cure disease. [13] In his *Harbinger of Health*, Davis equated this power with the odic force which Von Reichenbach believed he had discovered. [14] The view of Davis that this radiating force could be seen in various colors by clairvoyants [15] became a basis for the belief in auras, defined by the Spiritualists and Theosophists as etheric emanations from persons. Moreover, their be-

---

[9] Phineas Parkhurst Quimby, "Why I Do Not Cure All with Equal Ease," *Original Notebooks in Library of Congress*, March, 1862, Vol. 8, pp. 46–47. Since the author has used much material not found in the Dresser edition but taken from microfilm copies of the original manuscripts in the Library of Congress, reference to the latter will be hereafter cited as "Quimby MSS. in L.C."
[10] *Ibid.*, "The Christian Explanation of the Testaments," pp. 51–52.
[11] *Ibid.*, unnamed article, Nov., 1860, Vol. 11, p. 82.
[12] Quimby, p. 68.
[13] Davis, *The Great Harmonia*, Vol. 1, p. 286.
[14] Andrew Jackson Davis, *The Harbinger of Health* (Bela Marsh, first printed in 1861), p. 95.
[15] *Ibid.*, pp. 91–92.

lief that the various auric colors seen by clairvoyants indicate health or illness led to one Spiritualist method of diagnosing diseases.

Davis' additional belief that this " atmosphere," or magnetic force, could also be used to create ill effects upon the subject appears to be the seminal thought of the doctrine of evil animal magnetism. Quimby, likewise, when treating a patient, felt that he had to keep himself free from the influence of " mental atmospheres," and to realize the " protective presence of ' Wisdom,' or ' God's power.' " [16] Finally, many Spiritualists even today take measures to protect themselves from " auric emanations " of the sick whom they are treating.

Certainly not enough attention has been given to the possible contribution of Davis to the healing movements. Although few modern Spiritualists have read any of his books, which are long out of print, his principle ideas were already published before Quimby wrote his manuscripts. Moreover, for some years many American people were attracted to the phenomena of Spiritualism, whose basic philosophy the Spiritualist leaders expounded. Even though the exposure of fraudulent mediums drove some from Spiritualism, and other mediums explained the phenomena in many different ways, still the influence of Davis upon early metaphysical thought must not be entirely discounted.

Davis expounded a philosophy of healing in the first volume of his *Great Harmonia* in 1850 and in his *Harbinger of Health* in 1861, and Quimby's theories were developing in the same period. His manuscripts at the Library of Congress are dated from 1859 to 1865, although some may represent copies of earlier ones.

Parallels Between Quimby and Davis

Since no one has suggested that Quimby's philosophy and consequently that of the healing sects may owe a debt to the philosopher of Spiritualism, a brief comparison seems in order.

According to Davis, all illnesses are modes of discord in man's

[16] Quimby, p. 68; also, Davis, *The Great Harmonia*, Vol. 1, p. 286.

spiritual force or principle,[17] which he identified with soul, Spirit, and higher mind.[18] This spiritual disturbance causes a corresponding material imbalance to appear as disease,[19] which may be cured by the mind.[20]

In his early writings in 1859, Quimby, like Davis, wrote that " every phenomenon in the natural world had its origin in the spiritual world," [21] and " all effects produced upon the human frame are the results of a chemical change of the fluids, with or without our knowledge, and . . . accompanied by a peculiar state of mind." [22] Disease, he said, is " the name of the disturbance of these fluids or mind." [23] When the material mind entertains an idea of disease and communicates it to the spirit, the erroneous thought initiates a disharmony causing the spirit " to form disease, after the form the spirit gives the mind." [24] Therefore, Quimby agreed with Davis that health is harmony,[25] and disease is due initially to man's ignorance. For Davis, it is the penalty man pays for his ignorance of the divine principles of his inner life; [26] for Quimby, the ignorance of Wisdom or the mind of opinion.

Both Davis and Quimby identify God with Wisdom,[27] which is man's real self. The latter wrote in 1865: " The real man is God or the first cause. Every idea that man embraces comes through his natural senses, but this real man is not seen, but is truth or wisdom." [28] And since truth can only be apprehended clairvoyantly, according to both, medical and natural science is discredited in favor of a higher spiritual science founded on

[17] Andrew Jackson Davis, *The Great Harmonia: Being the Revelation of the Natural, Spiritual, and Celestial Universe*, 5th ed. (Bela Marsh, 1859), Vol. 1, pp. 103, 113.

[18] *Ibid.*, p. 105.

[19] Davis, *The Harbinger of Health*, p. 19.

[20] *Ibid.*, pp. 43–44.

[21] Quimby MSS. in L.C., "No. 14," Vol. 1, p. 18.

[22] *Ibid.*, "No. 17," Dec., 1859, p. 24.

[23] Quimby, p. 69.

[24] *Ibid.*, p. 182.

[25] Quimby MSS. in L.C., unnamed article, Nov., 1859, Vol. 11, p. 6; also *ibid.*, "Truth," 1866, Vol. 6, p. 139; also Davis, *The Great Harmonia*, Vol. 1, p. 43.

[26] Davis, *The Harbinger of Health*, p. 45.

[27] Davis, *The Great Harmonia*, Vol. 1, p. 16; also Quimby MSS. in L.C., "What Is God? " Aug. 9, 1861, Vol. 5, p. 68; also "Religion Analyzed," Nov. 15, 1861, p. 135.

[28] *Ibid.*, "On Wisdom," 1865, Vol. 6, p. 55.

causes rather than on effects.[29]

Other parallels between Quimby and Davis are the belief in the native goodness of man; the privative concept of an evil principle, while recognizing the necessity of moral goodness and love; the similar idea of death and the continual progression of the soul; the Swedenborgian and Hermetic view of the spiritual sun as God's self-manifestation, which Quimby equates with Wisdom.[30]

If Davis influenced Quimby indirectly, one should not infer that Quimby agreed entirely with Davis, even when their interests coincide; nor should one deny Quimby his distinct contribution to the healing methods. He put into practice a philosophy in which the cause and cure of disease was wholly mental. The magnetic healing theory, formerly held by Quimby, Davis still retained as late as his *Harbinger of Health* in 1861; whereas in Quimby's manuscripts, 1859 to 1865, there is only opposition to it. Davis also listed numerous diseases and their physical remedies in the *Harbinger of Health*, but Quimby denied the validity of both disease and medicines.

Throughout his manuscripts he emphasizes that disease is not self-existent, but only error of the " mind of opinion." This, however, does not mean that sicknes is only in the imagination. As Quimby explains:

" I never tell a man that he imagines his sickness and only thinks himself diseased, when really he is not. According to this very truth I am trying to explain, disease is what follows an opinion, and when a man says he has the heart disease or liver complaint, I do not deny it in one sense. I do not admit the disease and tell him that he has not got it, but I affirm that the disease is in his belief and his belief is in error. If he says I believe I have the heart disease, then he tells what he really believes and his feelings are the literal proof of his belief. This is the only way I reconcile the truth which denies disease with its real ex-

---

[29] Quimby, " Two Sciences," p. 196; also Davis, *The Great Harmonia*, Vol. 2, p. 277.

[30] Quimby MSS. in L.C., " The Trinity of Opinions and the Trinity of God or Wisdom," Oct., 1862, Vol. 8, p. 134. I cite only this one reference which refers to the last item in the list, because of its rarity in Quimby's manuscripts. The others may be documented in many places in both Davis' and Quimby's writings.

istence, but to acknowledge disease and deny the symptoms is to contradict myself." [31]

He clarifies this further by saying, " I always admit the sickness, for that is what I feel and that is real, but the disease is another idea that I deny as having any identity outside of the mind or belief." [32]

A concentrated study of Davis and Quimby will reveal apparent contradictions, but these are often resolved when one views their philosophies as a whole. A case in point is the status of matter in Quimby's thought.

The Natural Versus the Spiritual

Quimby sometimes displays a dualism of spirit and matter; at other times, a monism of God or Wisdom as the only reality. On the one hand, he says that matter is " eternal and cannot be destroyed," though its form may be changed; [33] on the other hand, he speaks of it as " a shadow of a substance . . . a vacuum to be filled by wisdom," when man learns the truth. [34] Most often he speaks of matter as ignorance or error, [35] and natural man, as a man of error to be distinguished from the man of Science or Wisdom. [36] Therefore, he means that natural man, including matter, exists phenomenally, but as an error of man's mind of opinion. Matter is an idea that Wisdom speaks into existence, he says, but its existence as matter is due to the belief of man, while " to wisdom it is nothing." [37] Thus its status is a semantic problem that depends upon whether one speaks from the standpoint of natural man or God.

31 Quimby MSS. in L.C., "Elements of Progress," 1863, Vol. 6, p. 33.
32 Ibid., "Disease and Sickness," Vol. 9, p. 254.
33 Ibid., "Concerning Happiness," 1865, Vol. 7, p. 157.
34 Ibid., "II," Jan., 1861, Vol. 4, p. 72, etc.
35 Ibid., "The Subject of Mind," Feb., 1861, Vol. 4, p. 113, etc.
36 Ibid., "An Introduction," 1864, Vol. 10, p. 13, and in many other passages.
37 Ibid., "Disease and Its Causes," 1864, Vol. 6, p. 151.

Ethics

Quimby's ethics stem from his doctrine of the man of Wisdom who is one with God, as opposed to the natural man of opinion and error who is ignorant of his divine nature. Since God fills all space, and matter and natural man are only shadows of the divine substance, there is then only a " vacuum ready to be filled by wisdom when man arrives at the truth of the substance that makes the shadow." Consequently, he said, " It is impossible to disobey God in any one thing." [38] The laws, whose transgression brings punishment to natural man, are of man's own making,[39] and their infractions are the sins that lead to disease and death.[40] However, God does not compel man to follow him, Quimby continues, but instead gives sanction to whatever man agrees.[41] The law, although fixed, gives punishment only so long as one believes it. Quimby's point here, which may appear untenable if generalized to include all laws, finds a rational basis in Quimby's experience. Although he makes no such illustration, he would have said that man regards as a law the statement that pain follows the jab of a pin into one's finger. Under ordinary circumstances all will confirm this to be a fact based upon scientific inductive reasoning, but Quimby would have said that it was founded on man's belief. Certainly one familiar with hypnosis like Quimby would agree, because the hypnotist may stick a pin into his hypnotized subject without causing any discomfort, because he can momentarily change his subject's belief through suggestion.

Quimby taught what he considered to be the real science embodied in the Wisdom of God, whose attainment would free man from the laws of his opinions. Then he would have a new freedom, " independent of all creeds and laws of man." And being subjected to only laws of his own agreement, he would be free from the laws of sin, sickness, and death.[42]

[38] *Ibid.*, " Christ Explained," Vol. 4, p. 72.
[39] *Ibid.*, " XI," July 11, 1862, Vol. 8, p. 66; also, " II," Vol. 4, p. 73.
[40] *Ibid.*, " The Subject of Mind," Feb., 1861, Vol. 4, p. 102.
[41] *Ibid.*, " II," Vol. 4, p. 73.
[42] *Idem;* also " Explanation of Matter," Jan., 1861, Vol. 4, p. 80; also " The Subject of Mind," Feb., 1861, Vol. 4, p. 110 (not in Dresser ed., but misdated by him).

Here is a type of mysticism according to which man might flee from the world of error to the free world of his subjectivity, the Wisdom of God, the higher Science of Health. Quimby explains what being in God and recognition of his Wisdom really means in the following lines:

"In the first place he puts no restrictions on me; in fact, he is in me and just as I know myself, I know him; so that I and God are one just as my children and I are one. So to please myself I please God, and to injure myself I injure my God . . . just as I measure out to you I measure out to myself. As you and I are one, you and your neighbor are one, and to love your neighbor as yourself is more than all the prayers of the priests. . . . So my religion is my wisdom which is not of this world, but of that wisdom that will break in pieces the wisdom of man, and man's wisdom is the superstition of heathen idolatry. All science is at variance with it." [43]

When Quimby tries to express this in Christian terms, the distinction between natural man and the man of Wisdom is ethically the distinction he makes between law and the Gospel.

"The law is a representative of the natural man; the Gospel or Science that of Spiritual man. So what the law or natural man cannot explain by his arguments, Science coming through the natural man and putting an end of his (common sense) or reason, introduces a higher law or reason and appeals to the higher elements or Christ." [44] Natural man, bound by law and error, is "superstitious, bigoted, overbearing, proud, vain, full of cunning, deceit, and all the passions of the beast." [45] Whereas sin or ignorance separates natural man from God or truth, attachment to God's Wisdom results in a new birth into this Wisdom, which entails freedom from disease and death, and responsibility for one's acts. [46] When "Science" is accepted, there is a new mode of reasoning, which Quimby calls the new heaven. "To enter into it is to be baptized in the blood or belief of Jesus

[43] *Ibid.*, "XXIV," Nov., 1860, Vol. 3, pp. 188–189.
[44] *Ibid.*, "Disease and Sickness," 1863, Vol. 9, p. 251.
[45] *Ibid.*, "What Is the Relation of God to Man?" Aug., 1861, Vol. 5, p. 88.
[46] *Ibid.*, "No. 15," Vol. 1, p. 22; also "What Is God?" Aug. 9, 1861, Vol. 5, p. 69; also "Death," March, 1861, Vol. 4, p. 120; also "On the Circulation of the Blood," Dec. 3, 1863, Vol. 9, p. 214.

which is Christ or Science." [47] To be converted from error or have error explained is his meaning of forgiveness of sin [48] and freedom from disease and death, [49] because Quimby believed " all evils are the result of false reasoning." [50]

Concerning natural evil, which causes misery through events of nature, Quimby offers the same explanation as Davis. God has no part in man's suffering occasioned by a burnt finger, etc. Man may suffer the consequences of a natural law, but he has not broken it. Natural evil is thus defined causally, but not purposefully, except to infer man's progression by recognizing his error. The following is his explanation: " If you throw a stone into the air, it returns with just as much force as it received; this is a truth and of course a law. But God had nothing to do with the reaction, for that was contained in the act. This is also a truth or law and contains no reward or punishment. But if you from your ignorance let the stone fall on your head, you have not obeyed or disobeyed a law and deserve no reward or punishment, but from your ignorance you have learned a fact. (A stone will come down on your head if you get under it when it is falling, and that is a fact.)" [51] Good and evil are truth and error.[52]

Quimby's Christology

Quimby was very critical of the traditional Christian churches. However, amid accusations that their religion rested on opinion rather than on God's Wisdom, he still credited Jesus with the discovery of the truth that would correct the error of sickness.[53] His own belief he referred to as " Science," in two or more passages, as " Science of Health," and in only one noted place, as " Christian Science." [54]

[47] Ibid., "Concerning the Use of Medicine," Vol. 10, p. 91.
[48] Ibid., "The Definition of Words," 1865, Vol. 7, p. 159.
[49] Ibid., "Death," March, 1861, Vol. 4, p. 120; also "XXIV," Vol. 3, pp. 162–163.
[50] Ibid., "Disease and Sickness," 1863, Vol. 9, p. 254.
[51] Ibid., "XI," 1862, Vol. 8, p. 66.
[52] Ibid., "Religion," May 1, 1864, Vol. 6, p. 175.
[53] Ibid., "X," April, 1862, Vol. 8, p. 60.
[54] Ibid., "Aristocracy and Democracy," Feb., 1863, Vol. 7, p. 94.

Like all later metaphysical leaders, he made a distinction be-tween Jesus and the Christ: " Jesus was the representative of man, while Christ was the Science which took away the errors or sins of man." [55] Christ or Wisdom, which was manifested in man,[56] was both the Father and the Son of God; [57] Jesus, the man, was the same as we are except that his embodiment of the Christ [58] upon receiving God's Wisdom made him both God and man.[59]

In at least two different passages Quimby writes concerning the Trinity. In one essay he says: " God is the word for that Substance called the father; Jesus or the Matter, the son; the explanation of the union of wisdom and matter is the Holy Ghost or Science." He explains further that the Holy Ghost is the " science of language that conveys the idea to the sick or associates the mind with the thing." [60]

In the other essay he writes: " The trinity of God is wisdom or God, the father; health, Science, or wisdom in practice, the son; and the explanation of the two, the Holy Ghost. These three are one and the same in power and wisdom. And to be born of the spirit of wisdom is to break from your wickedness or opinions and turn to the truth." [61]

The Quimby Manuscripts

During Quimby's stay in Portland, Maine, from 1859 to 1865, he became acquainted with the two daughters of Judge Ashur Ware of the U.S. Supreme Court. After becoming his patients, the two sisters suggested he write down his theories which were

[55] *Ibid.*, " The Definition of Words," 1865, Vol. 7, p. 164.

[56] *Ibid.*, " Defense Against Making Myself Equal to Christ," Nov., 1862, Vol. 9, p. 18; also "Disease and Sickness," 1863, p. 252.

[57] *Ibid.*, "Defense Against Making Myself Equal to Christ," p. 18.

[58] *Ibid.*, unnamed article, 1864, Vol. 9, p. 173; also "Christ Explained," Vol. 4, p. 9; also "Disease and Sickness," 1863, Vol. 9, p. 251. Davis also made an analo-gous distinction between Jesus the man and Christ the Principle of Love which is in man, while Jesus was our great *exemplar*. Andrew Jackson Davis, *Answers to Ever-Recurring Questions from the People: A Sequel to the Penetralia* (Austin Publishing Co., 1926, first published and copyrighted in 1862), p. 165.

[59] *Ibid.*, " Spiritualism," March, 1861, Vol. 5, p. 5.

[60] *Ibid.*, " Language," 1864, Vol. 6, pp. 117–118.

[61] *Ibid.*, " The Trinity of Opinion and the Trinity of God or Wisdom," Oct., 1862, Vol. 8, p. 134.

so different from current ideas of healing. Thus began the main portion of his manuscripts (1859–1865), which the Ware sisters read and discussed with him, and often corrections were made when the words did not express his exact meaning. Copies of these were then lent to his patients.[62]

After Quimby's death in 1866, permission was not given to publish the manuscripts until Horatio Dresser was allowed to edit and issue them as the *Quimby Manuscripts* in 1921. The originals at the Library of Congress comprise over twenty-one hundred pages written in twelve large journals; the Dresser edition is therefore very selective in spite of Quimby's repetition of thought and articles.

Although George Quimby did not want his father's manuscripts published until there was no danger of controversy,[63] Quimby himself had written: " It is impossible to give a work like this to the public like any other. It will be more like a court record or a book on law with the arguments of each case." [64] His reasoning was that each article spoke to a particular situation with some person in mind. On the other hand, although his essays often deal with current topics of the day, such as democracy, slavery, and the Civil War, each reveals something of his philosophy. Perhaps his only use of the words " Christian Science " in his manuscripts appears in such an unlikely article as " Aristocracy and Democracy," dated February, 1863, to which is appended a note by George Quimby that " Mrs. Eddy did not see Dr. Quimby till October, 1863." [65]

While living in Portland, he is credited with curing a number of patients who later became leaders in the practice of mental healing. Among these were Julius Dresser, Warren Felt Evans, and Mrs. Patterson, known later as Mary Baker Eddy.

[62] Quimby, p. 21.
[63] *Ibid.*, pp. 20–21.
[64] Quimby MSS. in L.C., " Supplement to an article in Book III," 1862, Vol. 9, p. 178.
[65] *Ibid.*, " Aristocracy and Democracy," Feb., 1863, Vol. 7, p. 94. Note is on the flyleaf, Vol. 7. George Quimby's date is erroneous. See pages 260–261.

Warren Felt Evans

Second only to Quimby in importance to New Thought is Warren Felt Evans, who first met the former in 1863, the same year Evans quit the Methodist ministry to become a follower of Swedenborg. After hearing of Quimby's remarkable cures, and journeying to Portland for two treatments, Evans' quick recovery of health led him to study the new therapeutics. As a result of Quimby's encouragement he tried the method himself and then devoted the rest of his life to healing and writing. *The Mental Cure*, which he wrote and published in Boston in 1869, became the first book embodying Quimby's ideas. The philosophy, which was expressed in Swedenborgian terms, included also much that would have been foreign to Quimby, for which reason, perhaps, Evans gave no credit to his teacher. However, in his next book, *Mental Medicine*, published in 1872, he used Quimby's phraseology and expressed his debt. *Soul and Body* was issued in 1875 and his most noted work, *The Divine Law of Cure* in 1881.[66]

Since Quimby's work had been quite local, and only a few articles about his theories had been published during his lifetime, one must give credit to Evans for disseminating Quimby's ideas through the printed word. These books and others became well known to American readers through their various editions, and *The Mental Cure*, which was translated into several foreign languages, spread the philosophy abroad.

Evans' Early Teachings

Evans' thought developed considerably during the period between his first book and *The Divine Law of Cure*, but though the philosophy was buttressed by references to Swedenborg, Fichte, Edwards, Wesley, or even later, Hindu monism, Quimby's structure is visible.

In his first book Evans stressed that disease resulted from the disturbance in the spiritual body, which affected the physical

---

[66] Dresser, *History of the New Thought Movement*, pp. 71-76.

body by the law of correspondences.[67] He said that man's physical and mental difficulties represented " the antagonism between the inmost divine essence in man and the selfhood, or the blinded and disorderly activity of the mind. . . ." If the inner life pervaded and controlled the more external side of man's nature, he would return to God, " as did the humanity of Jesus." [68]

Evans went beyond Quimby in delineating the spiritual causes of disease. He saw clearly, like recent scientific experimenters, that various stresses, such as fear and other emotions, e.g., melancholy, envy, anger, jealousy, etc., were disturbances that could lead to illness.[69]

While anticipating the work of Freud by noting that the sexual instinct could cause disharmony leading to trouble, he also recognized that sex had an important role in conjugal love. And further, since the life of God was love, man should open his heart to the divine influx and impart it to others as part of his purpose in life. If the divine impulse were perverted, however, by man's failure to keep in harmony with God's spiritual laws, selfishness would arise as a root of moral and physical evil.[70]

Evans also maintained that it was important to find the cause of sickness, which clairvoyant or intuitive perception could reveal. Upon its discovery the healer should use the " law by which mind communicates its spiritual states and forces to another. . . ." He should disregard the material body of the patient and " *speak as a spirit to his spirit.*" [71] This " law," already implicit in Quimby's thought, was the principle behind Quimby's " absent treatment," which later metaphysical groups employed. Thus modern practitioners believe they can treat a patient, even though miles away, by realizing that the person's true nature is of God instead of error. Mrs. Eddy gave much attention to the obverse of this idea, which she called " malicious

[67] Warren Felt Evans, *The Mental Cure Illustrating the Influence of the Mind on the Body Both in Health and in Disease and the Psychological Method of Treatment* (H. H. and T. W. Carter, 1869), p. 90.

[68] *Ibid.*, p. 23.

[69] *Ibid.*, pp. 90–91.

[70] *Ibid.*, pp. 214–217.

[71] *Ibid.*, pp. 268–269. Here Evans speaks of his practice as " magnetic healing," but here not to be confused with mesmerism or hypnotism.

animal magnetism." She believed that the evil thoughts of her enemies used against her caused many of her troubles and even the death of her last husband, Gilbert Eddy.

Evans' Later Development in Philosophy

In *The Divine Law of Cure* Dresser's point is well taken: the emphasis is not so much on a spiritual transformation stressing love and will as it is on a practical idealism advocating right thought.[72] Although the idealistic emphasis marked a difference in this later work, it was foreshadowed in *The Mental Cure*, where Evans attributed to the power of words the characteristic separating man from animal. He interpreted Jesus' use of it as follows:

" Jesus of Nazareth possessed this divine power in an eminent degree, and nature seemed passive under his hands. He comprehended the potential spiritual force of words, as a medium of communicating life and sanative psychological influence. He employed certain formulas or expressive sentences into which he concentrated and converged his whole mental force and made them the means of transmitting spiritual life to the disordered mind." [73]

Evans included a number of " pregnant utterances," which he claimed Jesus " used according to the nature of the case," for example, " Go in peace; Be of good cheer, thy sins are forgiven thee; Be it unto thee according to thy faith. . . . Peace be unto thee." [74] Here appeared for the first time the prototypes of the positive formula prayers which have dominated the practice of all later New Thought healing groups.

In *The Divine Law of Cure*, Evans inveighed against a priestly ecclesiasticism of the Christian churches. Instead of the pulpit describing what traditional theologians thought *about* God, he said that it should give to those desiring spiritual nutriment what it *knows* of him. This would point the way for the intuitional divine awareness, the potentiality of which all have,

---

[72] Dresser, *History of the New Thought Movement*, pp. 89–90.
[73] Evans, *op. cit.*, p. 306.
[74] *Idem.*

and would make possible the union of the soul with God, which he regarded as the central idea of Christianity.[75] But then as if to fortify himself against counterattacks from Christian theologians, he sought to base his idealism on philosophical fragments from Berkeley, Fichte, Schelling, Hegel, Schleiermacher, Wesley, Edwards, and others.

Starting with the belief that God was all and in-all, Evans propounded a monistic philosophy, which he compared to Fichte's Christian pantheism in *The Divine Law of Cure*, and to aspects of Hindu monism in *The Primitive Mind Cure* (1885), and in *Esoteric Christianity and Mental Therapeutics* (1886). But one should not infer that he had lost sight of the law of correspondences or would allow the individual self to be absorbed in the deity, although his vision is not always clear. He postulated the belief in distinction but not separation of the human soul from God. Man differed from God through his finitude, but since there was only one life in the universe, there was only one Being, which was multiplied in manifested existence as many.[76]

Correspondence in unity is also observed in Evans' doctrine of the Animus Mundi, held also by Davis [77] and Swedenborg, and stemming from earlier views of Neoplatonic philosophy and alchemy. This was the belief that God emanated as the Soul of the World, and Evans added that there was likewise an analogous relation between man and his body. Just as the latter were essentially one, so also was the action of God and nature. Therefore, the laws of nature were the uniform mode of the divine activity.[78]

" Nature is spirit visible, and spirit is invisible nature," quoted Evans from Schelling, and from this foundation he taught that matter was only spirit made visible to the mind. Material things were complemented by spiritual entities and together constituted one undivided and indivisible whole.[79]

[75] Warren Felt Evans, *The Divine Law of Cure* (H. H. Carter, 1884), pp. 33, 38, 44.
[76] *Ibid.*, pp. 16–23.
[77] Davis, *The Great Harmonia*, Vol. 2, p. 284.
[78] Evans, *The Divine Law of Cure*, p. 48.
[79] *Ibid.*, p. 147.

Since God, the Divine Mind and Spirit, comprehended all reality as an ultimate unity, Evans would not deny the reality of the material world, although he followed Bishop Berkeley in his refusal to grant it a separate existence outside the mind. Therefore, he reached a subjective idealism which accepted the phenomena of matter, but refused to ascribe to it noumenal existence outside the mind.[80] While recognizing scientific views of matter as forms of force, he taught that these were spiritual and that all causation was mental. Matter was then only a phenomenal manifestation of spirit with mind as the only real substance, i.e., underlying reality.[81] From Jonathan Edwards he found support for his view that matter existed only in the mind[82] — the Mind of God.

Evans believed that man, in whom divinity became human,[83] was an incarnation of the Divine Mind.[84] He formed part of the " Collective Man, the universal Divine Humanity," or the Christ,[85] an idea originating in early gnostic thought. His body was formed as a representation of mind which the preexistent soul continually created just as God through his thought projected the universe. It was not something superadded to the mind, but was a " presentation of the mind to itself," like an image in a mirror.

Since life itself was uncreated, " our individual life must perpetually spring from the Divine Being, and though never absolutely disconnected from its Source, yet we come to a distinct individuality in our conception. In this God comes to self-limitation, and the soul enters into time and space, and thus becomes an individual."[86]

The fountainhead of man's divine essence, the link between him and God, was the spirit which connects soul with body.[87] Since the spirit, which neither evil nor sickness could contam-

[80] *Ibid.*, pp. 150, 152.
[81] *Ibid.*, pp. 146–147.
[82] *Ibid.*, p. 169.
[83] Evans, *The Mental Cure*, p. 32.
[84] *Ibid.*, pp. 20–21.
[85] Warren Felt Evans, *Esoteric Christianity and Mental Therapeutics* (H. H. Carter & Karrick, 1886), p. 31.
[86] Evans, *The Divine Law of Cure*, pp. 163–165; 179–180.
[87] Evans, *The Mental Cure*, p. 59.

inate,[88] was equated with mind as the only substance underlying all material things, by changing the mental state there would be a corresponding modification of the form of matter, resulting in either health or disease.[89]

It would appear that Evans created his idealism to support his view that thought was the creative principle of God and man, the power of mind over the appearance of matter. He cited Fichte as his source for believing that the spheres of existence and thought were synonymous, and that the reality of the body lay in our thoughts and feelings. Therefore, to live truly meant to *think* truly.[90]

At this point Evans begins his Christian orientation. True thought, resulting in man's well-being and health, was the Logos. He said, " In the system which I adopt, the Logos, the Word, the Divine Thought, is that which creates and governs all things, and the universe as a whole, and in its parts is a manifestation of it, and a permanent expression of it." [91]

This Logos, or Divine Thought, was in all men, he continued, and the founders of all great religions had a harmonious blending of intellect and religious fervor by means of which their intellect was transported to a divine realm of thought. They were recipients of the indwelling Logos and became incarnations of God in a true sense. In a lesser sense, according to Evans, the Word was made flesh in all men.

The greatest example was Jesus,[92] who by means of the Christ-Principle, the living Word, or spiritual intelligence, became the Christ.[93] Its power, which Evans said was predominant in the healings of Jesus, appeared as " an intelligent mastery of nature by the soul." Man's former dominion over nature was recovered through Jesus, who brought the disturbed world order back to its original harmony. Thus Jesus lived in harmony

[88] Warren Felt Evans, *The Primitive Mind Cure: the Nature and Power of Faith; or, Elementary Lessons in Christian Philosophy and Transcendental Medicine* (H. H. Carter & Co., 1885), p. 187.

[89] Evans, *The Divine Law of Cure*, p. 148.

[90] *Ibid.*, p. 205.

[91] *Ibid.*, p. 64.

[92] *Ibid.*, pp. 120–121.

[93] *Ibid.*, pp. 137, 124.

with nature, which was God's will expressed as supreme law.[94] Evans wrote: " There is a law of the action of the mind on the body that is no more an impenetrable mystery than the law of gravitation. It can be understood and acted upon in the cure of disease as well as any other law of nature. Here Knowledge, and especially *spiritual intelligence,* is power, and in the eyes of the multitude, the results of its operation in the healing power of Jesus were deemed a miraculous potentiality. As a law of nature expresses the uniform mode in which the Divine force manifests itself, a conformity to law is to us the only source of power. It is thus alone that we can make the Divine power available for the cure of disease." This law, according to Evans, was available to all, and would someday be known as well as any law of nature.[95]

Acordingly, Evans, like Quimby, believed that behind every disease was an erroneous habit of thought which could be changed to positive truth resulting in health. One would be only supplanting the error of disease, which was not, with the reality of being, which is.

This philosophy has ethical implications. Since God's will was man's well-being, sin was a disorder, an error, a divergance from God's will. Appearing first in the mind, the error translated itself into an effect upon the body by the law of correspondences. Thus sin was connected with disease as an " error, a wrong way of thinking, feeling, and acting, the remedy for which was truth, the displacement of ignorance." [96]

Evans' Two Principles of Healing

In Evans' philosophy, as in Quimby's, there are both religious and psychological aspects, the latter of which need not presuppose the former. Concerning the religious side, first presented in *The Mental Cure,* health is equated with the recognition of one's Christ nature. Here it is expressed in what he later called Christian perfection, the transformation of man's fear,

94 *Ibid.,* pp. 125–126.
95 *Ibid.,* pp. 127, 129–130.
96 *Ibid.,* pp. 235–240.

anxieties, hates, envy, jealousies, etc., to love, sympathy, faith, etc. Also, in *The Divine Law of Cure*, he said:

" Man is the highest manifestation of God in the universe. . . . We have our being in him; he has existence in us. . . . To find God there, and identify our life with his life, is to be invested with a power over disease like that which was exhibited by the Christ." [97]

Having regarded life as coming from God, and God's life as love, Evans concluded in one place that man's degree of life and health were proportional to his expression of love.[98] At the same time, however, he was moving from his earlier Methodist heritage to the metaphysical, because faith, although spoken of often, was becoming secondary to knowledge through thought as man's way to salvation. Man's inner struggle, and the need for repentance and forgiveness, which Wesley and Swedenborg both recognized, were being transformed into the denial of error.

The psychological aspect follows Quimby's early idea. Disease is wrong thinking. Change the thought and you have health. If this is a law of the mind, what is the need for theology? The recognition of this law would suffice, whether one believed in God or not. With Evans begins the New Thought reliance upon affirmative prayer or positive thinking — the affirmation of the condition desired. Although most metaphysicians believe affirmations open the way to union of the self with its higher and real nature, the self-sufficient God, a few have felt no need for theology. In the latter case affirmations are simply the means of " working the law," which brings about desired results. Therefore, one finds grounds for both a religious and secular psychological approach to mental healing.

Evans' works initiated the trend toward the practice of mental science, but when Mary Baker Eddy introduced Christian Science with the publication of *Science and Health*, many more people became interested in mental or spiritual healing. The declaration that Christian Science was based on a new revelation, however, touched off a series of arguments between Mrs. Eddy and those who had learned Quimby's teachings through

[97] *Ibid.*, p. 256.　　　　　[98] *Ibid.*, p. 244.

Evans and Julius and Anetta Dresser. As a result, many broke away from Mrs. Eddy to join this other healing faction. Because of their published works on mental healing, both Evans and Mrs. Eddy must be credited with exerting the greatest influence upon those who later called their philosophy New Thought.

V

New Thought

THE MOVEMENT, later known as New Thought, developed slowly during the nineteenth century after Quimby's death in 1866. His ideas, interpreted first through the works of Evans, became the springboard for mental science, since New Thought as an organization did not originate until the 1890's.

Evans' books encouraged others to apply his teachings, and soon lecturers on mental science became authors who spread the new movement. Others, too, like Julius and Anetta Dresser, who had been healed through Quimby, aided the growth. The Dressers began their own mental healing work in 1882 and their classes in 1883. But still more important for the movement was the controversy they started about the alleged use of the Quimby manuscripts by Mrs. Eddy, whom they had known through their mutual association with Quimby. They first set forth their ideas in a circular in 1884, followed by Julius Dresser's work, *The True History of Mental Science*, in 1887. Anetta Dresser herself wrote *The Philosophy of P. P. Quimby, with Selections from His Manuscripts and a Sketch of His Life*, published in 1895.

Because of this controversy and the desire for greater freedom of belief, many renegade Christian Scientists swelled the ranks of the mental science movement in the 1880's and added their own interpretations of Christian Science to the developing New Thought.

Early Individualistic Aspects

This movement displayed the greatest individualism of any metaphysical group. The new teachers sought bases for their ideas in various philosophies. Charles M. Barrows, like some, first looked to India for an antecedent foundation, and then like others, turned also to Emerson.[1] Even today, although New Thought leaders recognize their debt to Quimby and Evans, most would probably quote Emerson far more frequently. Quimby and Evans are known historically, but Emerson is their perennial philosopher, who bolsters their doctrines of the divinity of man, the one reality of the Divine Mind, the privative concept of evil, their accent upon the affirmative, etc.

Because of their individualistic freedom, however, some, like Miss M. J. Barnett, in her *Practical Metaphysics* (1889), read Theosophical principles into the philosophy; others, like William J. Colville, in his *Spiritual Science of Health and Healing* (1889), set their ideas in the framework of Spiritualism.[2] Still others, who were closer to the philosophy of Evans and Eddy, were oriented toward Christianity. Although no one writer's works became the sacred textbooks for New Thought because of the cherished freedom of interpretation, Evans' works possibly came as close as any in the early period. His idea of thought as a creative force became New Thought's " healing power of thought." His use of the term " suggestion " as meaning something that could be visualized in the mind prepared the way for Henry Wood's theory of "ideal suggestion through mental photography." Thoughts came to be regarded by Wood as *things*, a view that was foreign neither to Evans nor to Theosophy. Prentice Mulford, one of the immediate forerunners of New Thought, utilized the idea in his widely circulated pamphlets.[3]

---

[1] Dresser, *History of the New Thought Movement*, pp. 127–135.
[2] *Ibid.*, p. 136.
[3] *Ibid.*, p. 149 and note.

Gestefeld and Hopkins

In the procession of early leaders contributing to the developing New Thought, Ursula Gestefeld and Emma Curtis Hopkins are very important. Both had been Christian Scientists who had left the narrow path of Mrs. Eddy in the late 1880's to tread the broader way of New Thought.

Mrs. Eddy had denounced Mrs. Gestefeld, whom she herself had taught, when her erstwhile student published a book, *Ursula N. Gestefeld's Statement of Christian Science*. Mrs. Gestefeld retaliated with a pamphlet, *Jesuitism in Christian Science*, and left the organization to become a leader in New Thought. Her controversy with Mrs. Eddy not only helped widen the gap between Christian Science and New Thought, but also drove from Mrs. Eddy many like Charles Fillmore, who had been formerly sympathetic toward her.

Still more important to New Thought was Emma Curtis Hopkins, who had been a teacher at Woodstock Academy from which she had graduated.[4] After studying with Mrs. Eddy in 1883, she rose rapidly in the ranks of Christian Scientists to become the Editor of the *Christian Science Journal*, which she served from 1884 to October, 1885.[5] For reasons not entirely clear, she left the Christian Science organization between October, 1885, and June, 1886, because by the latter date she had consented to teach her own classes in Chicago.

Mrs. Hopkins was evidently very gifted. Within the year she had taught six hundred students and had established the Hopkins Association, whose meetings were patterned after church services with Bible classes for both adults and children. Branch associations spread rapidly. By December, 1887, there were twenty-one spanning the United States from New York to San Francisco and from Seattle to Louisville. Although credited with teaching over fifty thousand during her lifetime, she, more than anyone else, became a "teacher of teachers" of New Thought. Through her many lectures throughout the United

[4] Margaret Cushing, "Emma Curtis Hopkins, the Teacher of Teachers," in the *New Thought Bulletin*, Vol. 28, No. 2 (Spring, 1945), p. 5.
[5] Charles Braden, *Spirits in Rebellion: The Rise and Development of New Thought* (Southern Methodist University Press, 1963), p. 140.

States and through her seminary, which she established in Chicago in 1888, she became the teacher of many noted New Thought leaders and founders of allied organizations. Among these were Charles and Myrtle Fillmore, who began the Unity School of Christianity; Annie Rix Militz, who started the Home of Truth Movement; H. Emilie Cady, author of the New Thought classic, *Lessons in Truth;* [6] Mrs. Frank Bingham, who taught Nona Brooks, cofounder of the Divine Science Church; Malinda E. Cramer, well-known New Thought leader; the poetess, Ella Wheeler Wilcox; and Ernest Holmes, who organized the Church of Religious Science.

Mrs. Hopkins called her teaching " Christian Science," and the first name of her seminary was The Christian Science Theological Seminary. " Christian Science " was to be understood in a generic sense and distinguished from Mrs. Eddy's organization. Thus many students of Mrs. Gestefeld and Mrs. Hopkins referred to their belief by that name until Mrs. Eddy threatened lawsuits.

Mrs. Hopkins had a wider basis for her philosophy than Mrs. Eddy would have allowed, and this may be a clue to her defection from her erstwhile teacher. For in the first announcement of her seminary, appearing in the June issue of *Truth,* 1888, she accepted the validity of other revelations than the Bible:

" The Christian Science Theological Seminary is founded to hold daily sessions for free expression of the extreme conclusions to which Scripture propositions lead.

" *The Bibles of all times and nations are compared;* their miracles are shown to be the results of one order of reasoning and the absence of miracles shown to be the result of another order of reasoning." [7]

Development of the New Thought Organization

The name " New Thought " designating the movement gradually displaced other terms during the 1890's. Dr. Holcomb,

---

[6] Cushing, *loc. cit.,* pp. 5–6.
[7] *Ibid.,* quoted by Cushing from *Truth,* June, 1888. Italics are mine.

a Swedenborgian, used the name in a pamphlet, *Condensed Thoughts About Christian Science*. *New Thought* then became the name for a periodical in 1894, and the term was coming into use in Boston in 1895.[8] Others elsewhere in the East began applying the name to the mental healing movement until it gradually replaced other terms, e.g., Christian Science, Divine Science, Mental Science, and Practical Metaphysics.

In 1887 the classes of Emma Curtis Hopkins first revealed its philosophy in San Francisco, from which it spread along the Pacific Coast most commonly under the name of Divine Science made popular by Malinda Cramer.

The International Divine Science Association, which began in 1892, held its first convention in San Francisco in 1894. In the succeeding years between 1895 and 1897 there were annual conferences in Chicago, Kansas City, and St. Louis respectively.[9] In the same year as the fifth conference held in San Francisco again in 1899, the first " New Thought Convention " using that name was held in February, 1899, in Hartford. This was followed by a second in Boston in October of the same year. It had been convened by the International Metaphysical League, whose name had perhaps been adopted at the first meeting. This was the first stage in the later development of the International New Thought Alliance.[10]

The Preface to the First Annual Proceedings of the International Metaphysical League expresses what the delegates believed to be the broad foundation of New Thought. It is " based . . . on the philosophy of practical idealism, the religion of spiritual development that leads to a conscious oneness with God, and the science that has for its foundation the universality of Love and Law; it has no hampering creed, no personal dogmas, no forms or ceremonials, no need for destructive methods. It is broad, tolerant, optimistic, constructive." [11]

The spirit of New Thought at that time was expressed in the address of welcome by President Charles B. Patterson at

---

[8] Dresser, *op. cit.*, p. 153.
[9] *Ibid*, pp. 192–196.
[10] Braden, *op. cit.*, pp. 171–172.
[11] International Metaphysical League, *Proceedings of the First Annual Convention*, Boston, 1899, p. 5.

this convention. Referring to the new organization, he said: "It has no desire to take away any good thing that people have acquired through their religious organizations. It has not come to destroy, but rather to fulfill — to make manifest, so far as possible, the perfect Law of God. It has no desire to build churches, or to start a new sect, or to formulate any creed or dogma. I believe that its one great thought is to bring a deeper knowledge of law and order into the individual — into the Universal Life. It aims at showing to the world the possibility of *recognizing* immutable Law, and through such recognition will come conformity to law and a higher standard both to the individual and to the race; that social and economic conditions will be changed, not in any arbitrary way, but through people seeing the right and then desiring to *do* right." [12]

New Thought began with no idea of establishing churches or sects. All people were invited to their national conventions held in various cities almost every year. When the meeting was held in Boston in 1907, Professor Josiah Royce and Dr. R. C. Cabot gave addresses on the opening day. All clergymen in Boston were invited the second day, because the subject was "The Relation of the Parochial Ministry to Spiritual Healing." The Chairman was the Reverend Albert B. Shields, an Episcopal priest. Ministers even attended the 1908 convention because of their interest in healing, and some held offices.[13] But gradually the independent churches of New Thought were organized and began having eleven o'clock services, and some leaders began forming separate sects.

"*What's in a Name?*"

Although the name "New Thought" had been used earlier than the Boston Conference, even then as now there has been some doubt concerning its fitness. To many the name has been a misnomer, because it implied something new about the truth that they believed even Jesus knew. These, like Quimby, maintained that they had merely rediscovered the true teachings of

---

[12] *Ibid.*, p. 17.
[13] Dresser, *op. cit.*, p. 201.

Jesus. Thus at the Boston convention the preliminary notice referred to the " so-called ' New Thought.' "

At the present time Dr. Fenwicke Holmes, an old-timer in the movement, disdains to use the name for his own philosophy. Although having been prominent at New Thought conventions and recognizing that many of his beliefs are held by New Thought, he prefers to call his own view " mental science." Many others of the movement, however, do not disparage the term " New Thought." Dr. Raymond Barker, a noted minister of the Church of Religious Science Churches, and former INTA president, felt no compunction about his identification with the name, but pointed to a problem of the movement, namely, the great diversity of ideas. He bemoaned the fact that the INTA included some who were radical enough in their individualism to be considered " crackpot." " Unfortunately for New Thought," he said, " when covering the conventions, the press seem to select the more sensational ideas of a few leaders and have stigmatized the name."

Probably most of the movement would agree with the justification given at the conference in 1895: " We call it new, while in a deep sense no truth is new. But eternal and immutable principles are constantly receiving fresh application and adaptation."

It was further explained that New Thought is new in the sense that it transcends the laws of materialistic science to discover " innumerable beneficent laws of undreamed of potency — physical, psychical, and spiritual," which it seeks to apply.[14]

In 1908 after several revisions of both constitution and name the parent organization was called the National New Thought Alliance, the name it retained until becoming the International New Thought Alliance in 1914.[15]

Guiding Principles of New Thought

At the annual convention at St. Louis in 1917, a *Declaration of Principles* was made, which was revised in 1919 and again in

---

[14] International Metaphysical League, *op. cit.*, p. 25.
[15] Dresser, *op. cit.*, p. 202.

1950. The last complete revision has suffered only one slight change in 1957.[16] The following represents the present list:

" We affirm the inseparable oneness of God and man, the realization of which comes through spiritual intuition, the implications of which are that man can reproduce the Divine perfection in his body, emotions, and in all his external affairs.

" We affirm the freedom of each person in matters of belief.

" We affirm the Good to be supreme, universal, and eternal.

" We affirm that the Kingdom of Heaven is within us, that we are one with the Father, that we should love one another, and return good for evil.

" We affirm that we should heal the sick through prayer, and that we should endeavor to manifest perfection ' even as our Father in Heaven is perfect.'

" We affirm our belief in God as the Universal Wisdom, Love, Life, Truth, Power, Peace, Plenty, Beauty, and Joy, in whom we live and move and have our being.

" We affirm that man's mental states are carried forward into manifestation and become his experience through the Creative Law of Cause and Effect.

" We affirm that the Divine Nature expressing itself through man, manifests itself as health, supply, wisdom, love, life, truth, power, peace, beauty, and joy.

" We affirm that man is an invisible spiritual dweller within a human body, continuing and unfolding as a spiritual being beyond the change called physical death.

" We affirm that the universe is the body of God, spiritual in essence, governed by God through laws which are spiritual in reality even when material in appearance." [17]

Flexibility of New Thought Through Individualism

Outside the above principles New Thought leaders may hold many different views including various interpretations of their common statements of belief. Freedom of belief and interpretation is the essence of New Thought. Therefore, it has both

[16] Braden, *op. cit.*, pp. 192, 195, 200.
[17] *Ibid.*, pp. 198–200.

profited and suffered because of its individualism. Its cherished freedom has allowed it to utilize the growing research in psychology, psychoanalysis, and medical science. At least as early as 1899 its leaders could fit into their philosophy the new theories of medical science concerning the relationship between mental and emotional attitudes and bodily health. Henry Wood could cite the findings of Dr. George E. Gorham, M. D., showing the role of faith in the " unconscious physical process," and the effects of " fear, anger, and other inharmonious mental states, upon the same wonderfully delicate mechanism." [18] New Thought made use of principles most Americans now accept as psychosomatic medicine.

It is also to the credit of most New Thought churches, whether organized or not, that they allow freedom to utilize medical services. This differs from the more conservative Christian Science practice, which with but few exceptions relies upon its own principles.

Whereas New Thought can easily reinterpret its beliefs in keeping with the growth of learning, Christian Science must read each Sunday without interpretation the words of Mary Baker Eddy, which reflect only the knowledge of her period. This is not to disparage whatever pragmatic truths Christian Science may contain, since that which healed then, still operates today. But Christian Science by its nature presents a more consistent interpretation. New Thought individualism, which accepts so much from such varied backgrounds, makes a very inconsistent contribution to philosophy. Therefore, one finds in New Thought some appealing ideas of well-educated, intelligent speakers and writers mingled very often with bizarre theories and wild, extravagant claims of the ignorant and simple-minded.

Individualism in the metaphysical movements has fostered many branches, which differ from one another in some respects. Out of the entire body of metaphysical doctrines some former New Thought leaders have made their own selections and emphases and formed separate sects. In some cases the organization has withdrawn from the INTA, e.g., the Unity School of

[18] International Metaphysical League, *op. cit.*, pp. 27–28.

Christianity, although part of its membership has not; in other cases, like the Home of Truth, it has remained in the INTA.

New Thought's diversity was characterized at its 1889 convention in a lecture entitled " After Christianity, What? " The Reverend Solon Lauer predicted that " ecclesiastical Christianity " would pass away because it did not fill the spiritual needs of a progressive race. He next considered whether religion would be represented largely by Spiritualism, Theosophy, Christian Science, or the type of Christian Science that generically New Thought represented. Quite to the point he said:

" Although I have spoken of Spiritualism, Theosophy, and Christian Science as separate movements, the fact is there are no very distinct lines of demarcation between them. All have certain things in common, and perhaps a broad and generous interpretation of each would remove most of the points of seeming antagonism. Certain it is that there are thousands of persons who read the literature and attend the public meetings of all these movements, and who find much to love and admire in them." [19]

With such possibilities for division, as early as 1899 there was a plea for unity to give strength to the movement. Jane W. Yarnall pleaded at the convention for a basis that would be above personal authority or traditional prejudices, so there would be no incentive for disagreement.[20] This hope, of course, was not realized.

If the broad ideas of New Thought are contained in its *Declaration of Principles*, an inspection of its literature will reveal greater contrasts within the system and also with traditional Christianity. Let us examine some of them more clearly.

First, New Thought tends to be pantheistic or close to pantheism. Most of its adherents would agree with Malinda Cramer that the only reality is God. She said:

" Until we see that the unity of Good is the unity of God, that the word *God* stands for the All-Omnipotence, Omniscience, and Omnipresence — and that we in no way differ from it, either in spirit, soul or body, we do not appreciate the

[19] *Ibid.*, pp. 54–55.
[20] *Ibid.*, p. 71.

true presentation of Divine Science." [21]

Here the extreme doctrine of God's immanence makes man divine in nature. On the other hand, there have been others, like Henry Wood, who criticize this dominant trend. Concerning God, Wood said:

" While he is in and back of all things, it would be pantheism to say that everything — as we behold it — as God. Immanence and transcendence are complementary aspects. To rate him as ' principle ' as that term is generally understood, is unworthy and such a concept will never fill the void in the human constitution." [22]

Horatio Dresser also defended Wood's statement and criticized extremists who might say, " I am God," or who would reduce the idea of God to an impersonal principle.[23]

Secondly, since New Thought believes the only reality to be God who is good, evil must be understood in a privative sense, i.e., the absence of good and consequently the absence of reality. Although historic Christianity has dealt with the problem of evil in various ways, it tends to recognize a reality of evil that is not to be eliminated by its denial, as New Thought is inclined to do.

Third, New Thought generally frowns on the use of the word " sin." Its use would seem to many to imply a dogma of orthodoxy. Yet it would be unfair to New Thought to say there is no concern for the moral life. Without expecting to hear many sermons on sin and forgivenes in New Thought churches, one notes an emphasis on the positive side, men's need to love one another. Even here, however, although the historic churches would agree with New Thought on the importance of love as a guide to action, they would stress the sinful nature of man and agree with Paul when he said: " I do not understand my own actions. For I do not do what I want, but I do the very thing I hate " (Rom. 7:15, RSV).

Concerning the moral life and man's duty to man, however,

[21] Malinda E. Cramer, "The Unity of Good," International Metaphysical League, *op. cit.*, pp. 137–138.

[22] Henry Wood, "Criticism of the New Thought," in *Spirit of the New Thought*, ed. by Horatio Dresser (The Thomas Y. Crowell Company, 1917), p. 199.

[23] *Idem.*

one again finds extremes in New Thought. Horatio Dresser, following the leads in Evans' earlier works, advocated the acquisition of purity within. To put the Word of God into practice was essential as proof of man's having found the Kingdom. As he said: " To seek it in absolute seriousness is to aspire to be perfect, even as the Father in heaven is perfect." [24] Man's duty to others was of paramount importance.

The opposite extreme is found in the statement of Prentice Mulford: " The government of your life is a matter which lies entirely between God and yourself. . . . Regarding others, ' ought ' is a word and idea with which we have nothing to do." [25]

The very influential Emilie Cady would solve the problem of doing God's will by affirming, " God works in me to will and to do whatsoever he wishes me to do; hence I cannot fail." [26] This last affirmation might seem to a traditional Christian as an oversimplification of the problem by omitting the inner struggle of trying to overcome one's sinful nature. But New Thought does not accept the doctrine of the fall of man.

Fourth, New Thought omits a doctrine of God's judgment upon man, which for the Christian is complementary to his love. Many New Thought adherents would probably agree with Prentice Mulford that ". . . the warning of penalty was necessary when humanity was cruder. The race was blind. . . . But when we begin to see clearer, as now the more quickened and sensitive of our race do begin to see, we need no rod, any more than you need a man with a club to prevail on you to go to a feast." [27]

Mulford's words, of course, were written before either of the two world wars and their concomitant suffering. They partook of the optimism that in a different way was also characteristic of much of Protestant Christianity of the same period. Liberal Protestants had hopes for the regeneration of mankind

---

24 Horatio W. Dresser, "The Sermon on the Mount," in Dresser, *op. cit.*, pp. 114–117.

25 Eva Martin, *Prentice Mulford*, *"New Thought" Pioneer* (London: William Rider & Co., 1921), p. 276.

26 Cady, *op. cit.*, p. 46.

27 Martin, *op. cit.*, p. 75.

through a social gospel. But the chastening of war has made them more pessimistic about humanity's progress. Neo-orthodoxy reaffirmed the sinful nature of man and his judgment by God.

Fifth, as a corollary to the above, New Thought has no doctrine of God's action in history. The traditional churches believe that God acts judgmentally through history in working out his purposes.

Sixth, although New Thought emphasizes love, its nature differs from the ideal of the traditional churches. While New Thought advocates the Golden Rule, there is no mention of sacrifice in loving action exemplified most highly by the death of Jesus Christ upon a cross. Christianity has taught that the type of love involved in one's bearing the cross of Jesus and following him sacrificially brings *pain* and *suffering*.

Henry Harrison Brown, one of New Thought's early leaders, showed the contrast in the following words:

" It is no longer a struggle for physical existence, but for spiritual expression. This demands not force, not sacrifice, not pain, not suffering, not labor, but love and love alone."

One should not be led to infer from this that all who are in this tradition are selfishly thinking only of themselves. There are certainly many whose lives are sacrificial witnesses to their faith. Still, *sacrificial* love, which means *suffering*, is not emphasized. Pain must logically be denied as a reality by New Thought.

Seventh, New Thought did not follow the interest of most traditional churches in a social gospel in the latter part of the nineteenth century, but there were some leaders, like Julius Dresser, who felt its reverberations. Dresser wrote:

" A fear for the New Thought people to put away out of their doctrine and out of themselves, is the fear the frankest self-examination and acknowledgement of what is true in personal defects in ourselves or in others can do the slightest harm so long as the mind is fixed upon, and dominated by, God and the true ideal from him. . . . We have only to set aside self-love, self-glory, and work earnestly in any cause, by every word and deed of love that opportunity offers, to find ourselves growing gradually in wisdom and understanding, and out of our ills and every form of unhappiness." [28]

His son, Horatio Dresser, believed likewise after the First World War that the secret of happiness was not in self-love and self-glory, but in loving service to others. On the contrary, however, Henry Wood's view at the close of the last century became more normal for New Thought. He spoke at a time when some, like the Dressers, were being influenced by the trend in the American churches. Speaking of the aim of New Thought, Wood said:

" It does not deal directly with surface phenomena, but with their inner springs of causation. I believe the danger that most threatens the New Thought of today is its more or less intimate amalgamation with other reforms, whether real or theoretical, upon lower planes. If we scatter our energies in the attempted repression of mere effects, the true momentum of the movement will be lessened or lost. Without uttering a word pro or con concerning political socialism, or theoretical land systems, tax systems, labor systems, and other political questions, I believe the New Thought should be kept above and distinct. A true moral socialism will result from a free spiritual individualism. . . .

" The New Thought believes in the potency of God and Law, and that an aggressive pessimism, emphasizing the evil of human conditions, is unscientific and harmful, even when well meant." [29]

Eighth, faith, although present in New Thought's idea of salvation, tends to be faith in its principles rather than in Jesus Christ as Lord and Savior preached by the Christian churches. New Thought's key to salvation is knowledge of one's unity with God and the realization of his divine nature, which is perfect. Thus it comes closer to the philosophies of Gnosticism or monistic Vedanta in this respect, but differs from these forms of mysticism in its emphasis upon the practical benefits of health, prosperity, etc., rather than upon the ecstasy of union.

Ninth, New Thought in agreement with traditional churches

[28] Dresser, *op. cit.*, pp. 291–292.
[29] International Metaphysical League, *op. cit.*, pp. 30–31.

that the Kingdom of Heaven is within, holds, however, that thought is responsible for one's heaven and hell. The traditional churches would see this as a great oversimplification. Moreover, they would believe the Kingdom is still imperfect and will only be realized in the world according to God's purpose in history.

Tenth, while New Thought, in common with many traditional Christians, believes in personal immortality after death, it is divided concerning its nature. Some leaders accept the belief in reincarnation like the Theosophists; probably more teach the doctrine of continual progression in the afterlife like the orthodox Spiritualists.

Eleventh, New Thought tends to separate the two natures of Jesus Christ rather than to declare the unity and inseparability of his divine and human natures. Jesus is likened to other men by having a divine nature, but differs from others in the degree of this realization. He was the way-shower pointing out the path of Christ-consciousness within. Therefore New Thought tends to be Unitarian rather than Trinitarian in the traditional sense, and at-onement with God or Christ-consciousness takes the place of the traditional doctrine of atonement.

Twelfth, since New Thought believes in the divine nature of man, it expresses no dependence upon a transcendent God. Man becomes the complete master of his fate, eliminating the need for a doctrine of God's divine grace.

Although many more contrasts could be made, any broad comparison runs the unavoidable risk of oversimplification. The genius of New Thought is its variety of beliefs, and therefore the above applies only to a general view. The same, of course, would be true in the case of the Christian principles, for many liberal Christians would share some of the New Thought doctrines.

Because of the individualism there are some New Thought students who consider themselves to be Christian, but New Thought is not obliged to define its doctrines in Christian terms. Its principles might actually be more suitable to the monism of either Buddhism or Hinduism.

Teachings of Emmet Fox

Since New Thought has been influential upon many in the denominational churches, it is fitting to examine briefly some ideas of Emmet Fox, one of the most renowned New Thought leaders in this century. Fox, like others of the movement, was an individualist, yet officially a minister of the Church of Divine Science. Although his beliefs fit into the New Thought and Divine Science pattern, he appealed to many Christians who were among the thousands in his daily New York audience, or who read his popular books. Fox referred to their cherished Christian doctrines, giving them usually new interpretations. He utilized theories of psychology and psychoanalysis, weaving them into his philosophy. In his library of over two-thousand volumes were the works of Martin Luther, John Wesley, George Fox, as well as many books on the non-Christian religions.[30]

Emmet Fox was born in Ireland in 1886, studied to be an engineer in England, and then gave up his profession to become a lecturer and writer in America. He had been reared as a Roman Catholic and studied in the Stamford Hill Jesuit College near London, but gradually his interest in New Thought drew him away from his Catholic faith.[31]

Christians have often criticized New Thought of manipulating God, who, like a kind of genie, is supposed to grant any selfish desires. But such would not strictly apply to Fox. If affirmation has seemed to be a kind of magic mantra putting God into operation, this would not be his view. Daily prayer and meditation were a part of his life and enjoined upon his followers. He interpreted the use of affirmations as the practice of God's presence in communion, and believed this devotional duty would transform people's lives and create a corresponding change in health and life conditions. He said: "*Holiness unto the Lord* means that there is nothing in existence but the self-expression of God — that and nothing more. It naturally follows from this that you yourself, and every condition in your

[30] Harry Gaze, *Emmet Fox, the Man and His Work* (Harper & Brothers, 1952), p. 26.
[31] *Ibid.*, pp. 18–19.

life today, are simply part of God's manifestation or self-expression, and therefore must be perfect, beautiful, and harmonious." [32]

Thus the affirmation was used to find God's presence and to discover his perfection. When through this practice one felt there had been some demonstration, he was urged to give thanks and really *feel* grateful.[33]

Like others of the New Thought tradition, Fox believed the Bible contained a hidden spiritual or metaphysical meaning not found in the literal interpretation.

Although his theological concepts of God and man were typically New Thought, he was not averse to the use of such traditionally Christian phrases as " God, the father " and " the Holy Spirit." If Fox did not believe in God as a person, he regarded him as having " every quality of personality except its limitation." [34] He taught that God manifests himself as Soul; as individualized in man, he is the Christ within each one.

Fox, more than most teachers of New Thought, seemed to emphasize the moralization of the spiritual like Emerson, whom he read avidly. He regarded evil as the consequence of violating the Law of Being. Evil, he said, does not always reveal itself through infractions of a strict moral code, but at times through man's false belief in his separation from God. Beginning with Adam, this belief is recapitulated in every man. According to Harry Gaze, Fox's interpreter, the original sin is repeated by every person whenever he gives power to anything but God, and accepts anything less than the Omnipresence of God. This is what was meant by choosing negatively. Through man's free will to choose between good or evil he has the choice of either recapitulating the fall of Adam or becoming reaware of his true spiritual nature.[35] However, if one elects to use his freedom negatively and " allows himself to think wrongly, selfishly, vindictively, he brings upon himself all the sorrows that afflict the human race." [36]

Fox taught, in his *The Sermon on the Mount*, that since God

[32] Emmet Fox, *Stake Your Claim* (Harper & Brothers, 1952), pp. 50–51.
[33] *Ibid.*, p. 29.
[34] Gaze, *op. cit.*, p. 43.
[35] *Ibid.*, pp. 41–45.
[36] *Ibid.*, pp. 56–57.

is love, by loving one can conquer any evil. Unlike most New Thought leaders, Fox not only recognized sin, but spoke often concerning it. He said that the feeling of guilt and the inability to accept absolution for past sins could cause physical illness. Sin is "the major tragedy of human experience," and has its roots in selfishness. Since he believed the Truth of Being to be one, the sin is the negation of this by thinking of our own personal existence. Its consequence is condemnation, resentment, jealousy, remorse, etc. So before seeking and receiving our own personal forgiveness, we are first obliged to forgive others.[37]

Fox's penchant for speaking in Christian categories doubtless reflects his early Christian training. But from a viewpoint of traditional Christian faith, his teachings are both an oversimplification and perversion of Christian beliefs.

If Emmet Fox tried to counter the stigma of the magical use of affirmations, other philosophical allies have likewise been critical of such use. Frederic Bailes, a popular New Thought writer, emphasizes the use of affirmations, but warns:

"Any affirmation is a statement of belief that embodies some particular truth. Written usually by a spiritually minded person, it is sometimes picked by a follower and repeated as a talisman. Unless this second person catches the consciousness of the writer, he will be repeating words only. This is superstition.

"A statement of spiritual truth is potent only when the inner-heart consciousness and the outer words coincide with each other. But when the person thus thoughtfully prays with both surface and deeper mind, he comes into a position of tremendous power, and a specific interaction of his mind and God's mind takes place."[38]

The Development of New Thought Beyond Healing

Although New Thought started as a healing movement, like Christian Science, its principles were soon extended to all

[37] *Ibid.*, pp. 110–111.
[38] Frederic Bailes, *Hidden Power for Human Problems* (Prentice-Hall, Inc., 1957), p. 89.

phases of man's life. Through the power of affirmation, i.e., affirming the state of being one wishes to have, it is believed one will be able to attain happiness, peace of mind, prosperity, etc., in addition to health. New Thought maintains that affirmations work according to spiritual law and reveal the divine nature of man which is one with God. Since God has no lacks, man is thought to have the potentiality of realizing this divine inheritance in his own life.

The first application of New Thought to the acquisition of prosperity remains a mystery. Perhaps this extension may have first come from Christian Science. The principles may be deduced from Mrs. Eddy's early writings, although emphasis upon their demonstration appears later. By 1888 Emma Curtis Hopkins recognized this phase. Among the purposes of her seminary recorded in the June issue of *Truth* of that year is the following statement: " We perceive that inherently there is one judgment in all mankind alike. It is restored by the theology taught here. With its restoration we find health, protection, wisdom, strength, *prosperity*." [39]

Charles Braden, in his recent book, *Spirits in Rebellion*, notes that there is a section on the subject in Frances Lord's *Christian Science Healing*, published in 1887.[40]

If Prentice Mulford was not the first to introduce the idea to New Thought, his many pamphlets, written between 1886 and the time of his death in 1891, had a great effect in emphasizing it. Mulford had been in California as a newspaper editor, journalist, and foreign correspondent for one of the San Francisco papers. He also added the lecture platform as an avocation, and his voice was heard in both Europe and America. In 1886 he retired to the mountains in New Jersey and began writing his series of essays covering a multitude of New Thought applications including prosperity. His biographer wrote: " If he seemed at times to advocate the use of this power for merely material ends, we must remember, again, that he was writing for businessmen and women, and that he himself, for all his theorising, never possessed even a moderate share of this world's goods."

[39] Cushing, *op. cit.*, p. 7.   [40] Braden, *op. cit.*, p. 152.

If Mulford himself did not make practical use of his own teachings, his biographer claims there would be thousands of people who would acknowledge they owed much of their success to his teachings.[41]

Although Mulford's treatments for prosperity and success may have helped to add this dimension to New Thought, this practice was not general even in 1904, since the constitution of the New Thought Federation (the name of the INTA at that time) that year confines the application of its principles "to health, happiness, and character."[42]

The Unity School of Christianity mentioned prosperity treatments in 1890, but did not stress them until 1898 after Charles Fillmore published his article "Overcoming the Poverty Idea."[43]

Perhaps this phase may be correlated with the growing American emphasis upon prosperity as a standard. Certainly concomitant with the rise of living standards through the growth of industry and business, the idea that prosperity is one of the rights and privileges of Americans has become prevalent.

New Thought Periodicals

The movement grew steadily, spread not only by lectures and books, but also by a larger number of its periodicals than appears today. The first mental science periodical, the *Mental Science Magazine*, although beginning under the title of *Mind Cure*, ran from 1884 to 1889 and was published by a former Christian Scientist in Chicago. The *Mental Healing Monthly* began in 1886, then united with *Truth* to become the *International Magazine of Christian Science*. It was edited by the Church of Divine Unity in Boston until discontinued in 1888. The *Christian Metaphysician* was published between 1887 and 1897; *Wayside Lights* began in Hartford in 1890; and *Harmony* was edited by Mrs. Malinda Cramer of San Francisco

[41] Martin, *op. cit.*, p. 276.

[42] "New Thought Constitution," *Unity* (Unity School of Christianity), Vol. 21, Nov., 1904, p. 276.

[43] James Teener, *Unity School of Christianity*, Ph.D. thesis (University of Chicago, 1939), p. 43.

from 1888 to 1906.[44] From the same city appeared the periodical *Now: A Journal of Affirmations*, edited by Henry Harrison Brown. Like others in the early period, it provided space for varieties of metaphysical thought other than mental science. It devoted a whole page in its first volume in 1900 to the annotated titles of many more periodicals in the healing field, of which most lasted a short time. The growing tendency in New Thought has been for only the separate organizations to publish such magazines.

Horatio and Anetta Dresser — New Thought Critics

Probably no family has been closer to the development since Quimby's time than the Dressers. Because Anetta Dresser had been a follower of Quimby, she criticized many phases of New Thought, especially its use of affirmations. Here she was most punitive. While admitting the effect of thought upon the body, she pointed to Quimby's "method of intuitive diagnosis and the endeavor to understand the entire condition of the patient, in contrast with mental healers, who, lacking this intuition, have depended upon affirmations." [45] Here, indeed, New Thought has departed not only from Quimby but also from Evans.

Horatio Dresser, the son of Anetta and Julius Dresser, and a follower of New Thought most of his life, was also a severe critic. He saw a change occurring in the nineties, when leaders, like Henry Wood and Ralph Waldo Trine, went beyond what he considered to be the deeper meaning of New Thought. He accused them of giving " thought " a power it did not possess, and of making it " a comprehensive theory for the whole of life." Such leaders had caught only part of the message of Quimby and Evans, and were overly influenced by the latter's idealism, so that emotions and will were neglected. What Dresser advocated was not a mental science, but a spiritual sci-

---

[44] Winifred Gregory, *Union List of Serials in Libraries of the United States and Canada* (The H. W. Wilson Co., 1943). The dates were verified in this reference. For the partial list: Dresser, *The New Thought Movement*, pp. 136–137.

[45] Anetta Dresser, "The Science of Life," in Dresser, *Spirit of the New Thought*, p. 208, note.

ence more in keeping with what he considered to be the true ideals of Quimby and Evans. This would involve a change of mind and will so that the spiritual cause of disease might be removed, i.e., that love might give place to hatred, a spirit of forgiveness take the place of condemnation, etc. Further, he traced these destructive emotions to selfishness which one had to eradicate before being completely cured.[46]

Although relying upon Quimby, he was no slave to his teaching *in toto*. He wrote:

" It can hardly be said that even with the experiences of half a century to draw upon the devotees of mental healing have proved that disease is ' an error of mind.' It has indeed been shown that inner states such as fear, anger, jealousy, worry, excitement, are instrumental in causing disease. But it does not follow that the accompanying physical states are merely ' shadows.' Nor has it been shown that mental treatment is a universal panacea, able to overcome all forms of organic and functional diseases. At best it has been established that suggestion is serviceable in its place, that mental treatment is one more method of healing added to those already possessed, and that spiritual healing can often accomplish results not achieved by merely mental healing." [47]

The change of will was more important than the secondary power of mind; disinterested love was rated higher than affirmations. He was especially critical of those who believed that the mere recitation of an affirmation magically brought corresponding change in the body, or prosperity without work.[48] With further castigation he said:

" The first misconception of the early enthusiasts was the assumption that thought can accomplish whatever we will, as if it were bodiless. The second point to be guarded against followed from it, namely, that the human individual is the center of attraction. This implies the exaltation of the finite above the infinite, the raising of the human self to the cosmic power. Carried to the extreme, it means putting the finite self above

[46] Dresser, *Handbook of the New Thought*, pp. 34–50.
[47] *Ibid.*, pp. 126–127.
[48] *Ibid.*, pp. 141–143.

law, nature, and God. Thus one may become affirmative in the extreme, self-satisfied and self-centered. . . . But thus to state the case is to realize the need for a right estimate of self-reliance and independence, lest one exceed the bounds of righteousness." [49]

Dresser added an amusing illustration of one New Thought leader who put the power of thought above that of love and will, and who therefore " expressed surprise at the outbreak of the Spanish-American War; for, he said, ' I supposed the New Thought had gained a greater hold in this country than that.' "

Although, like other New Thought leaders, Dresser would advocate silent meditation, he was quick to see the danger in exaltation of emotion. No emotion except the highest love was any guide in itself, but most emotions needed transformation.[50] While believing that orthodox Christianity had put too much emphasis upon sin, still he recognized there could be more to sin than just wrong thoughts: " No genuine Christian would be content to sit in silence in self-complacent optimism, sending out good and pleasant thoughts instead of going forth to learn the real condition of the needy. Where optimistic affirmations begin to reach their limit, the real work of life begins." [51]

Finally, Dresser inveighed against the metaphysical or allegorical interpretation of the Bible. He asserted that its application to mental healing, which began with Quimby, was continued by Mrs. Eddy and New Thought. He concluded: " As a result, we have so many variations and often such fanciful interpretations that the reader of works on mental healing is bewildered. When Scripture is said to mean so many things, it hardly means anything at all." [52]

Therefore, New Thought is far more than just the principles laid down by the International New Thought Alliance. It has its shallow places, but also its depths. If, on the one hand, it does not correspond to traditional Christianity and seems at times to oversimplify man's predicaments, to resort to magic,

[49] *Ibid.*, pp. 151–152.
[50] *Ibid.*, pp. 153, 157–159.
[51] *Ibid.*, pp. 162–163.
[52] *Ibid.*, pp. 69–70.

and to become self-centered, on the other hand, it has apparently helped many physically and has offered them a satisfactory philosophy. An idea that seems objectively false to some may have beneficial results to others who accept it subjectively and act upon it in faith.

Influence of New Thought

There are many exceptions to the rule that most New Thought churches are small, and that their more gifted leaders have hardly made an impact upon ministers and laymen of traditional Christian churches. Some have written best sellers carrying their influence far beyond their constituents. Emmet Fox's works have had great popularity, and Ralph Waldo Trine's *In Tune with the Infinite* has sold over a million copies.[53]

In a book entitled *Popular Religion*, two sociologists, Louis Schneider and Sanford Dornbusch, analyzed the contents of forty-six best sellers of American inspirational literature published between 1875 and 1955. Their research showed that the books with the greatest appeal usually contained concepts like those of New Thought.[54] This, of course, does not mean that every listed writer belonged to the New Thought tradition, but that some liberal Protestant, Catholic, and Jewish thinkers at times expressed views similar to it. The most popular title, Norman Vincent Peale's *The Power of Positive Thinking*, has sold over two million copies. As noted before, it exhibits techniques reminiscent of New Thought and the Unity School of Christianity. This claim for the greatest sale could still be challenged by the followers of Mary Baker Eddy, were *Science and Health* in the contest. The next three most popular works were Trine's *In Tune with the Infinite;* Marshall's *A Man Called Peter;* and Liebman's *Peace of Mind*. It is noteworthy that not a single author was listed who would be classed as neo-orthodox. Thus the influence of New Thought concepts

---

[53] Braden, *These Also Believe*, p. 142.
[54] Louis Schneider and Sanford M. Dornbusch, *Popular Religion: Inspirational Books in America* (University of Chicago Press, 1958), *passim.*

reaches the thinking and beliefs of millions throughout the United States and the world.

Next to be considered are some of the sects that are officially part of New Thought or closely related.

VI

The Divine Science Church

THE DIVINE SCIENCE CHURCH is a member of the International New Thought Alliance and according to its textbook, *Divine Science: Its Principles and Practice*, it is " a Christian religion based upon the teachings of Jesus." [1] Its present head, Dr. Irwin Gregg, characterized Divine Science as part of the metaphysical movement and " a revival of ancient teachings of early man, e.g., Diognetus," who, he said, had used the expression " Divine Science." He regarded it as being very much like the early form of Christianity that he said the church had rejected. It was a revival of " immanence philosophy." As already noted, New Thought has many followers who interpret their thought in Biblical terms and consider themselves to be Christians, whereas others who use the Bible to a lesser degree may not care to be so identified.

The Divine Science Church had several founders: Alethea Brooks Small, Fannie Brooks James, and Nona Lovell Brooks were responsible for the organization; Malinda Cramer, a teacher of the Brooks sisters, also supplied the name " Divine Science."

Malinda Cramer

Malinda Cramer claimed her teachings were the result of a revelation, the aftermath of years of suffering. In her quest for

[1] *Divine Science, Its Principles and Practice* (Divine Science Church and College, 1957), p. 190.

health she had finally moved to San Francisco upon the advice of her physician after having first gone from Indiana to New York. However, in 1855, when she was still pronounced incurable after fifteen years in sunny California, she resolved to stop taking medicines. And to her husband's question about her intentions, she simply replied, " Get well, of course." This positive answer so surprised her, however, that she meditated and prayed about it for an hour during which the truth was revealed. She had the intuitive realization of Omnipresent Spirit and knew that only through It would she recover. In this transforming experience she felt herself to be in God. She was aware of the oneness and goodness of life which was God in-all. Thus, she said, the ax was laid to the root of her infirmity, and as quickly as she changed her old habits of belief she became well.

She began healing others when urged by friends who had witnessed her recovery, and in 1887 she began to teach them the results of her meditations. In these devotional periods it was revealed that there was neither lower nor higher self, nor separation of body from Spirit. All was one in God, and apparent distinction was " a negative condition, a nonacceptance of Truth." Next came the realization that the bodily form was really a thought in her Mind, and that she was "that Omnipresence which lies back of all form; the Divine Mind which contains within Itself the things that are seen." [2] Therefore, a person's physical condition would depend upon his thought.

Knowing, then, her life's mission, in 1888 she chartered the Home College of Divine Science, among whose purposes was instruction in " the Christ Method of Healing." In the same year she began publishing the periodical *Harmony*, which made her teachings more widely known.[3] In 1890 she issued her first monograph, *Lessons in the Science of Infinite Spirit, and the Christ Method of Healing*, followed by her popular little pamphlet, *Basic Statements and Health Treatment of*

[2] Malinda E. Cramer, *Divine Science and Healing: A Textbook for the Study of Divine Science, Its Application in Healing, and for the Well-Being of Each Individual* (2d ed., published by C. L. Cramer, 1907), pp. 11–21.

[3] *Ibid.*, pp. 23–24.

Truth, which went through eight editions between 1893 and 1905. Her basic textbook, *Divine Science and Healing,* appeared in 1905.

The Brooks Sisters Establish Divine Science

In 1887, the same year Malinda Cramer began her teaching, the Brooks sisters of Pueblo, Colorado, became interested in "metaphysics." Emma Curtis Hopkins had just cured their friend, Mrs. Bingham, who had studied with the healer for three weeks before returning to Pueblo. Since the Brooks sisters were not well, they attended classes started by Mrs. Bingham, and during the fourth lesson Nona Brooks had a mystical experience:

" My whole being was completely flooded with a great light — a light brighter than sunlight, brighter than any I had ever seen. It filled me! It surrounded me! I was conscious of nothing but that intense white light! I thought that of course all in the room had seen the light too, but they had not. I alone had had this wonderful experience. I discovered that I had been instantly and completely healed.

" Though the actual healing was instantaneous, yet I truly believe that the months and months of praying that I might receive light had been a preparation for the healing which had actually come to me in the form of light."

Nona Brooks said all three were healed of their infirmities, their lives were changed, and their financial conditions improved.

Although agreeing with most of the teachings, the three sisters found some unacceptable. For example, they could not believe " the visible universe did not exist but was delusion and was to be denied." This seemed unreasonable. So they came to believe that " form was the product of God's creative activity, that this wonderful world was not to be denied but to be understood and interpreted," and that they should emphasize God's action in their lives. In their early formulation they taught:

" All creation is the expression of God and partakes of the same substance. All of the power and beauty in nature is the result of God's fiat going forth — ' Let there be light and it was so.' The universe of form is the Word of God. It is good from center to circumference, wholly good, like its Creator."

While continuing with their study, the sisters went to hear Mrs. Cramer, who came to Denver and started a class. They soon discovered that they agreed with her and received permission to call their own teaching Divine Science.

Nona Brooks' two sisters moved to Denver at the request of friends who were seeking help, and in 1896 Nona Brooks herself gave up teaching school to teach Divine Science with her sisters and to practice healing. Their work quickly outgrew the home of Mrs. James, and in the same year the Divine Science College was incorporated to train teachers, ministers, and practitioners, and to organize churches. After the death of Mrs. Cramer in 1907, Denver became the center of Divine Science.[4]

Basic Principles of Divine Science

Divine Science claims freedom from dogma and creed, so that it can give mankind an effective principle to overcome " limitations in thought, body, and affairs." It may be defined as the knowledge of God expressing himself as Creator in the creature, and though ostensibly creedless, it " stands for ":

" 1. The Fatherhood of God as Omnipresent Life, Substance, Intelligence, Power.

" 2. The brotherhood of man.

" 3. The unity of all life.

" 4. The highest thought in science, philosophy, and religion.

" 5. The power of right thinking to release into expression in each individual man's divine inheritance — health, abundance, peace, and power.

" 6. The goodness of the whole.

" 7. The transcendence and immanence of God as manifest in all created things, yet above and beyond all created things. God the Create and the Uncreate, the Visible and the Invisible,

---

[4] *Divine Science*, pp. 9-15.

the Absolute and the Relative, the Universal and the Individual." [5]

Even if most of its teachings are purportedly derived from the revelation of Malinda Cramer and the Brooks sisters, these founders seemed to have knowledge of the various strands of metaphysical thought which were being discussed in New Thought circles at the time. Mrs. Cramer, a former Quaker, developed a mysticism showing some evidence of Indian philosophy, Theosophy, and Christian Science, as well as of the Kabbala and Hermetic teachings. She claimed her "truth" was taken from no book, however, but from the "Omnipresent Source of all Truth." [6] Nona Brooks and her sisters, though abandoning traditional Christianity, still could not accept all the philosophy of Emma Curtis Hopkins. Although the biography of Nona Brooks mentions the names of Blavatsky, Cady, Eddy, Evans, Quimby, Trine, etc., the sisters disclaimed any influence.[7] In recent years, however, Divine Science has become interested in showing its relationship to ideas expressed by early mystics and Christian leaders, such as Dionysius the Areopagite (420–470 A.D.), Clement of Alexandria (150–215 A.D.), and Origen (185–254 A.D.). In a mimeographed lesson sheet published by the Divine Science Church, one may see many quotations from such early authors with whom Divine Science expresses its kinship.

Dr. Gregg's Explanation of Divine Science

Dr. Irwin Gregg, Divine Science leader, gave the following explanation of what his religion meant to him:

"Divine Science teaches complete faith in the intelligence and integrity of the Universe, and our emphases are to place ourselves in line with It. We differ from some of the other groups, who are doing very fine work, because we do not go in for visualizing or outlining what is our highest good. We be-

[5] Church of Divine Science, *Divine Science: The Cardinal Points of the Teaching Program of Divine Science*, n.d., pp. 5–6.

[6] Cramer, *op. cit.*, p. 23.

[7] Hazel Deane, *Powerful Is the Light: The Story of Nona Brooks* (Divine Science College, 1945), p. 108.

lieve that God knows best for us. Our belief is in the Omnipresence and our expression of It. We therefore do not try to have God conform to our personal view of what our good is.

" We believe in the law of spiritual evolution or unfoldment, and, like Christian Science, that we are sons of God, and aim to be ultimate expressions of God's plan.

" We believe then that any sickness, etc., is due to our own innocent blocking of the divine will. Since God is by nature the spirit of harmony and perfection, we do not set out to heal disease by working on that disease. Disease indicates a wrong expression of life, but by getting in harmony with God, we get healing. As we get in harmony with God and his will, we get results of health, abundance, etc., but we do not have to predetermine what that good is.

" The practice of the Omnipresence of God is the whole of Divine Science. To know that the Infinite contains all Its expressions — knowledge of this brings us back to the bridgepoint with life. It is risky and almost immoral to pray for anything but that the pure and right action of God should take place." [8]

Statement of Being and the Law of Expression

The chief cornerstone of Divine Science is its Statement of Being and the Law of Expression. The former states that there is only one Being, which is God, outside of which there is no reality. God is Spirit, Mind, Principle, Love, Truth, Substance, Soul, Intelligence, Being, Omniscience, Omnipotence, and Omnipresence.[9] Therefore, man, his body, and the whole visible universe are the direct expression of God, Mind, or Spirit. This is the Law of Expression, which, according to Mrs. Cramer, is Trinitarian in expression, i.e., the One All or Mind has a threefold nature as creator, creative action, and creation. There is no lower or mortal mind,[10] because there is only Mind, which emanates in creation as God's substance. There-

[8] Quoted from Dr. Irwin Gregg's statement during an interview by the author in 1958.

[9] Cramer, op. cit., pp. 272, 30–31.

[10] Ibid., pp. 23, 274–275.

fore, all created things are Spirit-Substance in essence, and are ideas held within God's mind.[11]

On the above premises Divine Science deduces that man's body, as the expression of Spirit, is real.[12] Man is divine, because he is one with God as his idea expressed in form.[13] Although the outer form may seem to change, the inner one of God's thought remains the same.[14]

Another way of expressing this is that God, the infinite Mind, manifests himself as living soul and body. Therefore, the Law of Expression gives the following Trinities: " Mind, thought, word," and " Spirit, living soul, body." [15]

When God as the source of creation is said to be related to it " as the bay is one with the ocean of which it is an extension," one is reminded of the Hindu monism of the Vedanta philosophy, but Divine Science tries to preserve the distinction of the individual self in the Absolute God. For while it attributes a divine nature to man and recognizes his oneness with God, it makes a distinction between man and God in the sense that they stand in relation to life as " Invisible and visible, Absolute and relative, Universal and individual."

Similarly, just as God expresses himself through the Absolute Trinity of Father, Son, and Holy Ghost; or through the Trinity of divine Mind, which is Mind, Idea, and Consciousness, there is a corresponding Trinity on a lower level of awareness. This is the Trinity of the Superconscious, conscious, and subconscious levels of man's mind. These are explained as follows:

" Superconscious, or Christ Mind, the Father expressing on the plane of the individual;

" Conscious level of Mind, the Son expressing on the plane of the individual;

" Subconscious level of mind, the Holy Ghost manifesting on the plane of the individual." [16]

---

11 *Divine Science*, p. 38.
12 Cramer, *op. cit.*, p. 86.
13 *Ibid.*, p. 35; also *Divine Science*, p. 41.
14 *Divine Science*, pp. 39–40.
15 *Ibid.*, pp. 62–63.
16 *Ibid.*, pp. 67–68.

Man's Use of the Law of Expression

Since Divine Science holds that thought is God's creative power working through man in accord with the Law of Expression, man has the choice of creating either good for himself and for others, or causing himself suffering. The law works in either case. Thus it behooves man to know the nature of God's good and abide by it. Each must know:

" 'My Father (the Universal) is greater than I,' yet each may also say, 'I am exactly what the Universal is. There is naught else to be, since man is the individualized expression of God.' " Man must learn that the purpose of individual creation is that God, the Creator, will find expression through and by the individual.[17]

Since Creator, creative action, and creation are really a tri-une expression of God's unity, and nature is God's manifestation in form, man must come to recognize this omnipresence of God. To become " conscious that we live and move and have our being in God is to find the Kingdom of Heaven here and now." [18] To seek the Kingdom of God and his righteousness means abiding by God's will, seeking full expression of his good, and learning to recognize the perfect soul-qualities in order to realize perfection and harmony. Then will all things be added to one.[19]

Now what does the above entail? First, one is to recognize that only the good is real by learning to change his thinking. This is done by affirming daily the truth perceived, for this practice will cause us to realize the truth. One must change his old patterns by losing all beliefs of dislike, prejudice, sickness, evil, and sorrow, and recognize their unreality as not being part of God. He must seek the good for all as much as his own; speak nothing but the truth; meet all obligations, no matter how great the sacrifice. Divine Science teaches that to the extent that he thinks and practices these things he realizes his unity with God.[20]

[17] *Ibid.*, p. 66.
[18] *Ibid.*, pp. 60, 137.
[19] *Ibid.*, p. 158.
[20] *Ibid.*, pp. 157–168, 85.

Prayer

Nona Brooks maintained that real prayer is not begging — even for more wisdom, supply, or good. It is realizing and accepting these things that are part of our real nature and of God's. Prayer again, according to her, is more than just thinking or speaking. It "includes the whole of one's life — every thought and feeling, the motive of every decision and of every action."

Prayer is said to be scientific. Its apparent failure at times is not due to God, but to the one who does not fulfill the law and realize he must express God's good in his whole personality and life.

The type of prayer used by Divine Science is the affirmation of that which it considers to be truth and reality. Since all good is ours and like produces like, it is believed the law will take care of the rest, if we continue to affirm the good until it is realized and made manifest.[21] True prayer then, would be the recognition of the omnipresence of God, acceptance of his good, thanksgiving for it, and "acting the true nature of God."[22]

Health and Sickness

Divine Science teaches that health is normal for man, since he has his being in God, who is spiritual harmony and wholeness, or health. It is God's liberated activity expressing through man. Healing is the process of making whole. To be healed or made whole is, however, more than just being free from a particular illness. The whole person is involved, including his *living* in the Spirit of wholeness.

Sickness occurs when thinking is separated from the truth of life's wholeness. False thinking and self-centeredness cause emotional disturbances that manifest as disharmony in the body. When such emotional problems as fears, worries, and

[21] Nona Brooks, *The Prayer That Never Fails* (Divine Science Church and College, n.d.), pp. 2–22.
[22] *Divine Science*, p. 81.

anxieties occur, one is breaking the law of life and losing the realization of life's unity. As man gives up these old ways, becoming conscious of God's omnipresence, it is said he becomes healed. Healing is defined as " the God-nature of man becoming visible by means of the great divine law of expression, like producing like or God's perfect health manifesting in the visible as man's health." [23]

Doctrine of Evil

Since God is the only reality and is good, evil must necessarily be only an appearance. It exists only as long as a person believes in it. This belief is a " misconception as to God's being infinite." [24] Still, Divine Science does not deny *apparent* evil causing *apparent* suffering. Man is said to give power to this unreality by failing to recognize the source of his existence as God, the good.[25] He does not know that he is " an individualized center of God-activity and that he is to share in fulfilling the Father's purpose of bringing love, peace, harmony, and good will to all." Without this knowledge he uses his mental power for selfish purposes. Just as long as he thinks and acts selfishly, i.e., expresses anything other than God's idea of good, he will experience suffering. As Emerson said, " Law obeyed or disobeyed brings opposite results." [26]

Therefore, man's lot is exactly what he makes it. Any apparent evil befalling him demonstrates his failure to understand and utilize the Law of Expression, his deficiency in working out his perfection by recognizing his true Self through right thinking. True thought, however, must not only be expressed in one's words but in his relations to others.[27]

Doctrine Concerning Orginal Sin and Sin

According to Divine Science, there is no original sin, since God is man's origin. Sin, it says, begins with the " belief of separation from God." In the Glossary of its textbook, sin is

---

[23] *Ibid.*, pp. 97–101.   [25] *Ibid.*, p. 43.   [27] *Ibid.*, p. 71.
[24] *Ibid.*, pp. 30–31.   [26] *Ibid.*, pp. 70–71.

defined as " Man's failure to unfold and express his real Self. Intentional or unintentional violation of spiritual laws." [28]

Although original sin is denied, the question might be raised by some as to whether Divine Science has really met the problem or explained it away. If it holds that this belief in one's separation from God has been characteristic of man through the centuries, is the problem not there, whether recognized or not? Otherwise, why is man ignorant of his true nature and relationship? Even though one judges the story of Adam's fall to be mythological, does he so easily escape the truth that this episode illustrates, whether he defines sin as real or apparent? In all major religious there is recognition that at least in some stage of man's life he has not attained the ideal of salvation in his religion. Does not this universal failure show man's predicament whether one denies or affirms original sin, uses the word " sin " or denies it, or the word " ignorance " or some other term? Traditional Christianity's explanation has been the doctrine of original sin.

The Christ, Jesus, and the Sons of God

The Christ, according to Divine Science, is the Christ Principle, the essential part of human nature. It is the perfect God-idea, or prototypal man, within each person. Thus " man *is* the Son of God, but as a son of man he has not yet put on that completeness which is latently his in God-Mind." He is in the process of unfoldment, spurred on by an innate urge to express the hidden wonders of the God-Mind. God, while holding his ideas in his consciousness, is zealous for their development and fulfillment, and Christ is this truth, the true Self that reveals and expresses the perfection of God's mind. Therefore, man is potentially perfect and may develop according to the Law of Expression.

Divine Science teaches that the Bible is the story of how man's consciousness of God and of his own divinity unfolds. Jesus, the way-shower, the perfect example of this unfoldment and of man's potentiality, revealed how the Christ might be

[28] *Ibid.*, pp. 149–150, 236.

manifested in the flesh. He demonstrated it so that man, the effect, might become " the true embodiment of the Christ, the indwelling Cause. In Jesus the inner and outer became one and indivisible — Jesus Christ! " Thus Christ, or Cosmic, Consciousness is the goal of man.[29]

Consequently, Divine Science can say that each man is a son of God, but lacks this awareness in proportion to his limited thought of self instead of unbounded consciousness of Self. When his realization is perfect, however, it is believed he may say with Paul, " It pleased God . . . to reveal his Son in me" (Gal. 1:15-16) or, "Beloved, now are we the sons of God " (I John 3:2). When this occurs, man's will merges with God's and he recognizes, accepts, and expresses the universal principle of Christ within himself.[30] Thus the " Christ is the impersonal idea of MAN in and of the infinite Mind before any individual existence, and is the substance of all individual existence." It is coexistent with Mind and is the only begotten Son.[31]

At-one-ment

It is the view of Divine Science that Jesus made no atonement, but revealed at-one-ment with God. Christ Consciousness is the redeemer and the truth, bringing conscious at-one-ment with God and overcoming the belief in man's separation from him.

With this realization, one becomes aware that he, like Jesus, has been immaculately conceived, because man originates from God, the spiritual parent.[32] This awareness is the meaning of the Second Coming of Christ, for one knows then that he is the Christ, the Truth, and God expressed in the flesh.[33] This entails the destruction of ignorance of one's true identity and its metaphysically interpreted as the baptism with fire and by the Holy Spirit, since " Fire is the light of understanding which consumes darkness of ignorance." Baptism by water is only a symbol of Christ's real baptism.[34]

29 *Ibid.*, pp. 116–127.   31 *Ibid.*, pp. 143–144.   33 *Ibid.*, pp. 154–155.
30 *Ibid.*, pp. 138–139, 141.   32 *Ibid.*, pp. 147–148.   34 *Ibid.*, pp. 150–151.

Communion

Divine Science recognizes communion as fellowship with Christ, the realization of the omnipresence of God, unity between Divine Spirit and body, and fellowship with all peoples as members of the Lord's body. The elements of bread and wine do not appear in its service, since they are regarded as substitutes for real Communion, which should be continuous rather than at separate times as in a Communion service.[35]

Divine Science Expansion

The organization has spread its teachings through its college in Denver, its special correspondence courses, books, pamphlets, and its monthly periodical, *Aspire*, which was first issued in 1902 as *Fulfillment*. It now includes articles of an inspirational nature, but also studies for each day in the month.

During her lifetime Nona Brooks did much to expand the organization. She was prominent in the conventions of the INTA and lectured in many different cities in the United States and abroad until her death in 1945 at the age of eighty-three.

Although Divine Science is apparently growing, perhaps its lack of organization has prevented knowing more about its number of churches and their memberships. Until the establishment of the Divine Science Federation International in 1957 there was little formal organization. Students might study at the College of Divine Science in Denver with no obligation to teach under the name of Divine Science. They might also be granted a charter to open their own college, whose students might again operate independently of the parent organization. Now that there is a more formal organization for mutual benefit, many churches are continually entering, although they are entirely self-supporting and autonomous.

[35] *Ibid.*, pp. 152–153.

VII

The Church of Religious Science

THE CHURCH OF RELIGIOUS SCIENCE was organized in 1952 by Dr. Ernest Holmes as an outgrowth and development of the Institute of Religious Science and Philosophy, which began in 1927. It must be characterized as a branch of New Thought because of philosophical similarities, although some, like Ernest's brother, Fenwicke Holmes, dislike associating it with that name and prefer to call it mental science. This would probably not reflect the majority opinion. Not only has Ernest Holmes often taken part in the INTA conferences, but many of his ministers and laymen are members of the INTA.

Ernest Holmes's Background

The story of the life of Ernest Holmes sounds almost like a Horatio Alger novel of the boy who reached both prominence and affluence after a long struggle from poor and humble beginnings. The founder, who died in 1960, was born in 1887, one of nine sons in a very poor family. His mother, a schoolteacher, taught the boys herself, because they lived a semipioneer life on a farm near Lincoln, Maine. The family attended the local Congregational Church, where Ernest played the organ for the Sunday morning services.

Although Ernest did not go to college, Fenwicke was graduated from Colby College, studied at Hartford Theological Seminary, and served as a Congregational minister for a few years. Ernest, however, increased his education by reading. Among the influential books, when he was young, were the Bible and Henry Drummond's *Natural Law in the Spiritual World*. At seventeen he began reading Elbert Hubbard's works and then gravitated to Emerson's *Essays*, particularly the one on " Self-Reliance." When he later moved to Boston, where he worked in a butcher shop, he attended the Powers School of Expression to study public speaking. Mrs. Powers, a reader in the Christian Science church, introduced him to her belief about 1905. He read the Christian Science literature avidly for a year and then enlarged his vista to include many other writers. Walt Whitman and Browning were followed by New Thought writers, e.g., Christian D. Larson, Orson Swett Marsden, Emma Curtis Hopkins, Emilie Cady, etc. The words of Freud also captured his fancy, as well as the Hindu mysticism of Ramacharaka, née William Walker Atkinson. Fenwicke explained his brother's interest in Atkinson as due to the latter's interpretation of Yoga in Occidental psychological terms.

By 1915, while Ernest Holmes was developing an eclectic philosophy from these various sources, his one great ambition was to discover the answer to this question: " What is the fundamental thing in them all that is *so* — something you cannot leave out? " To find the solution, he worked even harder to create a fusion of metaphysics, psychology, philosophy, and whatever he could utilize from the depositories of " Ancient Wisdom," such as the Hermetic teachings, the Bhagavad-Gita, and the Zend-Avesta. All of these would be harmonized with gleanings from Emerson, Whitman, Wordsworth, Browning, and especially Troward.

" I would like to make a synthesis of it all," he said. And that was what he did.[1]

He believed that truth could be found in all the great religious texts of various religions. From each he took what he considered to be in agreement and true. When asked by the writer in 1957 whether he regarded his teaching as Christian, he hesitated before saying that he was not sure this would be so. He, of course, referred often to the Bible in his lectures and books, and held Jesus Christ and his teachings in high esteem.

[1] Fenwicke Holmes, from an interview with the writer.

Nevertheless, he did not seem eager to be labeled a Christian or to be associated with a creedal faith. The same question brought a different response from quite a few of his followers who maintained they were indeed Christians.

Troward's Philosophy and Influence

When Ernest Holmes was pressed to name the one person influencing him most in his formative years, he pulled from a shelf a copy of *The Edinburgh Lectures on Mental Science*, by Thomas Troward. His view will now be examined briefly because it influenced not only Ernest Holmes, but also many New Thought leaders.

Thomas Troward (1847–1916), who had served as a Divisional judge in India, is far more noted for his lectures in London and Edinburgh, which in their published form became classics of New Thought. His last books, *The Law and the Word* and *The Hidden Power and Other Papers upon Mental Science*, representing material from unpublished manuscripts, were both published posthumously.

Troward followed the tradition of Evans, Mulford, and Wood in emphasizing the power of thought, which he fitted into a psychological system. In his tripartite division of man as body, conscious mind, and spirit, Troward equated spirit with Universal Mind or God and the subjective (subconscious) mind of man. The subjective mind, containing God's creative power, acted upon suggestions from the conscious mind to cause either health or disease. This was a mechanical operation in which Universal Mind created a corresponding form in the objective world according to what Troward regarded as the Swedenborgian law of correspondences.

Although he thought that Universal Mind was impersonal in having no recognition of Its individuality, It had the qualities of personality, infinite intelligence, and volition. Nature itself was infused with this personalness and power waiting to be used, but man had suffered from ignorance of its laws. Now, however, the human mind had evolved to the stage of evolution whereby an individual could express the personalness of Universal Mind and know that Its perfect mode of expression was in self-identification with man.[2]

" In this way, then the recognition of the community of *personality* between ourselves and the universal, undifferentiated Spirit, which is the root and substance of all things, solves the question of our release from the iron grasp of an inflexible Law, not by abrogating the Law, which would mean the annihilation of all things, but by producing in us an intelligence equal in affinity with the universal Law itself, and thus enabling us to apprehend and meet the requirements of the Law in each particular as it arises. In this way the Cosmic Intelligence becomes individualized, and the individual intelligence becomes universalized; the two become one, and the Law, which gives rise to all outward conditions, whether of body or of circumstances, becomes more and more clearly understood, and can therefore be more freely made use of, so that . . . we may reach degrees of power to which it is impossible to assign any limits." [3]

Since Troward believed that matter was only a form of God's creative manifestation produced by thought, man was one with Universal Mind. The apparent differences between subjective and objective mind were only modes of expression or the action of the same mind performing different functions. Man had only to make use of his creative thought.

Ernest Holmes accepted Troward as a foundation, but with his own creative mind he built a higher edifice with new building blocks of thought.

Holmes, like Troward, postulated conscious and unconscious minds, and he too did not really separate them. He believed them to be only different states of consciousness.

Subjective Mind as Universal Mind

According to Religious Science, the subjective mind is the " *creative factor* " in each of us, and acts as a " mental law

---

[2] Thomas Troward, *The Edinburgh Lectures on Mental Science* (Dodd, Mead & Company, Inc., 1943; first printed in 1909), pp. 1–53.

[3] *Ibid.*, p. 53.

working out the will and purpose of our conscious thoughts. This can be no other than *our individual use of that Greater SUBJECTIVE Mind, which is the seat of all mental law and action*, and is ' The Servant of the Eternal Spirit throughout the ages.' "

Through this subjective mind, man is thought to possess limitless power, because through it he is one with the Universal Subjective Mind. Therefore, according to Holmes, there is really only one Subjective Mind. What we have called *our* subjective minds has been only the use we have made of the One Law.[4] Like Troward, who would say that the " Great Guiding Mind " was not different from ourselves,[5] Holmes asserted that man's subjective mind had almost limitless power, depending on this consciousness of identity and use of the Law. To use the Law is to individualize it, he said. In reality, then, if there is only the Universal Mind, which is man on the subjective side of life, one would need to speak of the individual only at " the point of conscious perception." Therefore, whenever man uses his own mind, he is actually using the creative power of the Universal Mind, and all thought is creative.[6] A different way of expression would be that " the conscious mind is Spirit, the subjective mind is Law. One is a complement of the other and no real individuality could be expressed without a combination of both." [7] Thus the Universal Mind, which is good, finds " conscious and individualized centers of expression through us." Conversely, " man's intelligence is this Universal Mind, functioning at the level of man's concept of It. This is the essence of the whole teaching." [8]

At this point some might raise the question concerning how one can really speak of individuality. If matter is a form of God's creative manifestation and man's subjective and objective minds are only modes of God's expression, how does the combination of them give individuality? Is there not a need to ex-

[4] Ernest Holmes, *The Science of Mind.* Completely Revised and Enlarged (Dodd, Mead & Company, Inc., 1956), pp. 28–29.

[5] Thomas Troward, *The Hidden Power and Other Papers Upon Mental Science* (Robert M. McBride & Co., 1922), p. 201.

[6] Ernest Holmes, *op. cit.*, pp. 29–30.

[7] *Ibid.*, p. 31.

[8] *Ibid.*, p. 35.

plain the meaning of man's individuality having free will to choose positively or negatively? to make either right or wrong choices? Would not any choice which man might make be according to God's will?

Holmes' Collective Unconscious

According to this philosophy, the subjective mind of man is also the seat of memory. Here it goes beyond Troward to adapt Carl Jung's theory of the collective unconscious. Holmes said that man's subjective mind included race-suggestion and participated in a collective unconscious common to all men as the " One Subjective Mind." Therefore, man is subject to this collective thought, which includes all the erroneous human beliefs that bind, " until the individual mentally lifts himself . . . into the higher law of Spiritual Individualism." [9] Knowing this, his health, prosperity, peace of mind, etc., would depend on the thoughts of his conscious mind, which his subjective mind would create by the law of correspondences.

God and His Creation

According to Religious Science, God is threefold in his nature. It recognizes God as spirit; law and action; and body as the result. The Trinity is also expressed as the Thing, or Absolute Intelligence; the Way It Works, or Absolute Law; and What It Does, the result or manifestation.

Spirit, when thought of apart from its physical embodiment, is life or intelligence, the absolute essence of all, and the conscious mind which knows only itself. It has creation as a mode of its action, which represents its movement into form through the medium of law, its attribute.[10]

Man

Man is spoken of as being " one with everything physical in the physical world; one with the Soul of the Universe in the

[9] *Ibid.*, pp. 114–115.   [10] *Ibid.*, pp. 80–83.

subjective world and one with the Spirit of God in the conscious world," i.e., man is a self-conscious, thinking, choosing center of individualized God-consciousness in the great whole, according to Holmes. Man's spirit, equipped with volition, intellect, and purpose forms a microcosm within the macrocosm and is the image of God, the Christ or Logos.

According to Religious Science, the whole of Spirit is potentially in man's individual objective consciousness. Unfortunately, however, man is only slightly aware of this, because he approaches the Absolute through what appears to be finite. This is the consequence of his internal and external perception through the spirit. Internally the spirit intuits God; externally it perceives by appearance, and through opinion arrives at an estimate of reality.[11]

God's Will and Man's Realization of It Through Affirmative Prayer

Religious Science teaches that God's will for man is only good. If man could realize his oneness with God and find harmony with his law, he could demonstrate just as much as he could believe. Since undesirable conditions are due to self-imposed limitations, one must learn to expand this consciousness. As he becomes more unified with God, to that extent his conditions of evil and disease will disappear.

The method of realizing that God is one with our subjective minds as absolute power is through affirmative prayer and acceptance of this reality. As Ernest Holmes wrote, " Prayer is not an act of overcoming God's reluctance, but should be an *active* acceptance of his highest willingness." [12] The key to Religious Science is the recognition of the erroneous thoughts in our subconscious minds, and the changing of our minds to conform to God's goodness. This process is called a treatment; the results, a demonstration.

Religious Science teaches that since all thoughts and desires are really prayers, man should learn to pray correctly. To mis-

[11] *Ibid.*, pp. 112–113.   [12] *Ibid.*, p. 152.

use the law is to experience evil. This is a statement with moral impdictions. For example, if a man condemns others, he will suffer according to the law. Therefore, he should praise and show appreciation, because such acts have their good reward.[13] He should avoid negative emotions of hate, envy, jealousy, etc., which have evil consequences, whereas love has its corresponding good results. Although Religious Science has no formal doctrine of God's judgment upon man, would not the above precepts exhibit some of the elements contained in such a belief?

As important as affirmative prayer is to Religious Science, Ernest Holmes would not have thought of using it in the sense of " bossing God," according to Dr. Elmer Gifford. Dr. Gifford, a prominent minister of the Church of Religious Science, declared that Dr. Holmes always placed the accent upon the presence of God. He declared further:

" One does not treat to make something happen, but to provide an avenue through which something can happen. Ernest seeks to change a person's attitude toward life, coupled with the understanding of the law of Mind. Ernest Holmes said never to think of the power of positive thinking, but of affirmative acceptance."

Affirmative Acceptance

The idea of affirmative acceptance, which Ernest Holmes received from Troward's philosophy, means accepting the reality of the state one desires concomitantly with its affirmation. Troward, who claimed its roots were in Swedenborg's law of correspondences and in Plato's archetypal ideas, applied this principle to healing, prosperity, etc. According to him, one should conceive of the spiritual prototype of that which was wanted, and it would become " the root of the corresponding external existence. This prototype, being purely spiritual, can only be formed by the operation of *thought*, and in order to have substance on the spiritual plane it *must* be thought of as actually existing there."

[13] *Ibid.*, pp. 433–434.

Troward also asserted that this idea was proclaimed by Jesus Christ as recorded in The Gospel According to Mark. It has been quoted by nearly every metaphysician of this school ever since: " All things whatsoever ye pray and ask for, believe that ye *have* received them, and ye *shall* receive them " (Mark 11:24, R.V.).[14] The interpretation is that we are to *ask* God for something we do not have by *affirming* that we have it, *believing* and *accepting* it as so. Therefore, a Biblical basis is claimed and affirmative acceptance becomes an aspect of positive thinking.

Good and Evil (Sin)

Like other metaphysical teachers of New Thought, Ernest Holmes shared the belief that the Universal Mind embraces all reality, is absolute goodness, and finds expression through law. Evil befalling man is due to ignorance of his true nature and misuse of the law.[15] Because the law works, whether one is ignorant of it or not, man should change his thinking and put no limitations on its power. One must forget there is a force of evil, which is only experienced when one thinks falsely of duality rather than of God's unity of goodness.[16]

Ernest Holmes instructed his followers to develop a constructive program of thought and action. Man really knows right from wrong in the broadest sense, he said. But what is right? He answered that it is " right to live and to enjoy living. To be well, happy, and to express freedom, is to be in accord with Divine Law and Wisdom." [17]

Even if Ernest Holmes was disinclined to use the word " sin," he admitted that man could sin in the sense of making mistakes. The very meaning of freedom implied the possibility of suffering. If man did wrong, he suffered the consequences. This did not mean that there was any evil as a thing in itself, but only a " misuse of the Law of Freedom. . . . When the whole world sees the right and does it; then, and not until then,

[14] Troward, *The Edinburgh Lectures*, pp. 34–35.
[15] Ernest Holmes, *op. cit.*, pp. 36–37.
[16] *Ibid.*, pp. 38–39.
[17] *Ibid.*, pp. 45–46.

will the problem of evil be solved for the entire race." [18]

Again, while postulating that God is the only reality and is good, he also said that " God knows nothing of . . . sin. . . . Sin or mistakes are outside the province of Reality." [19] This, of course, does not deny morality, which, as in the case of Emerson, would be equated with the spiritual and with the goodness of God. It does, however, deny *reality* to immoral action or evil in man's existential place in the natural world. This is why Holmes could say that evil was unknown to God. It would follow then that in any action considered immoral and causing pain to others, both the action and the pain would have to be denied *essential* reality and relegated to an existence unknown to God, the only reality. Moreover, might one not deduce that existential man is not only being, but also nonbeing because of his participation in the nonbeing of evil? If that be so, would it not be more to the point to say that his existential individuality is in proportion to his participation in nonbeing?

Science, Salvation, and Redemption

Since both well-being and suffering are believed to be determined by thoughts according to law, the philosophy is considered to be scientific. Fenwicke Holmes explains that it is scientific because it is " founded upon the principle that the psychology of suggestion (affirmation, realization, treatment, etc.) provides the thought or ' word ' which, when it is implanted in the Universal Subjective Creative Intelligence, produces an objective form (or result) in exact correspondence to the seed-thought."

Because of this emphasis upon law and knowledge of one's reality, salvation is more dependent upon knowledge than upon faith. It might be said to be a progression to purity rather than from sin. Fenwicke Holmes again interprets his brother's thought in his unpublished biography as follows:

" Redemption is the restoration of the *primal purity* of *self* rather than a salvation from ' sin.' We do not look upon sin as hereditary, thus rejecting the conception of ' remission '

---

[18] *Ibid.*, p. 118.   [19] *Ibid.*, p. 438.

through suffering, or substitution, or through the virtue of second person — either in Jesus or the ' saints.' "

Immortality

Although Religious Science emphasizes man's well-being in this world, it also promises personal immortality after death. However, it is not dogmatic in interpreting what that existence may be. Ernest Holmes depended largely on the speculative approach, employing reason in arriving at his conclusions. To be sure, his view has been shaped to quite an extent by his knowledge and investigation of Spiritualism. Both he and his brother, having become friends of the medium, Arthur Ford, attended several séances with him as well as with other mediums. Like the Spiritualists, they accepted the Biblical miracles and visions as forms of psychic phenomena, the belief in continuous progression of the soul to higher states of consciousness, and the possibility of spirit-communication with the living.[20]

According to Religious Science, one need not fear any judgment in the afterlife, since God is love. Although it is true that man makes mistakes for which he has to suffer in this world and the next, he will gain enlightenment and understanding through them. He will continually progress.[21] Ernest Holmes, however, avoided using the words " sin " and " God's judgment."

Hudson's book, *The Law of Psychic Phenomena*, admittedly influenced him to believe that outside the possibility of fraud, all the psychic phenomena could take place. He would not agree with Hudson's thesis that they could also be explained by telepathy, etc., and thus eliminate the spirit as agent by Occam's razor. He thought that even though the appearance of a spirit form might be only a thought form, and a medium might reveal facts through telepathy, the spirits could

[20] Fenwicke Holmes. (The foregoing material was received from Dr. Fenwicke Holmes through interviews in part, but also includes quoted material from his unpublished manuscript of the biography of his brother. Hereafter cited as Fenwicke Holmes.)

[21] Ernest Holmes, *op. cit.*, p. 383.

still produce some of the manifestations. He reasoned that if spirits did exist, and we really lived in the One Mind, communication between the spirit world and ours would be possible.[22]

He taught that the spirit which held the true identity of man created the physical body — in fact, many bodies. Since our physical ones are changing continually, he suggested the possibility that the spirit might create others of finer matter. Thus the resurrection body would be nothing but a casting off of the physical instrument. There could be an infinite number of bodies composed of ether and even finer substances, which the spirit would use on a commensurate number of ascending planes of similar material. If so, the spirit would die on one plane to be resurrected on a higher one.[23] The Theosophists hold substantially the same view of man. Although this does not necessarily imply that Holmes was influenced by the Theosophists, conversation with him revealed his acquaintance with their beliefs.

Although he personally did not accept the theory of reincarnation, the doctrine of infinite progression in the spirit world has not yet become a dogma of Religious Science. Ernest Holmes was very liberal on this point, and since some of his ministers believe in reincarnation, one may even hear an occasional lecture on the subject at the annual conference held at Asilomar, California.

The Formative Years

In 1911 Ernest Holmes followed his brother, Fenwicke, to California, where Fenwicke served as minister in a Congregational church in Venice. Ernest, besides assisting in his church, worked with Boy Scouts, and was employed by the city as storekeeper and buyer. During his leisure time he spoke at the Metaphysical Library in Los Angeles. In 1915 when he began formulating his synthesis of teachings relevant to metaphysics, he and his brother published a magazine called *The Uplift*, which continued for two years. The influence of its articles

---

[22] *Ibid.*, pp. 378–379.   [23] Fenwicke Holmes.

caused people from many places to come to the home he established for treating the ill. Their initial success led to the rental of offices in Los Angeles and later a lecture hall where they gave ten lectures a week. As growth continued, they began using the Strand Theatre for their Sunday services under the name of the Southern California Metaphysical Institute. Then in 1917 they bought a sanitarium in Long Beach and named it the Southern California Metaphysical Sanitarium, and Fenwicke Holmes resigned from the Congregational ministry to work full time with Ernest.

This was a period when they expanded their thought. They studied psychic phenomena, which Ernest finally concluded was a separate field of research from theirs. Although the subject is treated briefly in the latest edition of *The Science of Mind*, the textbook of Religious Science, two chapters were devoted to it in the first edition, published in 1926. After his acquaintance with psychoanalysis in 1918, Ernest Holmes began to add concepts of applied psychology to his thought.

In 1918 Fenwicke and Ernest widened their appeal to the public by lecturing in other cities. They followed the pattern of William Franklin Kelley, whom Fenwicke Holmes credits with being the first to speak in various places about health after advertising in the newspapers. Ernest was invited to San Francisco, where some reporters made a feature of his lectures by saying that God was being advertised. In the same year Dr. Julia Seaton, world lecturer and founder of an organization called Church and School of the New Civilization, became acquainted with the brothers and invited Fenwicke to New York. After initial success there, Ernest joined him, and the two lectured at the Astor Hotel and later in Philadelphia. Upon his return to Los Angeles, Ernest wrote *Creative Mind* and *Creative Mind and Success*, which were published in 1919. Thus through the lecture platform and the pen the movement that Ernest Holmes called Religious Science expanded and grew. To its development his career was then totally oriented, while Fenwicke had mental science churches in New York and later in Oakland, California, until his retirement. Since then, he has affiliated himself with the work of his brother's church.

The Institute of Religious Science

In 1927 Ernest Holmes established the Institute of Religious Science and Philosophy, in which many people studied his ideas and began to put them into practice. According to Fenwicke, his brother was not interested in founding an organization, and did so only at the instigation of his friends. Some graduates of the Institute had become teachers in their own communities, using his books and employing his methods. They thought of their organizations as extensions of the Institute. The first to form an allied Institute was Robert H. Bitzer, a former minister of the Unity School of Christianity. Another similar organization began operating in Pasadena, but there was still no organic relationship with the founding Institute. Only loyalty to Ernest Holmes kept them together. Finally, Dr. Carmelita Trowbridge in Alhambra called her group a church. Although this move was at first opposed by Ernest, other Religious Science congregations followed suit. Thus an unofficial Church of Religious Science was begun, with Ernest Holmes as part of the movement.

The Founding of the IARSC

In 1948 Ernest Holmes initiated the idea of the International Association of Religious Science Churches, which became incorporated in 1949. Curiously enough, this organization caused a split within the group. In the words of Fenwicke Holmes:

" This association was qualified by its State Charter to grant organization privileges and to qualify leaders, but stipulated that they must first receive training in the Los Angeles Institute. Here a difficulty was encountered in that these churches had no representation on the Board of Trustees of the Institute which was a self-perpetuating body. To remedy the situation, it was arranged that the Churches should elect two members to the Institute Board and that the Board in turn should name two members of the Council of the International Association of Churches of Religious Science." [24]

[24] Idem.

According to Dr. Raymond Barker, minister of the First Church of Religious Science in New York, and a member of the IARSC, the first proposal was that the organization would be completely democratic, each church having an equal vote in the policies. When the plan was finally presented, however, a change had been made beforehand, so that the Institute in Los Angeles was given too much control. Many felt the founding church would become like the Mother Church of Christian Science in dominating the other churches.[25]

The Founding of the Churches of Religious Science

The continuing development has been narrated by Fenwicke Holmes:

" The Home Board was eager to seek a solution and hoped to find it through a change in its own organization from ' Institute ' to ' Church.' This decision was in line with the changing needs of the Headquarters Institute in meeting the requirements of a religious institution in regard to its assets and taxation. Therefore, a charter was obtained as ' Church of Religious Science.' It was apparently thought that the churches of the IARSC would now be able to become an integral part of the Founder's Church and that one complete church organization would result. However, the leaders of the IARSC felt they would surrender some of the freedom and authority which had developed over a period of time and they objected to what they considered to be in effect ' The Mother Church' rather than the ' Founder's Church.' They felt that the Founder's Church had a new name but not a new organization; in other words it had retained an autocratic board and they therefore refused to merge the independent IARSC with it."[26]

Thus an organization meant to unite the churches became divisive, so there are now two with the same teachings. Nineteen of the original sixty-nine churches remained with the IARSC; forty-six joined the Founder's organization. The IARSC established an eastern " Institute " in New York and

[25] Raymond Barker. Interview with author.
[26] Fenwicke Holmes.

another in Hollywood for teacher training. Its dominant leaders also began working more closely with the International New Thought Alliance and with a number of independent metaphysical groups, but the Church of Religious Science has continued by itself. Even though there are two organizations, there is no ill feeling between them; there are some exchanges of pulpits, and Ernest Holmes has been revered as their teacher by both sides. Recently there have been even some proposals for reunion.

To the question as to why Ernest Holmes frowned upon the purely democratic form, his brother has replied that it was a " protective measure to assure continuity of the message by forestalling the ultimate capture of the institution by demagogic process as has happened so many times in the history of other religious institutions." The plan was considered to contain a balance between autocracy and democracy, which prevented abrupt changes of policy, although the democratic factor would allow for slow change and growth of ideas.

In the organization of the Church of Religious Science, seven of the eighteen members of the Board of Trustees are elected by the Affiliated Churches for a term of three years and may be reelected. The others are elected by the Board of Trustees itself. The latter appoints the Editorial Board of the Department of Publication; selects seven of the eleven members of the Board of Regents of the Department of Education — the other four being chosen by the Board of Trustees from a panel suggested by the Church Council. The Board of Education passes upon the qualifications of prospective ministers and has charge of the curriculum for ministerial education. The Board of Trustees of the Founder's Church has control over the use of the church buildings, chooses the ministers, and judges those who may be invited to appear in their pulpits.

The other churches of the organization form the Affiliated Churches, which meet annually to discuss matters of mutual interest and to elect their quota of members to the Board of Trustees. They also select members for the Church Council, which determines the general ecclesiastical policy of the Affiliated Churches, makes necessary recommendations to the Board of Trustees, determines the requirements for ordination and authorization of practitioners, and names the Administrator and his duties.

Each individual church is autonomous as far as its debts, property, etc., are concerned. It has its own separate Board of Trustees, composed usually of nine members, which takes care of the church's internal affairs.

The Church of Religious Science has definite categories for its church development. First, there is the study group which may vary in size from two to forty-nine members, but must be under the supervision of a listed teacher. When there are fifty signed pledging members, it becomes a prechurch group. To be considered a church, there must be a minimum of one hundred signed and pledging members. In the list of practitioners of the Church of Religious Science there are many in places where they have no church at present, but they form nuclei for future churches through the interest of their patrons in the philosophy of healing.

Since the organization encourages religious education for its members, it provides classes which use the textbook, *The Science of Mind*, by Ernest Holmes. After a year of study a second year's course is offered leading to the degree of Fellow in Religious Science. In this year there is a special practitioner's training course for those wishing to heal. A third year's study is required of those interested in ministerial training. The latter, when called to a church after thirty hours of work, receive a licentiate, which is good for two years. Ordination follows, if, upon examination, their ministry has been approved by the Board of Regents.[27]

Adaptability of Religious Science

Although Ernest Holmes preferred to think of his movement as Religious Science rather than as Christian, its use of the Bible gives it a dominant Christian orientation in America. Ontologically, perhaps it may be closer to certain forms of Ori-

[27] The foregoing material was supplied largely through interviews with Dr. Elmer Gifford, authority and minister of the Church of Religious Science.

ental thought. Probably part of the strength of Religious Science is its ability to accommodate itself to a country's culture. Certainly this type of philosophy has been adapted even more readily to Buddhism in Japan than to Christianity in America. For example, in 1934 Masaharu Taniguchi founded one of Japan's New Religions, the Seicho-no-Ie, the House of Growth. Although ostensibly revealed, Dr. Fenwicke Holmes credits its inspiration and tenets to his two books, *Law of Mind in Action* and *Being and Becoming*, which are now translated into Japanese. One magazine of this organization claims a million subscribers, according to Dr. Holmes, and one of its basic books, enitled in English the *True Basis of Life*, has sold more than eight million copies. The basic philosophy, that of Religious Science, attempts to be both Buddha and Christ centered.[28]

According to the Directory of New Religions, published by the International Institute for the Study of Religions, the Seicho-no-Ie had 1,469,844 members in 1958. One may compare this number with the 657,348 Catholics and Protestants in Japan in 1959, and whose figure includes eighty-three Protestant denominations. In spite of the fact that Protestants in Japan increased from 121,004 in 1919 to 394,385 in 1959, and Catholics from 75,983 to 262,963 in the same period,[29] a metaphysical religion transplanted from the United States and adapted to a Buddhist culture has filled the need more widely. However, since this phenomenal growth has occurred largely in the few years since World War II, it is too early to predict whether or not this philosophy will add continued strength to an old culture.

If Religious Science is able to accommodate itself easily to a religion such as Buddhism, the church in the United States seems to be moving more closely to the Christian tradition through its rites and ceremonies. For example, Religious Science has a service of baptism in the manuscript edition of its new *Religious Science Ministers' Service Book*. Such a rite,

[28] Fenwicke Holmes.

[29] International Institute for the Study of Religions, *Directory No. 4, New Religions* (Tokyo, 1958), p. 34; also its publication *Contemporary Religions in Japan*, Vol. 3, No. 1 (Tokyo, 1962), pp. 81–85.

even though metaphysically interpreted, would be more fitting in the predominantly Christian United States than in the Buddhist version of Religious Science.

The introduction to the manual explains that the rites and ceremonies have been adapted from those of the traditional church, but although the original terminology is used, the interpretation has been changed to agree with the " spirit of Truth as we see it in Christian mysticism, metaphysics, Science of Mind or New Thought." It states:

" Specifically, the Minister of Religious Science has the obligation to fulfill a Christian Ministry, with the various duties which that involves, and yet the higher obligation to present that Ministry in terms acceptable to the science, philosophy, and religion of his own Church. We must lend every traditional dignity to the Church offices we perform, yet in choosing our wording we can put forth the things in which we believe." [30]

The service of baptism for children is explained as " a recognition of the loving Presence and Infinite power of the Spirit " in each child.[31] For adults it means the acknowledgment of " faith in the unity of God and man," and is to seal that union, which is also recognized as the " unity with the indwelling of Christ." [32]

Composition of Membership

Most metaphysical healing movements are largely composed of upper middle-class people, representing many professional and better educated persons. The leaders in the Church of Religious Science have come from varying backgrounds. Because one would expect the recruits to be mustered from those of a very liberal theological persuasion, it is surprising to learn that an evangelist has entered their ranks to put on a " healing crusade of Christ " under the banner of the Church of Religious

[30] Church of Religious Science, *Religious Science Ministers' Service Book* (unpublished manuscript), p. 1.

[31] *Ibid.*, p. 8.

[32] *Ibid.*, p. 18. Perhaps the fact that the new service book has not yet been published after its completion several years ago indicates a divided opinion concerning the inclusion of some of its parts.

Science. Other leaders also have been drawn from the denominational churches. The head of its Department of Education, for example, is a graduate of an Episcopal theological seminary, and the minister of the Founder's Church in Los Angeles is a former Methodist pastor. By and large, however, the majority have come from other metaphysical groups. The Unity School of Christianity has supplied a number of its ministers, such as Elmer Gifford and Ernest Wilson. Some, like Dr. Gifford, have felt they have had more freedom in the Church of Religious Science than in the Unity School of Christianity.

Ecclesiastical Structure of the IARSC

The International Association of Religious Science Churches is proud of its even greater freedom and autonomy. The Annual Congress of the organization becomes its legislative body, which is composed of delegates elected by the Affiliated Churches on the basis of one delegate for each fifty members. The maximum for any church, however, is twenty. Between annual conferences the Board of Directors, consisting of eight ministers and five laymen, meets once a month in Los Angeles, as the executive and judicial body.

The IARSC has the two stated objectives: " To spiritually unify, strengthen, and assist in the work of all member Churches, and secondly; To work to the end that Religious Science expands into an effective spiritual movement which encircles the globe." [33]

Basic Principles of the IARSC

As a summary of its beliefs, the following is the Declaration of Religious Science Principles:

" We believe — in God, the Living Spirit Almighty; one, indestructible, absolute and self-existent Cause. This One manifests Itself in and through all creation but is not absorbed by

---

[33] International Association of Religious Science Churches, *Origin, Organization, Objective, Declaration of Religious Science Principles,* Los Angeles, n.d. (leaflet).

Its creation. The manifest universe is the body of God; it is the logical and necessary outcome of the infinite self-knowingness of God. . . . We believe in the incarnation of the Spirit in man and that all men are incarnations of the One Spirit. . . . We believe in the eternality, the immortality and the continuity of the individual soul, forever and ever expanding. . . . We believe that the Kingdom of Heaven is within man and that we experience this Kingdom to the degree that we become conscious of it. . . . We believe the ultimate goal of life to be a complete emancipation from all discord of every nature, and that this goal is sure to be attained by all. . . . We believe in the unity of all life, and that the highest God and the innermost God is one God.

" We believe that God is personal to all who feel this indwelling Presence. . . . We believe in the direct revelation of Truth through the intuitive and spiritual nature of man, and that any man may become a revealer of Truth who lives in close contact with the Indwelling God. . . . We believe that the Universal Spirit, which is God, operates through a Universal Mind, which is the Law of God; and that we are surrounded by this Creative Mind which receives the direct impress of our thought and acts upon it. . . . We believe in the healing of the sick through the power of this Mind. . . . We believe in the control of conditions through the power of this Mind. . . . We believe in the eternal Goodness, the eternal Loving-kindness, and the eternal Givingness of Life to all. . . . We believe in our own soul, and our own spirit and our own destiny; for we understand that the life of man is God." [34]

Expansion of Religious Science

Since the beginning of Religious Science there has been a steady growth. If one were to compare the size of the several New Thought organizations, their relative strengths might be proportional to several different factors. First, there is the personality and ability of the leader; secondly, the existence of a solid organization which holds together the membership for

[34] *Idem.*

mutual benefits; thirdly, a training school or training schools under good leadership; finally, the number and quality of publications of the leader and of the association. With the exception of certain organizational difficulties, the position of Religious Science fulfills these requirements quite well.

The organization is particularly strong in its publications. Its monthly magazine, the *Science of Mind: A Practical Guide to Fuller, Richer Living*, began in 1927. Unlike many other metaphysical periodicals, it is to be found at most large magazine stands and is sold to many thousands each month. Besides the daily meditation and affirmations for each day of the month, it features articles, and often from writers outside the movement. In the June issue of 1958, for example, there were articles by Ralph T. Flewelling, Director Emeritus of the School of Philosophy of the University of Southern California, and by Samuel H. Miller, now Dean of the Harvard Divinity School. The correspondence course of Religious Science has been taken by both ministers and laymen from many Protestant churches. Moreover, the numerous books by Ernest Holmes, which have usually been published by most reputable companies, have greatly contributed to the interest in Religious Science. His *The Science of Mind* has now gone through twenty-four editions since 1958.

The IARSC has likewise grown steadily. From 1954 to March, 1961, it increased from nineteen churches to thirty-one. The Church of Religious Science, which was reduced to forty-six churches when the partition occurred, numbered seventy-one in 1961. Although about half the churches of the founder's group are in California, there are three in New York, two in Colorado, two in Washington, two in Hawaii, and one church each in Maryland, Florida, Texas, Idaho, Missouri, Minnesota, Oklahoma, Pennsylvania, as well as churches in Canada, South Africa, the West Indies, England, and France.

Although Religious Science is of recent origin, it has made an impressive beginning. What the future holds with the passing of its founder, and whether rivalries among the leaders will engender new splits, only the future will reveal.

VIII

The Unity School of Christianity

Geographical Locale

JUST A FEW MILES outside Kansas City, where the bottom lands of the Missouri River give way to higher ground, stands the Unity School of Christianity on the outskirts of Lee's Summit. Unity Farm, as it is more familiarly known in this region, sprawls over thirteen hundred acres of gently rolling countryside. It devotes two hundred acres to orchards, contains an excellent dairy fully equipped with modern machines for homogenizing milk and making ice cream. Its beautiful grounds, containing attractive buildings of Italian Renaissance and English Tudor, are complete with a tower rising one hundred and sixty-four feet. This tall campanile is more than just an imposing landmark, because it holds one hundred thousand gallons of filtered water from Unity's own twenty-acre lake.

As a village, Unity Farm has housing facilities, a swimming pool, an inn, a nine-hole golf course, a club house, and an amphitheater large enough to accommodate four thousand persons. But it is more than that. It is both a training school for those wishing to enter its ministry and a publishing company, whose printing plant requires forty-thousand square feet of floor space, making it one of the largest in the Midwest.

Unity's Influence

Of all branches of the metaphysical movements Unity must be regarded as being the most influential upon organized churches of the Judeo-Christian tradition. A glance at some statistics will show the size of its operation.

Unity employs over eight hundred people, with five hundred assigned to the administration and the publishing company, not counting one hundred in the printing department. This leaves approximately one hundred for Silent Unity and another hundred for the farm.

In 1957 Unity received over thirty-five thousand letters a week, or one million six hundred and sixty-seven thousand, seven hundred and eighty-six during the year. Its own first- and third-class mail count is more than twenty-five thousand a day.

Its most popular periodical, the *Daily Word*, is printed at the rate of three quarters of a million copies a month in the English edition. Besides the Spanish edition published also at the headquarters, it is printed abroad in Braille, Afrikaans, Dutch, Finnish, French, German, Japanese, Portuguese, Sinhala, Spanish, and Tamil. Its nine periodicals published at Unity Farm totaled twenty-three million, six hundred and twenty-nine thousand, eight hundred and sixty-six issues.

It has published more than fifty adult books, of which it sells hundreds of thousands of copies each year. These have been translated into one hundred and forty foreign languages, including among them Ibo, an African language, Japanese, Russian, Greek, etc. It is obvious that Unity has spread its influence far beyond the United States.

Whereas Protestant denominational literature is read largely by those in the particular denomination, most of Unity's periodicals are being read by people who are not classified in religious statistics as Unity students, but as Catholics, Protestants, or Jews. Although there are over two hundred Unity centers working in close cooperation with the school, these is no way account for the million and a half people who subscribe to the Unity magazines. Unity claims only seventy-five thousand attend these centers in the United States. The chart on page 231 shows in round figures the proportion between center attendance and outside influence in several sample states, drawn from estimates made in 1957.

Chart Showing Unity Audience by Three Major Classifications

	Subscribers to Unity Periodicals	Radio & TV Coverage	Center Attendance
State of New York	100,000	500,000	10,000
State of California	200,000	750,000	25,000
State of Missouri	40,000	100,000	8,000

The above figures do not take into consideration the fact that the periodicals might be read by more persons than the subscriber. If this is a close estimate, it would show that in these states the influence is roughly from eighty to ninety percent beyond the number of the Unity's own membership.

In 1957 Unity's radio programs were heard over more than fifty radio stations, reaching more than three million people; its television program of " The Daily Word with Rosemary Grace " was broadcast over twenty-six stations, reaching more than a million viewers.[1]

Unity publications are read by laymen in churches all over the United States. In New York a prominent laywoman, writer, and deaconess at the Riverside Church, said that in one church she had attended, a survey of the women's reading revealed that a majority were readers of Unity literature. She declared that although Unity did not put the proper emphasis upon sin, still she herself was a regular reader of the *Daily Word*.

A number of ministers in the United States are now preaching the Unity doctrine in their churches, although only a few will admit it openly. Among the more notable examples of Unity's influence has been Lewis Dunnington, popular writer and Methodist minister. In his book, *The Inner Splendor*, published in 1954, he tells of his indebtedness to the Unity School of Christianity for his " discovery of the great affirmations that work such wonders in human lives."

He had first noticed, when making calls on members of his church in Duluth, that the most poised and well-integrated ones among them seemed to be regular readers of Unity literature. Having sampled some of this material, he went to Lee's

[1] The statistics were prepared by the Unity School of Christianity, 1958.

Summit to visit the Fillmores. He was further impressed there by their records of the thousands who had claimed help from Unity. Among these was one from Starr Daily, who he discovered had been changed by Unity from a disgruntled prisoner in a state penitentiary to a person who made " a career of spiritual helpfulness that is almost without parallel in the annals of religious literature." The result was that Dunnington returned to prepare a group of sermons, which were published as *Handles of Power* and contained Unity's affirmations of faith and spiritual techniques. He said that because of just this one book he has received thousands of commendatory letters from ministers and laymen of all denominations. In the eleven subsequent years in the First Methodist Church in Iowa City, his congregation increased from four hundred to more than two thousand, and he held two identical services on Sunday mornings. Dunnington feels people want to know " how " to satisfy their spiritual hunger, which Unity's techniques give.[2]

While the writer was carrying on his research at the Unity School of Christianity he met the Reverend Robert Stevens, an alumnus of the School. He had been called to serve the Christian Chapel, a church of the Disciples of Christ at South Gate in the Los Angeles area. When the Reverend Charles Jarman began to preach the principles of Unity in his church, a split occurred. With part of his congregation he started a new church which called the Reverend Robert Stevens after Jarman's retirement. This church, although nine years old in 1958, had already over a half million dollars in assets, sponsored three daily radio programs entirely supported by offerings from the public, and cooperated fully with the Southern California Conference of the Disciples of Christ.

Unity's Missionary Effort — The Silent Seventy Department

Although the Unity School of Christianity sends no missionaries to foreign countries, the Silent Seventy Department takes their places. This branch, which was organized in 1910, was

[2] Lewis L. Dunnington, *The Inner Splendor* (The Macmillan Company, 1954), pp. vii–xi.

inspired by the tenth chapter of Luke, where one reads, " The Lord appointed seventy others, and sent them . . . into every town and place." Through Silent Seventy, free Unity literature is distributed to all types of institutions throughout the world. Thousands of volunteer workers in the field spread the literature through this department. At the request of any institution Unity's periodicals will be sent *gratis*. While there, I was privileged to look through its vast files containing the names of thousands of ministers and chaplains of various institutions who have requested literature and praised the work of Unity. They include the names of many hospitals, homes for the aged, public libraries, pentitentiaries, leper colonies, homes for the blind, homes for underprivileged children, and orphanages. In some prisons there are Unity classes under the direction of chaplains, whose letters testify to Unity.

Wee Wisdom, its periodical for children, has become popular in many public schools throughout the United States. Free subscriptions of it are sent to more than two thousand schools in the backwoods of Virginia and Tennessee as well as to underprivileged children in some of the mining districts. The director of a Navajo Indian reservation, where four hundred *Wee Wisdom* subscriptions are sent, wrote:

" Your gift subscriptions are indeed appreciated. The *Wee Wisdom* magazine will be the first magazine that many of the Navajo children ever had, and in many cases will be the only magazine introduced in many Indian homes."

Outside the United States the influence of the Silent Seventy Department has been noticed in many countries, most notably in Japan and in Africa, according to Unity. In Japan, where its materials have been translated into Japanese, the organization *claims* already a million followers for the " Truth movement," although this effect has not been noted in Japanese statistics. In Africa, from which hundreds of letters addressed to Unity arrive with every ship, Unity now boasts that its teachings are more widespread among the natives than are those of any denomination.

Besides the free distribution of Unity literature the Silent Seventy Department has busied itself with Christmas-card distribution to prisoners as an act of good will. Through the co-operation of the Hallmark Greeting Card Company, this department distributes over two hundred thousand free cards a year to prisoners, who send as many as they wish to friends and relatives.[3]

Unity's Stated Purpose

Although Unity must be described as a sect, since it trains and ordains ministers to serve its own centers, it still considers itself primarily as a publishing company.

Charles Fillmore gave the aim of Unity in the following statement:

" For many years the Unity School has looked forward to the time when it might do much of its work in the churches. Unity has never tried to establish another church or system of belief, but has endeavored to confine its teachings to the practical application of Christian principles as demonstrated in the life of Jesus Christ, and to give this teaching to all the people, independent of their church affiliations. It has never been the desire to take people out of the churches, but rather to educate them in the spirit of their teaching and thus help to restore the Christian spirit to the church." [4]

Background of the Fillmores, the Founders of Unity

Charles Fillmore, who died in 1948 at the age of ninety-four, was born in 1854 in a small log cabin on an Indian reservation near St. Cloud, Minnesota. His mother, Mary Fillmore, had a difficult time to supply her family with its bare necessities, after being deserted by her husband when Charles and his brother were quite young.

Charles had to go to work at an early age to help his mother when his brother also ran away. Although handicapped by a withered leg resulting from an improperly treated injury, he

---

[3] Unity School of Christianity, *Highlights of Silent-70* (leaflet).
[4] Charles Fillmore, " Unity and the Churches," *Weekly Unity*, Vol. 12, No. 48 (March, 1921), p. 3.

worked at various jobs, such as printer's devil, grocery clerk, and bank teller. If he consequently received very little formal education, an educated woman instructed both her son and his friend, Charles, in the works of Shakespeare, Tennyson, Emerson, and Lowell. The names of two sons, Waldo Rickert and Lowell, reflect the influence of the latter two. Particularly Emerson influenced the development of his thought.

After moving from job to job in various cities in his early manhood, in 1876 he met a young schoolteacher, Myrtle Page, in Denison, Texas. Myrtle, unlike Charles, had been born in an influencial family in Pagetown, Ohio, and had studied at Oberlin College. She seemed at first to be the very opposite of Charles except for a common interest in literature and philosophy, which had drawn them together in a study circle. Later they discovered their similar eclectic tastes.

Although Myrtle had been formerly a prominent worker in her home-town Methodist Episcopal Church, Charles had been only an occasional attendant with his mother at a Protestant Episcopal Church, and had not felt influenced by any orthodox teaching. Besides his love for Emerson, he had become interested in Spiritualism.[5] Although believing that mediums contacted spirits, he criticized the practice, because he said that it weakened man's control of himself and placed reliance upon spirits having no greater knowledge than before their transition.[6] Both the Fillmores from their study of Theosophy had accepted many of its principles, such as reincarnation and karma. It was therefore natural that after Swami Vivekananda came to America in 1893, they quoted him, advertised, and sold his works. The Rosicrucian influence also seems to be apparent from Charles Fillmore's response to Freeman Dowd's book, *The Temple of the Rosycross*. In it one finds the origin of the " Winged Globe," the symbol of the Unity School of Christianity appearing in its publications. Dowd's belief in the relationship between sin and sex and in the partial origin of sickness in lust was defended by Fillmore in an editorial in 1889 and

[5] James Dillet Freeman, *The Story of Unity* (Unity School of Christianity, 1954), pp. 19–40.

[6] James Teener, *Unity School of Christianity*, Ph.D. thesis (University of Chicago, 1939), p. 109.

became a basis for Unity's emphasis on continence.[7]

After the wedding of Charles Fillmore to Myrtle Page in a Methodist Episcopal Church in 1881, Charles gave up his position in a railroad freight office and was again on the move. Two unsuccessful business ventures followed before he became a prosperous real-estate broker during the Kansas City land boom in 1884, but this success was brief. The boom collapsed, a mining investment failed, and gone seemed the hope of prosperity. To make matters worse, Myrtle, who had apparently suffered from tuberculosis earlier, was now ill again, and the family thought of returning to Colorado from which they had come to Kansas City.[8] Then came the turning point in their lives.

The Path Toward Unity

In 1887 [9] after J. S. Thatcher came from Chicago to organize the Kansas City College of Christian Science, Eugene B. Weeks organized the first class which the Fillmores attended.[10] Weeks had been a representative of the Illinois Metaphysical College established by Emma Curtis Hopkins.[11]

The first lecture changed Myrtle Fillmore. She is said to have walked out with one thought in her mind: "*I am a child of God and therefore I do not inherit sickness.*" No longer did she think of herself as an invalid, and already the idea that God's will was perfect health was said to have begun its effect upon her body.[12]

The Fillmores later came under the direct influence of Mrs. Hopkins, who lectured twice in Kansas City in 1890. In the same year Charles became an ordained minister, after they studied in her seminary.[13]

Within two years after the first inspirational lecture on

---

[7] *Ibid.*, pp. 106–108.

[8] Freeman, *op. cit.*, pp. 33–39.

[9] Freeman, *op. cit.*, p. 44, gives the date as 1886.

[10] Teener, *op. cit.*, p. 7.

[11] Freeman, *op. cit.*, p. 42. Teener writes: "Christian Science Theological Seminary," *op. cit.*, p. 11.

[12] Freeman, *op. cit.*, pp. 44–45.

[13] Teener, *op. cit.*, pp. 10–11.

" Christian Science," Myrtle had allegedly recovered her health and was curing others. With Charles it was different. He was slow to accept the teachings fully, because inconsistencies in the views of various teachers bothered him. Seeing his wife's faith, however, he tried to determine whether it was true. Finally, he believed he was being guided by a higher power, God, the source of all truth, who could be realized through affirmation.

Changing times make changing fortunes, and during the depression in 1899 Charles Fillmore decided to give up his real-estate business and become a publisher. His first periodical, *Modern Thought,* was " Devoted to the Spiritualization of Humanity from an Independent Standpoint." [14] The first volume showed Fillmore's religious tolerance as well as criticism of the Christian churches. Concerning the purpose of his publication, he said that it advocated no one school of thought nor the view of any one person:

" It is a matter of indifference to us what the religious convictions of our co-worker may be, so long as he is aiming at the truth. . . . We shall express our views upon all questions according to the light we have today; if tomorrow's light is stronger, we shall shift our views to suit it, for we follow truth wherever she leads." [15]

Modern Thought accepted articles on Spiritualism, Theosophical subjects, etc., and Charles Fillmore declared himself to be a proponent of a " real spiritual church " rather than an " intellectual " one.[16] Nevertheless, his emphasis upon what he considered the " Jesus Christ standards " was one reason for his later separation from the less distinctive groups of New Thought and from other movements.

In the same issue of *Modern Thought* was the initial statement of his doctrine of everlasting life in the physical body. Theosophy had taught that after becoming a master through spiritual development, one might retain his physical body indefinitely, and Prentice Mulford had expounded the exact view

[14] Freeman, *op. cit.,* pp. 54–55.
[15] *Modern Thought,* Vol. 1, No. 1 (April, 1889), p. 5.
[16] *Ibid.,* p. 9.

of Charles Fillmore. Fillmore, like Mulford,[17] believed:

" There are those now living who will witness the advent of a society on this planet that will scientifically demonstrate the existence of the soul and the manner of its manipulation of matter. The scientific *modus operandi* of the so-called miracles of the past will be shown, for God works through universal laws, and those laws are just as operative today as in the time of Moses. This society will produce individual members who, through soul concentration, will have so spiritualized the atoms of their bodies, as to be able to make themselves visible or invisible at will; and who will have the power to live upon this earth plain any length of time they may desire. . . . These spiritual powers are latent in all, and must ultimately be unfolded in all, for we are the children of one God." [18]

Thus Fillmore thought that one could spiritualize his physical atoms by prayer and a spiritual life, by observance of sexual continence, and avoidance of sensual pleasures. In fact, he was once convinced that he himself would never die. Only among his last words did he show himself reconciled: the " Lord of my being has decided otherwise, and I am ready to do what has to be done." [19]

His passing still did not change the status of the view, because the school said in a letter to the Unity Centers on July 6, 1948, announcing his death, " He assured us only a short time ago that even if he were to pass on, it would not affect his belief or his teaching concerning eternal life." So Unity still accepts this doctrine as man's possibility, but reincarnation as the norm for those who die.

Although it is correct to call Unity eclectic, the organization

[17] Marin, *op. cit.*, pp. 62–63. She quotes Mulford: "Reincarnated we have all been many times. Regeneration is a step beyond reincarnation. . . . Regeneration means the perpetuation of an ever-refining spiritual body without that total separation of spirit and body called death. . . . A spiritualising and refining power has been and ever will be working on this planet. . . . It is ever changing him gradually from a material to a more spiritual being. It is carrying him through his many physical existences from one degree of perfection to another. . . . There will come in the future a more perfected life, when for the few at first and the many afterward there will be no physical death. In other words, every spirit will be able to use both its spiritual and physical senses through the continual regeneration of its physical body."

[18] *Modern Thought*, p. 10.

[19] *Bee-Picayune*, Beeville, Texas, August 9, 1948.

has maintained its independence from other such groups because of its own special interpretations. For example, while accepting the theory of karma, it teaches that the effect of one's deeds depends upon his submission to it, but through redirection of thought the Christ power will dissolve all karma.[20] Fillmore believed he and his wife had gathered and unified the good from many religions. He said: "We do not claim that we have discovered any new truths, nor that we have had any special revelation of truth. There is truth in every religion. It is my privilege to take Truth from any source, put it into my religion, and make it fundamental as a rule of action in my life."[21]

Relation to Christian Science

Although often associated with Christian Science, the Fillmores were never students of Mary Baker Eddy, nor did they join her church. Their main metaphysical thrust, which was related to Christian Science, came from teachers, such as Emma Curtis Hopkins and Ursula Gestefeld, who had already disagreed with Mrs. Eddy and left her organization.

Mrs. Gestefeld had been converted to Christian Science when Mrs. Eddy first came to Chicago to lecture in 1884. She became one of the directors of the Christian Science church there but did not fully agree with Mrs. Eddy. After publishing *A Statement of Christian Science: An Explanation of Science and Health* in 1888, in which she omitted the subject of malicious animal magnetism and declared that Mrs. Eddy's idea about matter was only half true, she invoked the founder's ire and was dismissed from the church. Her answer in a pamphlet entitled *Jesuitism in Christian Science* was heralded by Charles Fillmore in his magazine, and later the Fillmores used her lectures in a class.[22]

---

[20] Charles Fillmore, *Preserving the Unity of Soul and Body: Reincarnation* (Unity School of Christianity, 1921).
[21] *Unity, Devoted to Practical Christianity* (Unity School of Christianity), Vol. 59, Oct., 1923, p. 303.
[22] Teener, *op. cit.,* pp. 8–9.

Unity's Move of Separation

Fillmore had acknowledged his debt to Quimby as interpreted by Evans and declared Evans' works to be " the most complete of all metaphysical compilations." [23] Although similar in many respects to most of the metaphysical movements, already by 1897 Unity had made its first move to separate itself from the more diverse by limiting its pages in *Modern Thought* to those advocating and practicing " Pure Mind Healing only " as " taught and demonstrated by Jesus Christ." [24]

The Fillmores had joined their mental science friends at the Chicago convention in 1893, met them again at the meeting of the International Divine Science Association in 1895, and were hosts of the congress in 1896 at Kansas City. This group became the New Thought Federation and later the International New Thought Alliance. When the 1906 meeting in Chicago seemed too diversified for Charles Fillmore, he decided that Unity could not be considered as New Thought, but only as practical Christianity.[25]

This marked the separation of the ways for Unity until a brief period beginning in 1919. In that year the International New Thought Alliance asked for conditions on which the Fillmores would return. They replied that the association would have to accept Christ's message to the twentieth century, a message of works, not words, according to Christ's standards. Their terms were accepted, and Unity rejoined the Alliance until its final resignation in 1922. There were several reasons for this separation. In the first place, the INTA had not really accepted Unity's interpretations of truth; secondly, the INTA had set up a field lectureship in which various speakers would visit the centers, but unfortunately their views were often embarrassingly different from those of Unity; and finally, Unity had been asked to contribute teachers to a proposed INTA normal school. Since Unity already had its own, it felt that

---

[23] *Ibid.*, p. 109.
[24] *Ibid.*, p. 30. Quoted from "Explanation," *Unity*, Vol. 8, May, 1897, p. 393.
[25] Freeman, *op. cit.*, pp. 102–104.

the INTA was becoming a school instead of just a federation of organizations.[26]

Unity's Publications

As a publishing company Unity produces at its headquarters eight periodicals: *Wee Wisdom* for children; *Progress* and the *Unity Sunday School Leaflet* for teenagers; and for adults: *Weekly Unity*, *Good Business*, *Unity*, and the *Daily Word*, which is translated into Spanish as *La Palabra Diaria*.

The magazine *Unity* has continued publication since 1891 after consolidating with *Thought* in 1895. *Wee Wisdom*, which reaches almost two hundred thousand homes, claims to be the oldest children's periodical in the United States. It is also published in Braille and sent free to any blind person upon request.

Among its various books none has been so popular as Dr. H. Emilie Cady's *Lessons in Truth*, which was first published serially in *Unity* in 1892.[27] This was the first systematic presentation of much of the Fillmores' philosophy.

When one considers the number of free subscriptions given to people and institutions and the fact that *Unity* carries no outside advertising, one begins to appreciate the truth of Lowell Fillmore's words that probably only the *Daily Word* is self-sustaining. The explanation of Unity's great prosperity then lies not in its publications but in its Silent Unity Department.

Silent Unity

In 1890 Myrtle Fillmore announced the beginning of a new department, the Society of Silent Unity. It began with an invitation for any with ills or troubles to join with the Fillmores at ten o'clock at night for fifteen minutes of prayer. At that time Charles and Myrtle Fillmore would pray together with a small group of friends and bless those who might be with them in thought. The method was to meditate in silence " on the

[26] Teener, *op. cit.*, pp. 33–35.   [27] Freeman, *op. cit.*, pp. 67–77.

idea of God until the idea became a living reality in their minds and hearts and they felt Him as a living presence in themselves." Gaining this feeling of oneness, they would affirm God's goodness to be manifested in their minds, bodies, and affairs. Affirmations were printed in their magazine *Thought*, until their society organ, *Unity*, began to be published.[28] The idea seemed to catch on. More and more people began writing to the department for prayers, until in 1956 the department recorded the reception of five hundred and sixty thousand letters, twenty-six thousand, one hundred and sixty-six telegrams, and twenty thousand, seven hundred and twenty-five telephone calls for help. The department operates on a twenty-four hour basis, divided into three shifts and utilizing one hundred persons, of which twenty are its ministerial students. Every worker must take lessons in " Truth," " Bible," etc., twice a week, and every day begins with a prayer service using the affirmation given in the *Daily Word* for that week.

Unity answers each request by a letter with some helpful enclosures including an appropriate affirmative prayer. The problem is then quickly referred to the prayer room for proper attention along with many others. Each person is remembered in prayer for a month, unless notification confirms that the matter has cleared up. Although every kind of need is encountered, health problems are the most frequent, with domestic problems, prosperity, and guidance problems following in that order of importance.

When the question was raised concerning the cause of a prayer's failure, the reply was that such a question was never asked, because the issue was always between man and God. Unity does recognize that some prayers are not answered, however, but also realizes the difficulty of getting valid statistics on the ratio between answered and unanswered prayers. But since its services are free, the " love offerings " or gifts from thousands who every year feel they have been helped have contributed to its prosperity.

[28] *Ibid.*, pp. 81–88.

Prosperity — for Unity and Others

Although Unity began as a healing movement, it followed the trend of New Thought in its concern for prosperity. The Fillmores came to believe that God was the source not only of one's health but also of his supply. Through this awareness one could develop a prosperity consciousness. Unity teaches that poverty is due to man's failure to achieve the right level of consciousness.[29]

Such treatments were first begun in 1904, and the " Prosperity Bank " was introduced in 1910. Those wanting these services were asked to request a bank, which Unity would send free of charge. The recipients were directed to use Unity's " Prosperity Thought " for ten weeks and contribute a dime a week " as a reminder and earnest of the prosperity which was rightly " theirs. At the end of the period they were to send to Unity the dollar for a year's subscription to one of its periodicals for a designated person. By 1923 the School was sending out an average of eight thousand banks each month,[30] and the practice has continued.

Unity Becomes a Sect

When the Unity Society of Practical Christianity was established by Charles and Myrtle Fillmore, there was no thought at first of its becoming a church. Both Charles and Myrtle considered themselves as teachers rather than as ministers. Therefore, the Society was first incorporated as an educational institution in 1903. Its correspondence school, which began in 1909, had an enrollment of over two thousand within two years.[31] Then the Unity Society of Practical Christianity became actually the founding church in Kansas City, and the Unity School of Christianity was incorporated in 1914.[32] Although most of its students had first come from the Kansas City area, the broader basis of the training school was soon established to in-

29 *Ibid.*, pp. 118–119.
30 Teener, *op. cit.*, pp. 53–54.
31 Freeman, *op. cit.*, pp. 105–106, 166, 180.
32 Teener, *op. cit.*, p. 59.

clude others, when Unity began its summer course for intense study.[33]

It was only natural that those who had been interested enough in Unity to study its literature and take its correspondence courses might also want to teach and heal. Therefore, centers teaching Unity principles began forming in various cities. Although the Fillmores were reluctant to grant degrees or diplomas at first, even before the incorporation of the school a Field Department had been organized to contact the Centers and give suggestions about teaching.[34] Thus the growth of the Centers showed the need to organize a training school.

Difficulties soon arose, and try as it might, Unity could not escape some of Mrs. Eddy's problems. It was discovered soon that teachers in the Centers were holding séances, practicing numerology, etc. The Fillmores, while censuring these policies in their publications, were still not ready to dictate to the Centers.[35] Nevertheless, the die was already cast, so at the second Annual Unity Conference Charles Fillmore announced that all who had received diplomas would be ordained in the "Unity Church Universal." This was not ostensibly to be another sect, but was to recognize the need of an organization which could "interpret and demonstrate the spiritual realities back of the church symbols. All Christians could join such a church without breaking their present religious affiliations." At the same time the rites of Baptism and Holy Communion were established, but were to be administered "without the aid of the material symbols." This organization was soon laid aside, and no mention of it was made after 1924, because it was said that Mr. Fillmore realized that Unity was not interested in becoming another sect.[36]

Unity still needed a way to preserve its principles, and by 1933 the Constitution of the Unity Annual Conference showed further control over its ministers. It stated that after 1935 only those who had been ordained by the Unity School of Christianity, or had their ordination approved by the Field

[33] Freeman, op. cit., pp. 181–182.
[34] Teener, op. cit., pp. 62, 91.
[35] Freeman, op. cit., pp. 185–186.
[36] Teener, op. cit., pp. 94–95. Fillmore's statement was quoted from his article, "Unity Church Universal," Unity, Vol. 60, May, 1924, p. 438.

Department and the school could be accepted in the Centers. Membership in the Conference was to be renewed each year; Unity materials were to be used in all Centers; the course of teaching prescribed by the school should be followed; all Centers were to make annual reports to the Field Department; qualifications for ordination would depend on the completion of the Methods and Ideals Course by correspondence and two months training at the Unity School of Christianity.[37] According to Donald O'Connor, head of the training school in 1957, Unity now regularly requires four years of courses, each lasting a month, although this curriculum may be completed in two years.

Since Unity now has a Statement of Faith and ever growing Centers, whose services are held at eleven o'clock on Sunday mornings; a ministerial association, which has ties with the headquarters at Lee's Summit, even though the Centers are considered autonomous; one might now ask whether Unity has become sectarian in fact, if not by preference. One might question whether the foregoing developments do not indicate a change in position from that expressed in 1925, when Charles Fillmore wrote:

" The church of Jesus Christ still waits for a ministry that will represent it as it is — an organization in heaven without a head on earth, without a creed, without a line of written authority. This church exists, and must be set up in its rightful place — the minds and hearts of men. It can never be confined to any external organization, and whoever attempts such movement, by that act ceases to represent the true church of Christ." [38]

A similar view was once expressed by Mrs. Eddy.

Unity's Teachings

It would seem that if the individualistic characteristics of Unity were removed, the basic philosophy would be the same as the others. Its small variations in beliefs show that Unity has sometimes made a slightly different selection from the common

[37] *Ibid.,* pp. 96–97.
[38] Charles Fillmore, *Christian Healing: The Science of Being,* 12th ed. (Unity School of Christianity, 1925), p. 225.

sources of metaphysical thought. Unity does not seek authority in the early Gnostic writings as does the Church of Divine Science, but could so choose. It does not emphasize the psychological approach as much as the Church of Religious Science, although it is open to such. If it considers all religions as containing truth and has sought to unify and make a synthesis of this truth, the same is largely true of other metaphysical groups. Like these, it considers its faith to be scientific, believes that the only reality is God or Spirit, all and in-all, and does not deny the reality of matter, etc.

Its greatest strength, besides its organization, is probably that it considers itself to be Christian and consequently gives greater attention to Biblical interpretation than do most metaphysical sects. It does not frown on using the words " sin," " evil," and others familiar to traditional Christians. However, their meaning in the context of its philosophy differs from any traditional sense and fits the view of other metaphysical groups. It is indeed possible to listen to a Unity meditation and often hear a message that would fit into any person's Christian theology. Nevertheless, Unity's definitions of the terms might differ greatly from those of the traditional churches.

Unity's recognition of the power of the pen is also a fortifying factor. The articles in Unity's magazines are usually well written. It specializes in creative writing, and students at the training center are required to study and practice this art. The teachings in the popular *Daily Word*, besides their devotional setting, often give the superficial appearance of being traditionally Christian.

God

God is thought of in both personal and impersonal terms. As principle, the basis of spiritual science, God is spoken of by Myrtle Fillmore as " IT, neither male nor female." God as the " Principle of life, love, and intelligence," is also regarded as personal to each person.[39]

God, the Divine Mind, includes not only being, but appear-

[39] Myrtle Fillmore, *How to Let God Help You* (Unity School of Christianity, 1956), p. 25.

ance. As Charles Fillmore said: " Mind has two sides, being and appearance, the visible and the invisible. To say that mind is all and yet deny that things that do appear have any place in the allness is to state but half the truth." [40]

This view seems to lead to a paradox, however. By definition God is all-good and includes appearance as well as reality. He must logically include evil, which seems to be a contradiction.

Christ and Spiritual Man

According to Unity, the Logos, the Word, or Christ, is the " Revealer and Interpreter of the Hidden Being of God," and the medium of his manifestations in the world. God's being, an impersonal principle, sends out the idea that contains all ideas in the process of creation. This idea is the Logos, the Son of God, the Christ, and is also *spiritual man*.[41] This view is close to that of Christian Science.

Since Fillmore, like other metaphysicians, believed in an inner meaning of the Biblical words, the Bible, he said, could be interpreted as a history of man, and as a description of his spiritual faculties. The book of Genesis, for example, was explained as an allegory of what happened in a person's mind during his development from the idea to its manifestation. Fillmore's exegesis of Genesis also revealed his triune view of God who reveals himself as Mind and Creator, as idea in Mind, and then as the manifestation of idea. Therefore, the man God created and pronounced good is spiritual man, God's idea of perfect man, whereas Adam is the name God gave to manifest man.[42] Elsewhere it is said that there is only one mind, the Universal Mind, and we, in reality, have no independent minds, but only consciousness in that Mind, over which we have control.[43] The soul is one part of the Trinity of spirit, soul, and body comprising man.

[40] Charles Fillmore, *Prosperity* (Unity School of Christianty, 1938), p. 27.

[41] Charles and Cora Fillmore, *Teach Us to Pray*, 6th ed. (Unity School of Christianity, 1944), pp. 167–168. (Cora Fillmore was Charles' second wife, whom he married in 1933 after the death of Myrtle Fillmore in 1931.)

[42] Charles Fillmore, *Mysteries of Genesis*. Revised and Enlarged (Unity School of Christianity, 1956), pp. 10–13.

[43] Charles and Cora Fillmore, *Teach Us to Pray*, p. 138.

Psychology of the Soul

Charles Fillmore developed a psychology of the soul, which was divided into three elements: animal, human, and spiritual, representing man's thought and emotions on these planes. The highest or spiritual element includes all one's thoughts and aspirations concerning spiritual things and God, and becomes the connecting link between the human and the divine. Here the spiritual I AM is working to help man, even though he is unconscious of the process. Unity at this point unknowingly expresses a doctrine of God's prevenient grace.

Unity teaches that the soul at the time of death may pass to a realm where it functions feebly. This is the " spirit land " of the Spiritualists. Others, however, who have had a hard and strenuous life, may spend this period in sleep. All still must eventually reincarnate back to earth again.[44]

Fillmore was influenced by Rosicrucianism to believe that man has twelve seats of power situated in various parts of his body. These correspond to the twelve disciples of Jesus Christ. When man begins to develop his spiritual awareness, he can activate these consciously by his thought, so they will function in the universal as well as in the personal. This attainment, Fillmore believed, is the second coming of Christ.

" The first coming is the receiving of the Truth into the conscious mind, and the second coming is the awakening and the regeneration of the subconscious mind through the superconscious of Christ Mind."

Charles Fillmore also asserted that Jesus, the I AM, had his throne in the top of the head, where, according to phrenology, spirituality was located. These powers or centers are:

" Faith — Peter — center of brain

" Strength — Andrew — loins

" Discrimination or judgment — James, the son of Zebedee — pit of stomach

" Love — John — back of heart

" Power — Philip — root of tongue

" Imagination — Bartholomew — between the eyes

[44] *Ibid.*, pp. 48–51.

" Understanding — Thomas — front brain
" Will — Matthew — center front brain
" Order — James, son of Alphaeus — navel
" Zeal — Simon the Canaanite — back head, medulla
" Renunciation or Elimination — Thaddaeus — abdominal region
" Life Conserver — Judas — generative function "

The above scheme, we are told, can be expanded for a better understanding of its nature. For example, Philip, situated at the root of the tongue, not only governs taste, but also the action of the larynx and all vibrations of power throughout the organism.[45] And so on with the others.

Man's Goal and Method of Attainment

Man's goal is to join himself in consciousness with the one Christ Mind, his real being. His difficulty, according to Fillmore, has been that he has unconsciously separated himself from others and assumed an individual personality.[46]

When man reaches this state of unity, so that he has really found his being in God, it is believed he will not be of the world; his interest will be in spiritual things; he will have the realization of his oneness with eternal good to the extent that he will be impregnable to evil. He will become so good in purpose that he will unselfishly produce good in everything he does. This is Unity's meaning of sanctification. This unity with God is explained as one's expansion into the divine rather than an absorption of man's consciousness. Charles Fillmore thought this to be the true meaning of unity taught by Hindu philosophy.[47]

Unity teaches that man must realize within himself both the Kingdom of God and the Father revealed through Jesus, a truth to be experienced rather than intellectually imparted. Even though no two individuals are believed to be alike due to

[45] Charles Fillmore, *The Twelve Powers of Man* (Unity School of Christianity, 1930), pp. 15–16.
[46] Charles and Cora Fillmore, *Teach Us to Pray*, p. 138.
[47] Charles Fillmore, *Mysteries of John* (Unity School of Christianity, 1957), pp. 150–151.

the diversity of ideas appropriated from the Divine Mind, still, according to a person's ability to make God's ideas his own, he has the potentiality of becoming the "only begotten son."[48]

This experiential knowledge of man's reality, we are told, comes through man's will. He must learn to claim his Christ Understanding and affirm his oneness with Infinite Understanding. By keeping in the Spirit through affirmations man will *know* through his intuitive faculty, which is a direct influx from God's mind.[49]

Like the other metaphysical schools, Unity regards Jesus as the way-shower. According to Fillmore's interpretation of the Gospel of John, Jesus recognized that the Christ, the divine-idea man, was actually his true self, and consequently, he was the Son of God. Because of his perfect recognition he was able to transform his physical body into a spiritual substance that became his resurrection body. It is also believed that all mankind has this same creative power. As man accepts through faith in Christ this higher consciousness, he is saved and transformed by this higher spirit of the law taught and practiced by Jesus. Thus an important part of the regenerative process for Unity is the recognition of ourselves as Sons of God. This awareness through affirmation is the door through which we may enter into the fullness of the Godhead. As a preparation for this, Unity believes one must deny himself, i.e., put away any "undue devotion to personal aims, which are always narrow and selfish," and deny all error thought, including the forgiveness of sins.[50] This is the meaning of "putting on Christ," of being born anew, which involves a transformation from the human to the spiritual plane of consciousness.[51]

Doctrine of the Fall of Man

In order to explain why man does not have this realization of his true nature, Unity has a doctrine of man's fall. Adam was created as a spiritually illumined creation, according to

[48] Fillmore, *Christian Healing*, p. 17.
[49] *Ibid.*, pp. 105–106.
[50] Fillmore, *Mysteries of John*, pp. 13–18.
[51] Fillmore, *Christian Healing*, p. 26.

Fillmore, who interpreted the word " Adam " metaphysically as the soul, intellect, and body of man.[52] Man fell because he departed from spiritual consciousness by seeing both good and evil. Had he stuck to the good, that would have been the only manifestation. His salvation, however, is through Jesus Christ, the Word, which is interpreted as " perfect man," i.e., the spiritual mind of man, the Christ. Through Christ in this sense we are believed to be saved from the Fall.[53]

Fillmore attributes lust as the reason for Adam's departure from the good, or regenerative love. In this case, Adam and Eve are interpreted as the innocent and uneducated powers of the masculine and feminine in every person. The serpent symbolizes sensation and desire tempting the male and female elements of man to lust, or symbolically, to eat of the tree of good and evil. Fillmore believed it was this sin which eventually brought the dissolution of man's physical body.[54] Then because of Adam's sins, man is ignorant of his true nature, which Fillmore regarded as a short definition of sin.[55]

Restoration of Man Through Christ

Unity teaches that the suffering on the cross lowered Jesus' consciousness to that of the human race, so as to give man's soul and body the properties of being which could restore man to his divine place. Thus it can say that through Jesus Christ man is guaranteed eternal life, and through at-one-ment (atonement) man's life is united with that of Jesus Christ. Through unity with the indwelling Christ, the Savior, man is raised from his Adam consciousness.[56]

Meaning of the Cross

The cross too has a meaning in Unity, that differs from any traditional interpretation. It is " a symbol of the forces in man

[52] Fillmore, *Mysteries of Genesis*, p. 68.
[53] *Ibid.*, pp. 43–44.
[54] Fillmore, *The Twelve Powers of Man*, pp. 57–58.
[55] Fillmore, *Mysteries of John*, p. 90.
[56] Charles and Cora Fillmore, *Teach Us to Pray*, pp. 64–65.

adjusted in their right relation." Man must be raised into the harmony of the Spirit and become adjusted to its fourth dimensional plane, even as Jesus was lifted on the cross, whose four branches represent these four dimensions.[57]

Knowledge and Right Action

Although man is enjoined to demonstrate his true being, Fillmore warned against his attempt without having first the requisite knowledge. The personal mind that tempts man to try experience without knowledge is defined as Satan,[58] and the devil is man's adverse will that tries to make him keep his personal freedom instead of submitting to divine guidance.[59]

It would naturally follow that man should pray that not his will but God's be done. God's will is followed by understanding the God-given law — a " law through which we can make any conditions that we desire." [60] But first man's lack of knowledge, selfish action, and failure to surrender his personal will to God's through prayer, underlie his difficulties,[61] according to this philosophy.

Although right thinking is of great importance to Unity, right action too has an important place. Charles Fillmore once heard the complaint of a number of students that they were unable to demonstrate what they desired, even though they had an understanding, and had both denied and affirmed for years. He then explained to them that one should learn also to " walk by the Spirit." In other words, a requirement for the new birth is not only right thinking, but also following the way laid down by the Sermon on the Mount, and learning to love our enemies, blessing them that curse us, and doing good to them that hate us, etc.[62]

[57] Fillmore, The Twelve Powers of Man, p. 154.
[58] Fillmore, Christian Healing, p. 53.
[59] Ibid., p. 107.
[60] Ibid., p. 73.
[61] Ibid., pp. 102–103.
[62] Ibid., pp. 202–203.

Sin (Evil), Repentance, and Forgiveness

Although enjoining one to walk the way of the Christ, Unity, in keeping with the other groups stemming from Quimby's thought, denies the reality of evil as a power in the world, unless one gives it force through belief. On the other hand, Fillmore affirmed that man was subject to error and fell short of God's ideal. Man had to learn to cross out his errors and conform to the " Jesus Christ Standard." Repentance for sin became a form of denial. With the cleansing of the mind by the denial of sin, he believed that an inflow of divine love would express itself as the joy that came but once to the orthodox Christian through the conversion experience, but could be produced at will by the metaphysician who practiced affirmations and denials as a science.

Both he and his second wife, Cora, gave similar meanings to the concept of forgiveness. He believed that forgiveness of sins meant " an erasure of mortal thoughts from consciousness," an equivalent to his concept of repentance,[63] while Cora Fillmore considered forgiveness as " the act of putting something else in place of the thing forgiven." It meant setting the " positive realization of the Truth of Being in place of the appearance of negation and adversity which your sense and your intellectual training report." [64]

Traditional Christianity, like Unity, would enjoin the reestablishment of a broken relationship through forgiving love rather than through holding a resentment. But, unlike Unity, it would recognize the sinful act as real rather than as an appearance, and would teach to forgive, not *by denial* of the sin, but rather *in spite* of the sin.

Law and Will

The philosophy of Unity is a type of mystical idealism and humanism, in which, through the apotheosis of man, one depends wholly upon himself — a self and the law of the self,

[63] *Ibid.*, p. 55.
[64] Myrtle Fillmore, *How to Let God Help You*, p. 68.

which are regarded as divine. In such systems principle or law is substituted for a doctrine of God's grace, and knowledge equated with God's will. Therefore, Unity declares that man attains his good by the knowledge and use of God's spiritual law, described also as his unity with God, the Christ, or his real self. The means to this end is through affirmative prayer and a spiritual life. But even though God's will is to be sought, Charles Fillmore said that " God is the potential, unformed will; man is manifest God-Will, or good-will." [65]

Spirit

Unity and allied metaphysical thought differ distinctly from traditional Christianity by believing in man's possession of the Spirit as the inner self. Here it is close to the early Gnosticism. Traditional Christianity teaches that the Spirit is a gift of God, and through the Spirit, man participates in the crucifixion and resurrection of Jesus Christ, and through it Jesus Christ is made present to man. Thus the reception of the Spirit would be interpreted as a gift of grace rather than the realization of man's being as Christ, the Logos. The traditional Christian would hold that the metaphysical ideas emphasize the pneumatic side of man at the expense of recognizing the reality and nonappearance of man's sinful flesh.

Communion with God

Although Unity speaks of communion with God, it would have a different theological import from traditional Christianity. Though Unity may speak of God in personal terms and teach that God becomes personal to the individual, still it makes God an essence rather than an actor, and reserves action for the individual person, the manifested idea of God. For example, Fillmore would not say God loves anyone, but only that " God is love: man is loving," or " God is wisdom: man is wise." [66] This follows from Fillmore's theological concept that

---

[65] Fillmore, *Christian Healing*, p. 103.
[66] Charles and Cora Fillmore, *Teach Us to Pray*, p. 13.

God as creator makes use of the Logos, the Christ, or spiritual man as his idea concretely expressed. In other words, God as love becomes finitely manifested by the action of man's loving, and man becomes one with God through this act. Man's thoughts and actions bring into expression that which is of God. According to this philosophy, one should love and not fear. One should not " behold evil as real and agonize over the evils of the world," because Love " taketh not account of evil." [67]

Health and Disease

Unity, like New Thought, regards health as the real, " the God-given condition, and disease the unreal, the abnormal, from which we are all seeking to escape." It teaches that if we deny disease as real and affirm our true nature as healthful, we will demonstrate health. So we are enjoined to have daily meditation, in order to open up the current of thought that manifests desired conditions.[68] This follows from the belief that man's nature is of God, who is perfect and has no lack. We are to make this affirmation and deny the reality of disease, and through the realization of our unity with God we will acquire health, prosperity, and other desired conditions.

Even though there are still great differences between traditional Christianity and the Unity School of Christianity, many members of denominational churches have found reassurance in Unity's optimism, its spirit of devotion, and its affirmative thought. As for the bona fide Unity student, one must admit that if he spends a few months at the Unity Farm he cannot leave without the impression that these people are doing their best to live the life they profess.

[67] *Ibid.*, pp. 112–114. [68] *Ibid.*, pp. 130–131.

IX

Christian Science

Writing Pro and Con

IN THE ANNALS of American religion probably no one's life has been so obtrusively laid open to criticism and defense as that of Mary Baker Eddy, the founder of Christian Science. Works such as Edwin F. Dakin's *Mrs. Eddy: The Biography of a Virginal Mind*, although offering much interesting material, are too polemical and often insufficiently documented. Georgine Milmine's book, *The Life of Mary B. Eddy and the History of Christian Science*, is valuable for the wealth of letters and recorded statements. Since she interviewed former friends and acquaintances of Mrs. Eddy who had known her in the formative period of Christian Science, the evidence is important. Nevertheless, all testimony cannot be taken at face value. Jealousies and former animosities could easily have colored the statements taken long after Mrs. Eddy reached success. Hugh A. Studdert-Kennedy's book *Christian Science and Organized Religion* is more sympathetic, and even more so the recent work by Norman Beasley, *The Cross and the Crown*. *Mary Baker Eddy: The Truth and the Tradition*, written by Ernest Sutherland Bates and John Valentine Dittemore, was censured by the official Christian Science Board, even though it depended largely on church archival records, and Dittemore had been a former member of the Board of Directors. For the Christian Scientist the official biography is still *The Life of Mary Baker Eddy* by Sibyl Wilbur.

Because of the vast gulf separating the official biography

from the very critical works, one may be led to believe that the true life of Mrs. Eddy must have lain somewhere intermediately. From the mass of evidence it would seem that she was a person who had her share of faults, whose recognition may be inversely proportional to the degree of sympathy one has for the movement. Certainly the years have magnified the halos of saints in the eyes of believers, while the goodness of rogues, like Caesar's, was " oft interred with their bones."

Recently more attention has been given to the organization, which has been critically treated in a book by Charles Braden, *Christian Science Today: Power, Policy, Practice* (1958).

Although much has been written concerning the possible influence of Hegel and Berkeley upon the thought of Mrs. Eddy, I shall limit this discussion to associations with the major philosophies already mentioned in this work. To treat only the common ideas, however, would be to distort the view of Christian Science. Critics have often dwelt so heavily on such doctrines as the denial of matter, evil, and illness that they have given little attention to the fact that Christian Science claims to be Christian. If Mrs. Eddy's interpretations do not agree with traditional views, there is still a place for a more rounded perspective of her doctrine.

Christian Beliefs Metaphysically Interpreted

Mrs. Eddy had been a member of the Congregational Church and had been reared in a Calvinistic, God-fearing family. If it was her choice to reject the orthodoxy of her time, she utilized, nevertheless, more Christian categories than any other metaphysical organization, even though she gave them a twist that would make them unacceptible to traditional Christianity. Let us turn to some of the Christian allusions.

Christian Science accepts for its basis the Bible as interpreted by Mary Baker Eddy. If it does not adhere to an orthodox Trinitarian theology, it has the concept of a triune God, believes Jesus Christ to be the Son of God of virgin birth, and embraces a doctrine of the Holy Ghost. Christian Science has its own belief in Christ's atonement which includes man's redemption from sin (and sickness). It holds that the wages of sin are disease and death, and that Jesus suffered for man's sins. It accepts a doctrine of the crucifixion, resurrection, and ascension of Jesus Christ. It teaches that a Christian should be willing to pursue the way of the cross and endure suffering and persecution. It believes repentance and suffering will help us to understand Jesus' atonement for sin and includes a doctrine of God's forgiveness of sin. It teaches that man should forsake sin, seek God's will, and follow it by subjugating the human will, self-will, selfish motives, self-righteousness, envy, revenge, etc., and man should seek first the Kingdom of Heaven, believing all other things will be added unto him. It advocates the Golden Rule, enjoins man to return good for evil and to love all mankind, because through love man is transformed. It accepts the belief in man's immortality after death and also the belief and hope of Christ's imminent return, when all men will love their neighbors as themselves. These views and many more which certainly sound like those of historic Protestantism are the beliefs of Christian Scientists and are found in Mary Baker Eddy's works. Still their full explanation places them outside traditional Christian theology and allies them more closely with other metaphysical movements.

Even though Christian Science gives more attention to the Bible and its interpretation than most other metaphysical sects, it is further separated from the traditional Christian churches because of its belief in the final revelation of Mrs. Eddy. As the one and only true interpretation of the Bible, and ostensibly a return to primitive New Testament Christianity, it must exclude the continuing witness of all Christian writers from the Church Fathers to the present day. Mrs. Eddy's book, *Science and Health with Key to the Scriptures*, is the definitive explanation of Biblical truth for Christian Scientists. Each Sunday it must be read alike in every Christian Scientist church, but with no interpretation. Mary Baker Eddy must have not only the last word but the only word of Biblical exegesis.

Life and Background of Mary Baker Eddy

Mary Baker Eddy was born as Mary Baker on July 16, 1821, in Bow, New Hampshire, the youngest of six children. All accounts agree that she had little formal education. She herself related in *Retrospection and Introspection* that her father believed her brain was too large for her body and so kept her out of school much of the time. She said that she became interested in natural philosophy, logic, and moral science, however, and had learned something of Hebrew, Greek, and Latin from her brother Albert, although most knowledge from books disappeared after her discovery of Christian Science.

Her later calling and the revelation of Christian Science was foreshadowed and seemingly preordained by voices she heard when eight years old. On various occasions during a twelve-month period she heard her name called three times in quick succession. Each time it occurred she thought it was her mother's voice. Finally, one day her cousin, who was playing with her, heard it too and said, " Your mother is calling you! " After verification by her cousin, later that night her mother read to her the story of Samuel and told her to reply as he had: " Speak, Lord; for thy servant heareth." When the call was repeated, however, she was afraid to answer, but praying for forgiveness, she promised to respond the next time. One final time the voice came, and after speaking the words of Samuel, she said she heard the call no more in her " material senses." [1]

After the death of Grandmother Baker in 1835, the family moved the following year to a farm near Sanbornton Bridge (now called Tilton). It was here at the age of twelve, according to Mrs. Eddy, that she was admitted into the Congregational Church, although the official biographer, Sibyl Wilbur, notes the church records show her acceptance was not until she was seventeen. [2]

Mrs. Eddy had apparently been a sufficiently sensitive child

[1] Mary Baker Eddy, *Retrospection and Introspection* (Christian Science Publishing Society, 1892), pp. 8–9.
[2] Sibyl Wilbur, *The Life of Mary Baker Eddy* (Christian Science Publishing Society, 1929), pp. 29–30.

for the effect of circumstances to cause illness. In her reminiscences she said that when preparing for her public confession in the Congregational Church, she became so bothered about the doctrine of unconditional election that she became sick. After taking her mother's advice to lean on God's love and to pray for guidance, however, the fever left and she was again in normal health.[3]

A brief but happy marriage to George Washington Glover in 1843 was terminated the following year when her husband died of yellow fever in Wilmington, North Carolina. Mrs. Glover returned to live with her family in Tilton until 1850, and then for three years she stayed with her sister Abigail.

During this period Spiritualism began to have its effect upon American thought, and mesmerism, Emerson, and Andrew Jackson Davis became topics of drawing-room conversation. The official biographer of Mrs. Eddy comments that she lived both fully and deeply in that environment, and although never seriously connected with Spiritualism, she admittedly associated with Spiritualists as she did with Universalists and Unitarians.

Mrs. Glover had been in delicate health for some time, and while living with her sister she was often in bed for long periods. It was alleged that she had a weakness in her spine which had caused spasms and then nervous prostration. Her marriage in 1853 to Dr. Daniel Patterson, a dentist and a homeopathic physician, although promising at first, ended in divorce twelve years later.[4]

During this period she heard about a healer, Phineas P. Quimby, of Portland, Maine, who was intending to visit Concord, New Hampshire. Dr. Patterson wrote to him his intention of having him see Mrs. Patterson, if he were to come. Quimby did not, but the next year on May 9, 1862, Mrs. Patterson wrote to him herself, begging him to help her. Finally, in October, 1862, she went to him in Portland.[5]

All sources agree that she believed she had been cured by

[3] Eddy, op. cit., p. 13.
[4] Wilbur, op. cit., pp. 36-55.
[5] Georgine Milmine, *The Life of Mary Baker Eddy and the True History of Christian Science* (Doubleday, Page & Co., 1909), pp. 42-44.

Quimby at that time. The official Christian Science biography tells how she was assisted to his office because of extreme feebleness, but yet returned well to Tilton.[6] It is also admitted she wrote articles defending Quimby,[7] but it is denied that his philosophy had influenced the content of Christian Science. Officially, Quimby was little more than an uneducated hypnotist.[8]

Her critics have cited the article she wrote in the *Portland Courier*, November 7, 1862, in which she acknowledged his ideas as a science, the "result of superior wisdom which can demonstrate a science not understood," and defended him against charges that he employed electromagnetism and animal magnetism (mesmerism). She implied that his cure had been through the discovery of "the truth which he opposes to the error of giving intelligence to matter and placing pain where it never placed itself."[9]

Later in another article published in the *Portland Courier*, she defended him against the accusation that he was being compared to Christ, but said that Quimby healed as never one has healed since Christ. She concluded: "And is not this the Christ which is in him? We know that in wisdom is life. . . . P. P. Quimby rolls away the stone from the sepulcher of error, and health is the resurrection."[10]

The official biography explains Mrs. Eddy's position by declaring that her attitude toward Quimby was like that of a daughter who idealized her father even when the whole world thought differently. Out of gratitude to Quimby for improvement in her health, she gave him credit for a system that he did not have.[11]

In 1864, according to Wilbur, Mrs. Patterson again returned to visit Quimby with the hope of enlightenment, since she felt she had neither a clear understanding nor a sound philosophy.[12]

In her later *Miscellaneous Writings*, published in 1896, Mrs.

---

[6] Wilbur, *op. cit.*, pp. 77, 102.
[7] *Ibid.*, p. 102.
[8] *Ibid.*, pp. 85–86.
[9] Milmine, *op. cit.*, pp. 58–59.
[10] *Ibid.*, p. 60. Quoted from the *Courier*.
[11] Wilbur, *op. cit.*, p. 103.
[12] *Ibid.*, p. 106.

Eddy wrote that the sum of what Quimby had taught her was that manipulation could benefit the sick by conveying electricity to them,[13] a charge against which she had earlier defended him.

Beginning of Christian Science

After the death of Quimby in 1866, Mrs. Patterson, subsequent to a severe fall, began the development of Christian Science. The official position is that during the period from 1862 to 1866 she had been trying to reconcile her faith with the ideas of Quimby; her own earlier thought had been influenced by animal magnetism, of which she was ignorant. While still in this state she had believed she had been cured by Quimby, but his thought and personality threatened her religious peace and faith. The fall and her miraculous cure on the third day brought an end to this state. According to Wilbur, Mrs. Patterson was knocked unconscious and severely injured by the mishap, and was still only semiconscious the next day. On the third day she opened her Bible and read the story of Jesus healing the palsied man. The truth was then revealed to her. Through this revelation she was instantly healed. She arose from bed and walked about the room, to the surprise of the clergyman and others who had gathered to be with her when she died. This was the discovery of Christ Science for which she had been preparing, for then she learned that Mind was all and matter nothing.[14] This is the official belief.

Critics have made much of the letter she wrote to Julius Dresser, a follower of Quimby, who, like her, had been cured by him. The letter dated February 14, 1866, inquired whether he would take the place of Quimby since he was the most capable to carry on Quimby's work. After telling of her fall and of her determination to get well, she wrote: " Now can't *you* help me? I believe you can. I write this with this feeling: I think that I could help another in my condition if they had

[13] Mary Baker Eddy, *Miscellaneous Writings, 1883–1896,* 3d edition (published by Joseph Armstrong, 1897), p. 378.
[14] Wilbur, *op. cit.,* pp. 121–129.

not placed their intelligence in matter. This I have not done, and yet I am slowly failing. Won't you write me if you will undertake for me, if I can get to you? Respectfully, Mary B. Patterson."

With this letter was enclosed a sonnet that she had written in memory of Quimby and that had already been published in the Lynn newspaper. It was entitled: " Lines on the Death of Dr. P. P. Quimby, Who Healed with the Truth That Christ Taught in Contradistinction to All Isms." [15]

Wilbur speaks for the Christian Scientists in declaring the letter to be Mrs. Eddy's final glance back to Quimby and his thought. The fact that help was refused, she said, closed the door on Quimbyism and ended the work for which she had hitherto given him credit. She was thereby forced to have recourse to God. [16]

From then until the publication of *Science and Health with Key to the Scriptures* in 1875, Mrs. Eddy was busy in the formulation of her thought, while moving from place to place, living with various people. When staying with Mrs. Sally Wentworth, in Stoughton, she taught her what she knew of the Quimby method. She also lent her the manuscript, which Wilbur said had been prepared by Mrs. Eddy while at Portland. [17]

Her first convert, Hiram Crafts, abandoned his shoemaking trade to demonstrate her teachings by healing others. His training forced her to systematize her thoughts and to compose a new manuscript, not too different from the one allegedly written for Quimby. She had searched the Scriptures and found in them a " spiritual signification " which she felt revealed the Principle of Christian Science. Wilbur, however, said that at this time Mrs. Eddy still felt Quimby shared with her the truth about healing, but her writings were now the product of her own experiences. [18] Critics have claimed she had not discredited Quimby as the author of the manuscript until after the publication of *Science and Health*, but they base their arguments

[15] Milmine, *op. cit.*, pp. 69–70.
[16] Wilbur, *op. cit.*, p. 130.
[17] *Ibid.*, pp. 174–175.
[28] *Ibid.*, pp. 151–152, 161.

upon much later statements from her earlier associates.

From 1870 to 1875 Mrs. Eddy spent her time in teaching, healing, and writing. She taught her methods to Richard Kennedy, who sent her patients interested in the philosophy of healing, so that she was soon able to form her first class. The testimony from all sources indicates that her early period of teaching was rather unpleasant. Many of her students did not create a good public image for her. For some years she suffered lawsuits involving them, often as a plaintiff to recover unpaid tuition or as a defendent against their demands for refunds. Even Richard Kennedy departed from her when she demanded he stop the practice of manipulation associated with mesmerism, but which he said she had taught him. Thus arose the necessity to write a textbook to which the publication of *Science and Health* was the answer.

Whereas the pressure to get her magnum opus recorded on paper had caused her to curtail teaching, now that only proofreading remained she began a new class in 1875. On May 26 of the same year a committee of her students met to pledge funds for renting a suitable hall and for hiring her to preach or direct their Sabbath meetings. So the nucleus for her first church was formed, and on June 6, 1875, the first public meeting of about sixty students was held [19] in Lynn, Massachusetts.

In the first edition of *Science and Health*, Mrs. Eddy expressed a disdain for church organizations and claimed Christian Scientists had no more need for them than Jesus Christ had. Nevertheless, on August 6, 1879, she applied for a state charter under the name of " The Church of Christ (Scientist)" [20] with headquarters in Boston. In 1881 she established the Massachusetts Metaphysical College, which taught pathology, therapeutics, moral science, metaphysics, etc.[21]

In spite of serious difficulties she had with recalcitrant students, resulting in expulsions from the church, and despite more trials and arguments, these tribulations seemed to increase the solidarity of the faithful. Her churches multiplied, as did the

[19] Ernest Sutherland Bates and John V. Dittemore, *Mary Baker Eddy: The Truth and the Tradition* (Alfred A. Knopf, Inc., 1932), pp. 163–164.
[20] *Ibid.*, p. 207.
[21] Wilbur, *op. cit.*, p. 262.

editions of her textbook. Missionary activities by Mrs. Eddy and her students carried Christian Science to major cities of the United States, and the *Christian Science Journal*, beginning in 1883, helped to increase her prestige. By 1886 Christian Scientists showed their importance by organizing the National Christian Scientist's Association.

Further steps were necessary, however, before her organization was to reach its present character. Mrs. Eddy desired to consolidate her church into a unit. She had no control over some students who had established Christian Science churches but were presumedly teaching variations of her philosophy. And there was also dissension in her own local church. Therefore, in 1889, Mrs. Eddy dissolved both the Metaphysical Institute and her Boston church. Then, in place of the latter, she dedicated the Mother Church in 1895. She did this after first buying the original mortgage for land on which the local church had intended to build, and then deeding it over to the Trustees of the new church.[22] According to the Deed of Trust, the church was to have a self-perpetuating Christian Science Board of Directors incorporated under the laws of Massachusetts. Elections held by the Board would be used to fill vacancies in its ranks. The terms of the deed, however, gave Mrs. Eddy or her heirs the right to recover possession of the property, if for any reason it seemed expedient to discontinue the work of the church.[23] It was Mrs. Eddy's church by law, even though the Trustees held the deed, because neglect of conditions named in the Deed of Trust would cause the property to revert to her.

Mrs. Eddy drew up the rules governing the new organization and published them as the *Manual of the Mother Church* in 1896. According to its laws, the President was to be elected for a one-year term subject to the approval of the Pastor Emeritus, Mrs. Eddy. The five-member Board, which was to handle business matters of the Mother Church, was also responsible for the satisfactory performance of all church officers and for

[22] *Ibid.*, pp. 312–330.
[23] Mary Baker Eddy, *Manual of the Mother Church of the First Church of Christ Scientist in Boston, Massachusetts*, 89th ed. (The Trustees, 1934), pp. 130–133.

the dismissal of any who failed in their duties after due notification. Conversely, if the Board of Directors failed in its obligations, it was to resign so that the Pastor Emeritus might choose a new Board. To ensure that no rules would be changed, the Manual provided that revisions required the consent of its author, Mary Baker Eddy.[24] The Manual, while ostensibly only for the Mother Church, applied also to the branch churches. Thus Christian Science consists of really only one church with many parts.

In order to protect her teachings from adulteration, in 1895 she passed a law forbidding individual sermons in her churches. From that time on, she ordained the Bible and *Science and Health with Key to the Scriptures* to be Pastor of the Mother Church. Therefore, the same lesson-sermon, prepared and read in the Mother Church each Sunday, is read also in each of the branches.[25] This gives a unique character to the Christian Science form of worship. It requires one reader for appropriate sections of the Bible. He is followed by a second reader, who gives the spiritual interpretation of the Scriptures, after announcing that he is reading from *Science and Health*, by Mary Baker Eddy. Such a method, of course, ensures greater uniformity of belief.

After the death of Mrs. Eddy in 1910, the church was immediately faced with new problems. The Manual, which could not be changed, was to be the guide for the administration of the church. Unfortunately, however, many of the rules required the personal sanction of Mrs. Eddy. The Board could not function, if it held strictly to the Manual, and for a time it was assumed these demands would have to be disregarded.[26]

Then a struggle for power arose between the Board of Directors and the Trustees of the Christian Science Publishing Society. The latter organization controlled the publication and distribution not only of Mary Baker Eddy's own works, but also of the Christian Science periodicals. Among these were

[24] *Ibid.*, pp. 25, 28–29, 104–105.
[25] *Ibid.*, pp. 58–59.
[26] Hugh A. Studdert-Kennedy, *Christian Science and Organized Religion: A Plea for an Important Consideration and the Examination of a New Point of View* (The Farallon Press, 1930), pp. 139–140.

the *Christian Science Journal* and the *Christian Science Monitor;* the *Christian Science Quarterly*, which gave the daily Bible studies for the Sunday services; and the *Christian Science Sentinel*.

Mrs. Eddy had set up the Christian Science Publishing Society as an independent entity with its own separate Deed of Trust and subject only to her. Although the Society was empowered to fill its own vacancies, the Board of Directors, together with the the " First Members," might declare vacancies to exist for expedient reasons. Since the deed demanded the Trustees be loyal and consistent believers in the principles of Christian Science, the problem concerned whether the Board of Directors should be the authority to question the " Trustees' " loyalty. After ensuing difficulties between these two agencies of Christian Science, the right of the Board to dismiss a Trustee of the Publishing Society was taken to the Massachusetts courts in 1919. The first decision favored the Trustees, but the Board of Directors carried the case to the Supreme Judicial Court of the state and emerged victorious in 1921. The issue was permanently decided. The Board of Directors was to have complete and autocratic power over the Christian Science Church.[27]

A part of the Board of Directors' authority is its sovereign judgment concerning statements made either about the life and work of Mary Baker Eddy or about her teachings. The branch churches have their own local elections, but since all officers must also be members of the Mother Church, their words and actions are held accountable to the Board of Directors. Those failing to keep the standards of the Board are liable to suspension or excommunication from the church.[28] The public image of its founder is also the concern of the Board, whose local control is invested in the Committee on Publication, its authoritative representative. An example of the great care taken by the Board occurred recently when a television station wished a lecture on Christian Science for its series on religious beliefs.

[27] Charles Braden, *Christian Science Today: Power, Policy, Practice* (Southern Methodist University Press, 1958), pp. 66–91.
[28] *Ibid.*, p. 98.

Even the local Committee on Publication, which prepared the lecture and the answers to predetermined questions that were to follow, had to send a copy to the Board of Directors for official approval.

The Board of Directors supervises the Department of Education which passes on all Christian Science teachers, and it rules on the authenticity of classroom instruction, if questioned. Those who desire their names in the register of the *Christian Science Journal* must take a primary and a normal course. This instruction, which is completed in twelve days, presupposes the qualified applicant has practiced Christian Science for three years and has studied the textbook, *Science and Health*. Taking class notes is discouraged, and in no case are they to be referred to in any publication. Thus the work of Arthur Corey entitled *Christian Science Class Instruction,* which purported to be the interpretation given by various Christian Science teachers, came under the proscription of the Board of Directors.

So careful is official Christian Science to keep its doctrine pure that any teacher not currently in favor does not suffer alone. All his former students must be retaught by someone qualified, after they have again shown proof that they are worthy and have paid another fee. The final authority for the correct interpretation remains with the Board of Directors.[29]

The Board of Lectureship, which enjoins each branch to call upon it for a lecturer at least once a year, is under the Board of Directors too. The former also provided authorized speakers for other public occasions. Through these controlled public lectures Christian Science presents a unified doctrine to an ever-increasing public.

The Revelation of Christian Science

One of the touchiest subjects officially has been the question of the validity of Mary Baker Eddy's independent revelation versus the influence of Quimby upon her, as alleged by her critics. Christian Scientists accept the originality of Mary

29 *Ibid.,* pp. 106–116.

Baker Eddy's divine revelation, now dated officially as the year 1866 following her fall,[30] but foreshadowed by her calling when she was a girl.[31] Christian Science would seem to regard itself as a final revelation making explicit that which was only implicit in the Bible.

Although Mrs. Eddy believed that Christian Science healed in the same way Jesus healed, she said in *Science and Health* that Jesus Christ " left no definite rule for demonstrating this Principle of healing and preventing disease. This rule remained to be discovered in Christian Science." [32] Similarly in *Retrospection and Introspection* she wrote:

" Even the Scriptures gave no direct interpretation of the scientific basis for demonstrating the spiritual Principle of healing, until our heavenly Father saw fit, through the Key to the Scriptures, in Science and Health to unlock this ' mystery of godliness.' " [33]

Her unique position as receiver of a new revelation is again disclosed in the same work: " No person can compass or fulfill the individual mission of Jesus of Nazareth. No person can take the place of the author of *Science and Health*, the Discoverer and Founder of Christian Science. Each individual must fill his own niche in time and eternity.

" The second appearing of Jesus is, unquestionably, the spiritual advent of the advancing idea of God, as in Christian Science." [34]

In her interpretation of the tenth chapter of the book of Revelation, she said that the angel or message from God mentioned was " divine Science," and she queried whether the " little book," which was opened, contained the revelation of " divine Science." [35]

[30] Mary Baker G. Eddy, *Science and Health with Key to the Scriptures* (published by the Trustees under the Will of Mary Baker G. Eddy, 1934), p. 107. Hereafter cited as *S. & H.* Georgine Milmine notes that the first edition of *Science and Health* in 1875 gives the date of her discovery as 1866 (Milmine, *op. cit.*, p. 77).

[31] *Supra*, p. 259.

[32] *S. & H.*, p. 147.

[33] Eddy, *Retrospection and Introspection*, p. 37.

[34] *Ibid.*, p. 70.

[35] *S. & H.*, pp. 558–559.

Again in her explanation of Rev. 12:1, she alluded that the "woman clothed with the sun, with the moon under her feet, and on her head a crown of twelve stars," referred especially to our present age.

Finally she wrote: "John the Baptist prophesied the coming of the immaculate Jesus, and John saw in those days the spiritual idea as the Messiah, who would baptize with the Holy Ghost — divine Science. As Elias presented the idea of the fatherhood of God, which Jesus afterwards manifested, so the Revelator completed this figure with woman, typifying the spiritual idea of God's motherhood." [36]

Thus only divine Science was able to reveal God, according to her,[37] and this Science she equated with the Holy Ghost,[38] or the Comforter which led one to truth.[39] This would certainly seem to make Christian Science an exclusive religion, if the final revelation is through Mrs. Eddy.

The Quimby Controversy

The two books on Quimby's teachings by Warren Felt Evans, which were published prior to Mrs. Eddy's revelation, precipitated no trouble for her until after the appearance of her work, Science and Health, which made her claims more widely known.

The real controversy between Mrs. Eddy and her outside critics did not come into public view until February, 1883, when the Boston Post published a letter by Julius Dresser setting forth the claims for Quimby. To this Mrs. Eddy replied in the same paper. She said that the year 1853 was the date of her "first experiments in mental healing." In a further exchange with Dresser, in which he had declared Quimby to be the originator of mental healing, Mrs. Eddy answered in the Christian Science Journal, setting the date of 1844 as the time when she was certain "mortal mind produced all disease." [40] Thus the battle was joined.

[36] Ibid., pp. 560–562.
[37] Ibid., p. 292.
[38] Ibid., p. 562.
[39] Eddy, Miscellaneous Writings, p. 174.
[40] Milmine, op. cit., pp. 78–79.

If the more than two thousand pages of Quimby's writings in the Library of Congress are authentic, certainly some acknowledgment of her debt to Quimby might have been in order, because they contain much that is quite like the teachings of Mrs. Eddy. Most of the essays are dated and have many interlinear corrections. Although without systematic arrangement, many of the articles have contemporary events and problems as their background. Moreover, any impartial person who examines the manuscripts carefully will certainly note a uniformity of style, even though they were written in several different modes of handwriting.

Nevertheless, the problem concerning the manuscripts is still more complicated than often observed. Mrs. Eddy had claimed in *Science and Health* that there were only a dozen pages of Quimby's manuscripts which she corrected for him. Horatio Dresser admitted she saw only the first volume, which he said his father had lent her, and which was a copy of a copy. He said further that there were over eight hundred closely written pages of manuscript, and presumably based his printed edition on these. The Library of Congress, however, now has almost three times as many pages of manuscript.

The claim that Mrs. Eddy borrowed the words " Christian Science " from Quimby, cannot be supported on the basis of the present manuscripts. Even though the article containing these words had been written after the first meeting of Quimby and Eddy, it does not appear in the same journal as " Questions and Answers," which critics have alleged Mrs. Eddy copied and used as the basis of Christian Science. This, of course, does not preclude the possibility that Quimby used the term in conversation or that Mrs. Eddy saw more of the manuscripts. But neither Julius Dresser nor Warren Felt Evans used these words when describing Quimby's philosophy. Only careful study of a critical edition of the manuscripts might hope to clear up many of the problems, which are beyond the scope of this work.

Christian Science scored a point when E. J. Arens, a former student of Mrs. Eddy, plagiarized some of her works and was sued. He lost his case when George Quimby refused to produce his father's manuscripts as evidence. Four years later, in 1887,

Mrs. Eddy made a public offer in a Portland paper to publish Quimby's writings, provided, of course, that she be allowed to examine them. This provision was ostensibly added so as to determine whether they were really his, or some of hers, either left with him years ago, or stolen from her published works. George Quimby refused to let them out of his hands.

Julius Dresser tallied next in the same year by publishing *The True History of Mental Science*, in which he reprinted the eulogies of Quimby which Mrs. Eddy herself had written and allowed to be published. She replied in the *Christian Science Journal*, June, 1887, that she must have been mesmerized, if she wrote the articles.[41] Thus the battle continued.

It is unfortunate that Christian Science has made such an issue concerning the uniqueness of Mrs. Eddy's revelation. If one examines the inspired sayings or revelations of all great historical religions, he will see that every historical religion may have distinctive features, but each has been built upon the religio-cultural blocks of the past. One cannot study primitive Buddhism without seeing the influence of Hindu philosophy. One may also witness part of the Judeo-Christian tradition recorded in the Koran of Islam. Even Christianity rests upon the earlier foundations of the Old Testament. Parts of the Old Testament bear the marks of Canaanite, Babylonian, or Persian influence, etc. Each religion is unique as a whole, and yet its strength derives something from the past. Therefore, the allegations of some dependence upon Quimby need not discredit the revelation of Mary Baker Eddy for those who honestly believe in Christian Science. Even if it were proved conclusively that Quimby contributed to Christian Science indirectly, it would not mean that Christian Science is nothing but Quimbyism. Even as Evans' philosophy and later New Thought have unique qualities, so Christian Science too has distinctive characteristics.

Christian Science in Its Milieu

The question of Quimby's influence upon Christian Science is only part of the problem. One may possibly view Mrs.

41 Bates and Dittemore, *op. cit.*, pp. 240–243; also Quimby, pp. 437–438.

Eddy's philosophy as an outgrowth of the whole welter of thought that was akin to American transcendentalism. I have already noted that in this milieu the current ideas of Emerson, Mesmer, Davis, Swedenborg, Quimby, and Hindu monism, etc., were mingling to form a cultural ethos, separate from that of orthodox Christianity, which has continued to the present day. It has been the genius of Christian Science to weld two traditions into an unorthodox but metaphysical Christianity which is unique.

Since possible contributions of Davis and Swendenborg have already been discussed in a previous chapter, only additional material needs to be added. For example, Mrs. Eddy's separation of the human Jesus from the Christ as Principle in every man, a doctrine held by all metaphysical sects, is not a first for Mrs. Eddy. Liberal Protestantism had already viewed Jesus only as a way-shower, and Andrew Jackson Davis was the first of the metaphysicians to write about the distinction between Jesus and the Christ. Professor Herman Ficke pointed out Davis' contribution, which appears in his work, *The Penetralia, Containing Harmonial Answers to Important Questions*, published in 1856. Principle rather than person was the predilection of both Davis and Eddy in referring to God, as it has been among all other metaphysical groups. Many other comparisons would be equally inviting.

Quimby followed Swedenborg in believing that Biblical words had a spiritual interpretation differing from their literal meaning. It seems strange, however, that Quimby's spiritual definitions vary from those of both Swedenborg and Eddy. This would seem to prove the originality of at least some of Quimby's manuscripts, even though the interpretive principle may have been influenced by Swedenborg. Some of Mrs. Eddy's definitions are very close to those of Swedenborg, although the majority differ.

In 1847 *A Dictionary of Correspondences, Representatives and Significatives Derived from the Word of the Lord* was first printed in Boston with many successive reprintings. This work had extracted Swedenborg's spiritual meanings of words derived from his works and listed them in the form of a glossary.

Mrs. Eddy's *Science and Health with Key to the Scriptures* contains also such a glossary of spiritual meanings. The following tabulation may be suitable to compare some of the definitions:

Emanuel Swedenborg	*Mary Baker Eddy*
" By the Ark going Forward, were represented combats and temptations."	". . . The ark indicates temptation overcome and followed by exaltation."
" Dan. All kinds of error."	"Dan (Jacob's son). . . . Error, working out the designs of error."
"Fan . . . signified separation of the false from good."	" Fan. Separator of fable from fact."
" Urim . . . signifies the light which is from the divine truth proceeding from the Lord." [42]	"Urim. Light."

Christian Science Teaching

God

Mrs. Eddy, while not accepting an orthodox Trinitarian view,[43] still considered herself as a theist believing that God was triune. This concept she expressed in various ways. She interpreted God or divine Principle as Life, or the Father; as truth, or the Son; and as Love, or the Mother.[44] Often she spoke of God as the Father-Mother God. She said that Love, which was the divine Principle, was the Father and Mother of man and the universe.[45] In still another place she said that Life, Truth, and Love representing the triune God, were essentially the same, but occupied multiformed offices: God was the Father-Mother; Christ, the spiritual idea of sonship; and divine Science, the Holy Comforter.[46]

[42] Herman S. Ficke, " The Source of Science and Health," *Bibliotheca Sacra,* Vol. 85, No. 340, Oct., 1928, pp. 417–423.
[43] *S. & H.,* p. 256.
[44] *Ibid.,* pp. 568–569.
[45] *Ibid.,* p. 256.
[46] *Ibid.,* p. 331.

Christian Scientists may speak of God in personal terms. He is personal, but only in the sense of infinite personality.[47] As divine or immortal Mind, he has other attributes which are synonymous with his nature, such as Soul and Spirit.[48] He is finally the only reality, is all and in-all, and good.

Creation and Matter

Christian Scientists teach that creation was God's infinite idea, which emanated from Mind, when God acted as Infinite Mind, the creator.[49] Since Mind is one, it includes both noumenon and phenomena, which has been interpreted as God and his ideas.[50] Atomic action or material force has nothing to do with creation. The universe, including man, is the reflection of God's Mind, and man is God's image and likeness.[51] What one might call atomic action is Mind rather than matter.[52] Since God as Mind pervades all space, the atom and molecule cannot be matter, it is reasoned. They must be the result of Mind, which is its own cause as well as its effect.[53] Thus nature and God are one, according to this philosophy, and so-called material law, a contradiction. There are really only spiritual laws,[54] and only one Science, the law of Mind.[55] This means that all objects in the world, e.g., trees, plants, etc., are merely the ideas of Mind, which are multiplied by it.[56] Since God is believed to be all, then matter is *nothing;* there can be nothing more than all.[57] This is the Christian Science dialectic.

In a section entitled " Questions and Answers " in her *Miscellaneous Writings*, Mrs. Eddy qualified this in response to the question about whether material objects exist only in one's

---

[47] *Ibid.,* p. 116.
[48] *Ibid.,* p. 115.
[49] *Ibid.,* pp. 256–257.
[50] *Ibid.,* p. 114.
[51] Eddy, *Miscellaneous Writings,* p. 23.
[52] *Ibid.,* p. 189.
[53] *Ibid.,* p. 173.
[54] *S. & H.,* p. 118.
[55] Eddy, *Miscellaneous Writings,* p. 173.
[56] *S. & H.,* p. 280. For a more explicit statement than this reference, one should consult earlier editions such as the 100th published in 1896, p. 176.
[57] Eddy, *Miscellaneous Writings,* p. 26.

imagination. In answer she recognized that even the *human* conception of beauty and grandeur is more than that; it is next to *divine* beauty and the grandeur of *spirit*. What one sees, feels, tastes, hears, and smells constitutes our *mortal* environment, the environment of *mortal* mind. She said that one did not label this beauty of the world nothing and make a caricature of God's creation. Nevertheless, she believed that matter was a poor conception of mortal mind, and mortal mind was a still poorer representative of the beauty and grandeur of immortal Mind.[58] Here Mrs. Eddy would seem to agree closely with Emanuel Swedenborg that *so-called* matter is of God, since God is all; but matter, however, is not in any way to be considered as God, but as only a shadow, a lower and poor correspondent of God's true reality. Such was not only Quimby's view, but also that of Andrew Jackson Davis. But Mrs. Eddy went far beyond this, and to understand the full view, it is first necessary to understand her conception of man.

Immortal Man

One must carefully differentiate between immortal man, " God's man, made in his image, and the sinning race of Adam," which represents mortal man.[59] I shall try to make clear the distinction, even though, according to Mrs. Eddy, eternal and immortal man cannot be perceived until understanding of truth destroys mortal and material error, which finally disappears.[60] As an idea in God's Mind, immortal man is forever perfect in God.[61] Therefore, there would really be no material creation, because " all that really is, always was and forever is; for it existed in and of the Mind that is God, wherein man is foremost." [62] If this view is true, the question remains, whether there would be *any* creation in time, and whether even time exists except as the error of mortal mind.

[58] *Ibid.*, pp. 86–87.
[59] *S. & H.*, p. 345.
[60] *Ibid.*, p. 252.
[61] Eddy, *Miscellaneous Writings*, p. 5.
[62] *Ibid.*, p. 57.

God's oneness is his allness, and man " coexists with God and the universe," [63] wrote Mrs. Eddy. Because God as infinite principle is reflected by the infinite idea expressed in *immortal* man, finite *mortal* man could not be the image of the infinite God. But even though *immortal* man infinitely reflects God, he is not absorbed in the deity, thereby losing his individuality. Nevertheless, Mrs. Eddy also wrote that man still " represents infinite Mind, the sum of all substance," [64] which must be considered in the sense of man as a microcosm, because even though God and man " are inseparable, harmonious, and eternal . . . God and man are not the same." [65] There is here a doctrine of God's transcendence, even though he is also wholly immanent, because it is written that man is only a reflection of the divine substance of Mind, just as man's image may be reflected in a mirror.[66] Therefore, man is not the same as God, but depends upon God for his existence, even as his own reflection in a mirror depends upon the existence of his image.

In line with the above, Mrs. Eddy separated Spirit from the spiritual. According to her, Spirit as a proper noun is the name for God, who is one and infinite. It refers exclusively to God. Spiritual, however, alludes to the quality of Spirit, but is not God. Thus man may be said to be spiritual as reflecting infinite Truth, Life, and Love, but is not Spirit; man is the image made by Spirit in the likeness of Spirit and not matter.[67]

Soul

The word " soul " has a unique meaning for Christian Science. Soul is God with whom man coexists and reflects, but it is not in man's body.[68] There is not a multiplicity of souls, but only one, just as there is but one Mind, and only one Ego, according to Mrs. Eddy. Man then is not Soul or Ego,[69] but man is its representative and cannot be separated from it or from God, whom he reflects.[70] One cannot therefore speak of a finite

[63] *S. & H.*, pp. 266–267.
[64] *Ibid.*, p. 259.
[65] *Ibid.*, p. 336.
[66] *Ibid.*, pp. 300–301.

[67] *Ibid.*, pp. 93–94; also p. 468.
[68] *Ibid.*, p. 120.
[69] *Ibid.*, pp. 249–250.
[70] *Ibid.*, p. 306

soul or spirit,[71] because Soul, the infinite creative principle, is outside finite forms, which only reflect it.[72] Also one cannot speak of a sinful soul, because sin and sorrow mean an absence of God.[73]

Mortal Man

Mortal body and mind as a unity have been called man, but man is not mortal, according to Mary Baker Eddy. Mortal existence is only a dream having no real entity.[74] Thus Mrs. Eddy would be able to say that God, who is all, is being and *is;* immortal man is a reflection of being, but not identical with it. Mortal finite man exists as error, but *is not,* i.e., he has mortal erroneous existence, but not being.

According to Mrs. Eddy, both matter and mortal mind are strata of man's human belief, which appears to be a tautologous statement. The grosser, she named matter; the more ethereal, the human or mortal mind.[75] The mortal body is but one's mortal erroneous belief, and matter itself is only error.[76] Since matter has no sensation, according to her, man has a body without feeling.[77] His five physical senses are only the beliefs of his mortal mind affirming that he is material rather than spiritual.[78] It follows that pain too is only the product of mortal mind due its belief in pain.[79]

Original Sin

This raises the problem of why man is as he is, caught in the illusion of mortal mind and not reflecting the goodness of God. While traditional Christianity explains man's sinful condition through the myth of Adam's fall, in one sense there is no fall, according to Mrs. Eddy, since immortal man remains perfect as

[71] *Ibid.,* p. 466.
[72] *Ibid.,* p. 71.
[73] *Ibid.,* p. 215.
[74] *Ibid.,* p. 250.
[75] *Ibid.,* p. 293.

[76] *Ibid.,* p. 372.
[77] *Ibid.,* p. 280.
[78] *Ibid.,* p. 274.
[79] *Ibid.,* p. 153.

the image of God.[80] Mortal man, however, is related to Adam, but not as a fallen man, since he has never had a perfect state of being from which to fall. Mortals " were, from the beginning of mortal history, ' conceived in sin and brought forth in iniquity.' " [81] The beginning of this discord " was the Adam-dream, the deep sleep, in which originated the delusion that life and intelligence proceeded from and passed into matter." This error was occasioned by the serpent, who caused man to think that he could be like a god, that spirit was in so-called matter, and that matter had as much life as God.[82] This original sin of Adam, which seems more amoral than immoral, expressed itself in many forms, according to Mrs. Eddy: " passion, appetites, hatred, revenge, and all the et cetera of evil." [83] Since the way out of sin to redemption is through Jesus Christ, his place in Christian Science is important.

Jesus Christ

Jesus, the son of a virgin,[84] while not God, is believed to be more spiritual than other men. Because of his great understanding he was able to demonstrate how spiritual truth could destroy material error. He " was the mediator between Spirit and the flesh, between Truth and error," and became the way to salvation by his explanation and demonstration of Divine Science. Jesus, the corporeal, the only begotten son of God, the Father, must be distinguished from Christ, the Son of God, the incorporeal, spiritual idea representing divine good. It is this Christ which Christian Science believes it has revealed.[85] Thus God's nature expressed in Christ Jesus is deemed to have given mortals the truer reflection of God and the real image of their likeness,[86] of which they had lost sight. Then through the goodness and grace of Jesus Christ was " purchased the means of

80 Eddy, *Miscellaneous Writings*, p. 182.
81 *S. & H.*, p. 476.
82 Eddy, *Retrospection and Introspection*, p. 69.
83 Eddy, *Miscellaneous Writings*, p. 114.
84 *S. & H.*, p. 313.
85 *Ibid.*, pp. 315–316; also *Miscellaneous Writings*, pp. 163–164.
86 *S. & H.*, p. 259.

mortals' redemption from sin." Nevertheless, the sinner can only pay for this through divine love, when he is " ready to avail himself of the rich blessings flowing from the teaching, example, and suffering, of our Master." [87]

The Crucifixion and the Cross

Christian Scientists believe that the crucifixion was efficacious because of the " affection and goodness it demonstrated for mankind," and through it they have seen the truth that " enabled their Master to triumph over the grave." [88] Mrs. Eddy said that " Jesus bore our sins in his body. He knew the mortal errors which constitute the material body, and could destroy those errors." [89] When he prayed, " Not my will, but Thine, be done," this was his request that the Spirit rather than the flesh should be represented in him, and it gave a " new understanding of spiritual Love." Christian Scientists are enjoined to drink of his cup, to be able to share the " blood of the New Covenant, the sufferings . . . which attend a new and higher understanding of God." [90] Rather than commemorate the eucharistic cup with natural symbols, Mrs. Eddy enjoined her followers to observe communion by emulating the example of Jesus, healing the sick, casting out error, preaching Christ to the poor in order to bring in the millennium.[91] They are to take up the cross and pray they will be delivered from evil or error, until they can demonstrate through Science that evil has no power or existence, since God is good and is all-in-all.[92]

The Resurrection and Ascension

According to Mrs. Eddy, Jesus' resurrection and ascension " showed that a mortal man is not the real essence of manhood, and that this unreal mortality disappears in presence of the

[87] Eddy, *Miscellaneous Writings*, p. 165.
[88] *S. & H.*, p. 24.
[89] *Ibid.*, p. 53.
[90] *Ibid.*, p. 33.
[91] *Ibid.*, p. 34.
[92] Eddy, *Miscellaneous Writings*, p. 115.

reality." [93] Thus " the divinity of the Christ was made manifest in the humanity of Jesus." [94]

Salvation

Salvation for Christian Scientists is not through faith alone, but is the result of following Jesus' example. This means that " all have the cup of sorrowful effort to drink in proportion to their demonstration of his love." [95] Mrs. Eddy wrote that if we remember the " sweat of agony which fell in holy benediction on the grass of Gethsemane, shall the humblest or mightiest disciple murmur when he drinks from the same cup, and think, or even wish, to escape the exalting ordeal of sin's revenge on its destroyer ? " [96] This willingness to suffer may seem inconsistent with the idea that pain is to be denied as an error of the mortal mind. But while a Christian Scientist may say that he has the freedom to reflect God in his body as in his mind, thereby becoming the Word made flesh, he still recognizes the pain caused by mortal mind before attaining the goal. For example, " if he says, ' I am of God, therefore good,' yet persists in evil, he has denied the power of Truth, and must suffer for this error until he learns that all power is good because it is of God." [97]

Atonement (At-one-ment)

Christian Science has a doctrine of the atonement promising redemption from both sickness and sin.[98] This does not mean vicarious suffering, but rather at-one-ment with Christ through the law of justice. Therefore sinners must suffer for their sins, " repent, forsake sin, love God, and keep his commandments." Mrs. Eddy said salvation from sin was through a divine life, which was our Redeemer.[99] Atonement is equated with one's unity with God, through which he reflects Truth, Life, and

[93] S. & H., pp. 292–293.
[94] Ibid., p. 25.
[95] Ibid., p. 26.
[96] Ibid., p. 48.
[97] Eddy, Miscellaneous Writings, pp. 183–184.

[98] Ibid., p. 96.
[99] Ibid., pp. 123–124.

Love. Man is indebted to Jesus for teaching and demonstrating it.[100] Therefore, he must get rid of false individuality, and by means of Love must free himself of self-will and self-love, which are the " law of sin and death." [101] He must liberate himself of self-ignorance, self-righteousness, lust, covetousness, envy, and revenge.[102] Through pangs of repentance and suffering, Mrs. Eddy believed we are aided in understanding Jesus' atonement for sin.[103] Here Mrs. Eddy was perhaps farthest from other metaphysical healing groups, which have borrowed from her, and closest to traditional Christianity.

Baptism of Spirit or Regeneration

Man's goal is his regeneration, which is defined as " the appearing of Divine law to human understanding." [104] Its last stage is called the third baptism, i.e., the baptism of Spirit, in which human consciousness is immersed in infinite love. When man attains this state, his repentance and abandonment of sin will dissolve his material life, so that he reflects only Spirit or good, and is cleansed from his sin.[105] He must first understand that evil holds no abiding pleasure, and neither pleasure nor pain exists in matter. These beliefs of pleasure, pain, and fear, which are false, as well as all our sinful appetites, the Divine Mind can destroy.[106] So Christian Science teaches the temporality of mortal man and claims to reveal the eternality of the spiritual man, who is the perfect image and reflection of God.[107] While such a belief in the possibility of perfection is present in some forms of denominational Christianity, the realization of this state would not be associated with the alleviation of suffering and pain.

100 *S. & H.*, p. 18.
101 *Ibid.*, p. 242.
102 Eddy, *Miscellaneous Writings*, p. 118.
103 *S. & H.*, p. 19.
104 Eddy, *Miscellaneous Writings*, p. 73.
105 *Ibid.*, p. 205.
106 *S. & H.*, p. 327.
107 *Ibid.*, p. 302.

Evil (Suffering, Death, and Sin)

Christian Science reasons that if God is all-in-all and good, and man is God's perfect image, it naturally follows that mortal man, evil, sickness, and death are only errors of man's mortal mind, which, beclouded by sin or error, is ignorant of immortal man's true condition. Evil then would not come from God, but only from the false belief of mortal man.[108] This means that immortal man would never be sick, because Mind cannot be sick and matter is not real. Mortal man's false belief is the disease and its cause, as well as the sinner and his sin, an error to be dispelled by truth.[109] Since it is believed that the Divine Mind never suffers, only mortal mind feels pain.[110] Immortal man, who is always in accord with God, is never thought to suffer or sin.[111] In a similar way Mrs. Eddy could say that the suffering of Jesus was due to the sins of others, but the Christ, the spiritual idea of divine love, did not suffer.[112] Jesus' mission was to save man from the illusion that he is a sinner, and that sin is real.[113]

Eschatology

Although Christian Science recognizes that immortal man cannot die, but merely experiences a change called death, it does not hold that sinners are suddenly pardoned when this takes place. They must still be punished in the world beyond.[114] Because they still have material thoughts after death, they must continually progress until God's truth removes their ignorance and sin. As long as mortal mind creates its own conditions on that plane, error will bring self-destruction, offering the possibility of even a second death.[115]

[108] Ibid., p. 356.
[109] Ibid., p. 393.
[110] Ibid., p. 108.
[111] Ibid., p. 202.
[112] Ibid., p. 38.
[113] Mary Baker Eddy, Unity of Good (Christian Science Publishing Society, 1908), p. 59.
[114] S. & H., pp. 35–36.
[115] Ibid., pp. 290, 77; also her Miscellaneous Writings, pp. 2, 14–15.

Second Coming of Christ

Mrs. Eddy held a belief in the Second Coming of Christ, when God's universal kingdom would appear on earth. The view is that man will slowly advance from his materiality until love will be supremely expressed, so that God's will shall be done here as it is in heaven. Just prior to this, however, there will be much conflict, famine, pestilence, etc., but " as this consummation draws nearer, he who hath shaped his course in accordance with divine Science will endure to the end." When evil reigns during the final conflict, those who understand Christian Science will help in getting rid of error, checking crime and maintaining law and order while happily waiting for the " certainty " of final perfection.[116]

Primacy of the Individual (Spiritual Man) and His Welfare

Although both Theosophy and the Arcane School have shown sporadic interest in social reform, Christian Science and other metaphysical sects have been almost entirely involved in the welfare of the individual. This may be another reason for the growth of these movements in our day. Perhaps their very philosophies enhance this lack of larger social concern, although less than a hundred years witness a Protestant social emphasis. These metaphysicians seem more interested in what they believe to be man's spirtual reality. Many are more concerned with man as a participant in eternity than in what they consider to be the illusory sphere of time and history. Paradoxically, however, this does not mean that they are like Hindu world-denying ascetics. On the contrary, they believe that the goodness of God is reflected not only in personal health, but also in *material* prosperity, which the American way of life has defined as good.

[116] S. & H., pp. 96–97; 55; also her *Miscellaneous Writings*, p. 213; also her *Retrospection and Introspection*, p. 70.

Curiosa

Since Mary Baker Eddy's death theoretically precludes changes of view in her philosophy, her works contain statements now unacceptable to many people. Mrs. Eddy lived in a period when medical science was in its infancy. It was true in her time that many remedies actually weakened the power to cure. Certainly the practice of bloodletting and the use of medicinal leeches would not be considered therapeutic today any more than many patent medicines of her time. Nevertheless, Christian Science must still exclude the use of all antibiotics and antitoxins that have been discovered, because Mrs. Eddy taught that no drug was efficacious to produce health.[117] Hygiene, too, she thought was worse than useless; he who knew no hygienic laws was believed to be more receptive to spiritual power.[118] One may criticize *Science and Health with Key to the Scriptures* and her other writings for such statements, yet the growth of Christian Science should make one more aware of the place that thought, emotion, and spiritual values can have upon mental and bodily health. Christian Science and other metaphysical sects that stress the place of religion in health have helped spur the traditional Christian churches to greater concern in this direction.

In this outline of Christian Science taken from the works of Mary Baker Eddy, I have purposely avoided most statements that might appear contradictory. Their presence, however, may partly explain why Christian Scientists avoid free discussion, which might promote variant interpretations leading to schisms in the church. That even authorized teachers of Christian Science have differed from one another has been made evident in Arthur Corey's book, *Christian Science Class Instruction*, which has not been approved by the Board of Directors.

[117] Eddy, *Miscellaneous Writings*, pp. 8, 53; also S. & H., p. 154.
[118] *Ibid.*, p. 17; S. & H., p. 381.

Growth of Christian Science

Christian Science has steadily grown and spread to Canada, Europe, Australia, and Great Britain. Since the Manual forbids publishing the number of Christian Scientists, it is difficult to know the size of the organization. During World War II, however, when the size of a church determined the number of its army chaplains, the Christian Scientists reported a membership of 268,195 in the United States. Using these figures and the knowledge that there were 2,284 local churches or societies reported in 1941, Dr. Charles Braden projected these figures to their world coverage in estimating a total of 3,115 churches and 367,570 members.[119]

Dissenters

Christian Science has had many dissenters who have been excommunicated or who have resigned over policy decisions. Although renegades from Christian Science, such as Emma Curtis Hopkins and Ursula Gestefeld, had been very influential upon New Thought groups, the only important schism resulting in a separate church was caused by Annie C. Bill, who organized the Central and Universal Church of Christ, Scientist, in London in 1912. This " Parent Church " had a number of branches in England and America until the death of its founder, but has now apparently ceased to exist.[120]

In recent years other noted members have left the church, some of whom rebelled against the strictness of the Christian Science oligarchy in matters of philosophical interpretation.

Joel Goldsmith

The late Joel Goldsmith, a very successful Christian Science practitioner for sixteeen years, had been allegedly healed of an incurable disease through Christian Science when he was a young man. His interest in his newly found faith led him to give up his clothing business to become a practitioner.

Walter Starke, his New York representative, said that dur-

119 Braden, *Christian Science Today*, p. 272.
120 *Ibid.*, pp. 381–389.

ing the years Mr. Goldsmith's ideas had slowly developed beyond the official Christian Science position: " Joel Goldsmith
realized his oneness with God and with all humanity in meditation. This meant that he did not need to treat a person for a particular illness. He did not even treat a person as an individual,
but realized his oneness with him and with God within himself.
He then began writing mimeographed letters of his thoughts at
the request of his students, and finally in 1947 he had the substance of these published as *The Infinite Way*. Since he could
not get permission as a Christian Scientist to do so, he left the
church to go on his own. It was not, however, Joel's desire to
form any organization, since that would lose the spirit.

" Mr. Goldsmith does not believe in fighting an evil, because
that brings one down to that level; but all should be treated
with the love of God. We do not try to decide what we want
and work for it by prayer, because we do not know God's will
for us or for others. We might try to demonstrate a Cadillac
by visualizing it completely as Mr. . . . teaches, but if we
got it, we might have a bad accident or lose it for nonpayment.
Seek first God within, and all we need will be supplied to us
according to God's will for us. We must not decide for ourselves. It is not our will, but God's will that is to be done."

Goldsmith's *The Infinite Way* contains the essence of his
later works. Though differing slightly from the official view of
Christian Science, it can be largely documented by Mrs. Eddy's
works. The most noticeable difference is Goldsmith's even
greater monistic emphasis, which he likens to Hinduism, Buddhism, and Taoism, while trying to express it in Christian terms.
His teaching is that there is but one life, one mind, and one
soul, which is the life of individual being.[121] Since man's spiritual sense reveals this reality, sin, disease, and death are only
its misperception by finite sense [122] — Mrs. Eddy's mortal mind.
What one's material sight can see is not the real life, which is
Christ, but only an illusion or false sense of existence.[123] If one
forgets about his selfish desires and becomes receptive to the

[121] Joel S. Goldsmith, *The Infinite Way* (Willing Publishing Co., 7th ed.,
1957), p. 52.
[122] *Ibid.*, p. 44.
[123] *Ibid.*, pp. 59, 62.

divine wisdom, the resources of the soul will pour forth more than one can accept.[124]

His philosophy relates persons to God like individual waves in an ocean.[125] Although Mrs. Eddy said that God was all-in-all and the one mind, she still recognized his transcendence and maintained that man was not spirit but a reflection as God's perfect idea.

The Spiritual Interpretation of Scripture, 1947, contains his metaphysical meanings based on the same hermeneutical principle as that of other groups studied herein. This book was followed by others, among which were *Practicing the Presence*, 1958, and *The Art of Meditation*, 1956.

Certainly *The Art of Meditation* has reached an audience far beyond the circle of Christian Scientists and displays a different emphasis from his earlier writings. As a devotional piece, more in the tradition of Meister Eckhart than most current mystical works, it has caused difficulties for many to recognize Goldsmith as a renegade Christian Scientist. It is perhaps ironical that Edmund Fuller, review editor of *The Episcopal Churchman*, while criticizing Norman Vincent Peale and Pealeism in the *Saturday Review*, in the same issue contributed a " Protestant Reading List " for Lenten reading, in which appeared *The Art of Meditation*, by Joel Goldsmith.[126]

On the dust jacket of Goldsmith's book, *Practicing the Presence*, Fuller recommended *The Art of Meditation* as " An able manual of introduction to the declining meditative art and an elaboration of its vital and productive role in Christian living and worship."

My purpose is not to criticize, but rather to note once again the growing influence of metaphysical literature upon the traditionally orthodox churches. Although Peale's techniques are similar to those of the Unity School of Christianity, how interesting that an Episcopalian of orthodox Christian tradition should denounce Peale, minister of America's oldest church, which is Dutch Reformed, and at the same time recommend

[124] *Ibid.*, pp. 88–89.
[125] *Ibid.*, p. 99.
[126] *Saturday Review*, March 9, 1957, pp. 28–31.

to Protestants a book by Goldsmith, former Christian Scientist, and still a metaphysician.

Although Joel Goldsmith was not interested in forming an organization, in many places throughout the world small coteries of people have formed Infinite Way groups. Mr. Goldsmith often visited these, when called, in order to give lectures to closed classes, which met six days a week for two weeks. According to Mr. Starke, meditating with him helped the groups to realize the Christ because of Goldsmith's own experiential knowledge.

About fifty percent of those attending his lectures were estimated to have been Christian Scientists, while the rest were from churches of the Catholic, Protestant, or Jewish traditions. It is said that many Christian Scientist practitioners are using his material, and quite a few are joining his groups.

Before his death Mr. Goldsmith moved to Honolulu, Hawaii, leaving authorized representatives in the United States, Canada, and England. He sold tape recordings of his lectures to various groups and offered a monthly *Letter* that included some new phase of his philosophy in each issue. A foreign edition was published in England for distribution to groups in Europe, Africa, India, Australia, and New Zealand. Had he lived longer, perhaps a new organization would have been formed, as has been the case with so many of the metaphysical sects, whose founders had no such original intentions.

X

The Church and Health

IN THE PREVIOUS CHAPTERS were presented various beliefs of the American religious philosophies which I have designated as the metaphysical movements. Their similarities of thought, their origins, and to some extent their influences have been noted in particular instances. There still remains, however, the question of their combined effect upon Protestantism's growing interest in its ministry to the ill. But before attempting an answer, it is necessary to reexamine one aspect of these sects which is important to their growth and influence in these times of crisis.

All metaphysical sects promise experiential knowledge in some way. They endeavor to give meaning to life not only through the mind but also through emotions or feelings. Believing their philosophy to be capable of scientific proof, they aim to demonstrate their beliefs through the exhibition of psychic phenomena, development of occult powers, a mystical awareness of God, or recovery of one's health. Although present in all these movements, the belief in God's healing power best epitomizes the *raison d'être* for those sects related to the thought of Phineas P. Quimby. The belief of the adherent that God has acted in his behalf to cure his disease and indeed to remedy other problems is an experience that may change his life. It may also give emotional support to the intellectual tenets of his particular sect. He is able to testify to concrete experiences that have happened to him personally. This reinforces faith, dedication, and commitment to the philosophy, which in turn gives meaning to his existence.

All religions, real, or pseudo such as Communism, contain three elements in varying degrees: the mental, the conative, and the emotional. Thus each religion contains a body of philosophy, which may or may not be based on logical reasoning. Still it directs the adherent's will toward certain patterns of action, the conative aspect, and gives him a way of life. These two elements, the mental and conative, must find support in an emotional aspect, a feeling that one's beliefs are true. This becomes the driving force behind the will, engendering commitment to the faith. The basis for this aspect, however, usually lies in one or more kinds of experience. It may be the supreme ecstasy of union with the Godhead, an emotional conversion, speaking in tongues, or simply the feeling that God has made himself known through the experience of healing. These, of course, do not begin to exhaust the ways in which man feels an awareness of the numinous. Each type of experience becomes authoritative, however, and bolsters emotional validation of belief. One *feels* that his belief is true through experience. To the extent that this emotional aspect is weak, his religion tends to become a mere intellectual body of thought and an ethical system. Therefore, a religion must be in some sense experiential and have an emotional appeal.

Among the major Protestant denominations deriving their traditions from Puritan sources, there has been a decline in the experiential element from the time of the halfway covenant, when the second generation of Puritans was not required to testify to a conversion experience. This waning of the emotional side led to an imbalance, tipping the scales toward the mental and ethical aspects. Against the intellectualizing process the Great Awakening revolted in favor of a religion of the spirit with concomitant emotional excesses. The continuation of the experiential emphasis among some led to the rise of the Pentecostal sects at the beginning of this century with their stress upon speaking in tongues. Although differing theologically, the metaphysical movements meet a similar experiential need.

While the metaphysicians were busy accommodating their philosophies to the accelerated interest in science, the theory of evolution, and later, the new psychologies, the traditional churches became concerned with new problems of interpretation. When Biblical scholars became engrossed in the application of scientific methods to the interpretation of the Bible, a new focus emerged for intellectual heirs of Puritanism — the social gospel. But while the major Protestant concern for the reformation of *society* overshadowed its ministry to the individual, the metaphysical sects still continued their emphasis upon meeting *personal* needs.

Because of the severe crises of the twentieth century, the intellectual and social emphases have been insufficient to the needs of many. Some have wondered about the efficacy of theological reasoning and social ethics when there was such a pressing need to experience God, to be aware of his presence, and to satisfy personal needs when on the brink of eternity. Therefore, some have sought new meaning to faith and life in various forms of religious experience. Certainly the fastest growing churches in America lately have been among the Pentecostals and conservatives, who have placed their accent upon meaning through experience. This phase has been seen in many of the more staid churches recently with the increasing practice of speaking in tongues, a return to a more literal interpretation of the Bible, and a warmer reception to evangelists such as Billy Graham. To the extent that there is an overemphasis upon the emotional side, the mental aspect is occluded, and theology declines. Without depreciating what the experience of speaking in tongues may mean to the individual spiritually to change his life, the phenomenon may be psychologically akin to practices found in other religions. There are at least similar manifestations brought on by disassociation and suggestion among shamans in some primitive religions, whose familiar spirits or gods speak through them; or perhaps among entranced mediums, if authentic; or in the spontaneous nonverbal utterances of the followers of Subudh in this country, when purging themselves in their *latihan*. When the pieces of one's life in times of crisis cannot be put together with reason and logic, this sometimes irrational but always emotional approach may bring about at least a temporarily healing catharsis.

Others who cannot find meaning this way are seeking experiential assurance through mystical ecstasies from hallucinogenic drugs, or they are searching for experiential values through Zen Buddhism, Vedanta, Yoga, the Self-Realization Fellowship, the Ruhani Satsanga, etc. All of these, including the metaphysical sects, are experiential forms of religion.

Such are the signs of the times. The pendulum has been swinging back toward the satisfaction of emotional needs in the traditional churches as a whole. When many in the churches are finding their meaning to life in beliefs and practices outside what has been considered normal for the church, the church is being forced to change its focus. Prayer groups are becoming more popular again, and prayer therapy has been having its vogue. Many of the ancient devotional classics and works of early mystics are being reprinted. A liturgical revival is taking place in many churches with its emphasis upon making the devotional life more meaningful. And renewed attention is being given to spiritual healing, or at least to the care of the sick in a ministry of healing.

With a shift toward meeting the needs of the individual, one often sees a theological approach to an existential psychology. The words of Martin Buber, the Jewish philosopher, and Paul Tillich, the Protestant theologian, and others, are being applied to man's existential situation both theologically and psychologically. Salvation is now often being equated with healing and wholeness. Even psychiatrists and medical doctors are speaking to man's spiritual need. Probably never before have the Biblical interpretations of a medical doctor and psychiatrist, such as Paul Tournier, been received with such acclaim. Still another psychiatrist appears on the horizon to play a stellar role in the practices and theories of pastoral psychology. This is Victor Frankl, the Viennese psychiatrist, who interprets man's salvation in terms of the will to meaning in his life. And Selye, Wolf, and others in medical sciences are proving theories that throw new light upon religious values and their relationship to health. With this increased interest in the application of psychology to the problems of religion and health, a number of important periodicals related to this subject have appeared

in little more than one decade. Notable among these are the
*Journal of Religion and Health, Journal of Existential Psychia-
try, Journal of Pastoral Care,* and *Review of Existential Psychology.* With this trend toward the practical and psychological values, the church is turning in the same direction as the
metaphysical movements. Because of this increasing rapport
between psychology and religion, some churchmen have looked
for possible contributions from the metaphysical healing groups
which likewise have made use of certain psychological principles. Let us turn to a brief outline history of the church's
interest in the mental and bodily health of the individual during this century, and to influential aspects of metaphysical
thought.

The Church and Health

In America the active concern of the minister for the sick
owes something to the short-lived Emmanuel Movement and
to the efforts of its founders, the Reverends Elwood Worcester
and Samuel McComb. They began their ministry in Emmanuel Episcopal Church in Boston in 1904 with two things
in common. They both had studied psychology, and they
shared the belief that the minister could be of assistance to the
physician in the cure of disease. They had seen the role that
Christian Science and metaphysical healing were playing. They
not only believed in the therapeutic value of such practices,
but also perceived the lack of concern for a healing ministry
by churchmen. They studied the methods of the metaphysicians and noted the effects of the power of suggestion. After
much consultation with Drs. Richard C. Cabot, Joseph H.
Pratt, Isador Coriat, and others, they began their experiment.
Believing God could cure through the mind or spirit in addition to medicine, and that the Gospels had a therapeutic value,
they concerned themselves with the poverty-stricken tubercu-
lar patients who could not afford to go to a sanatorium. In addition to the prescription of fresh air, sleep, and nourishment,
they had weekly meetings at the church for all who could attend. There the patients were given milk and pure olive oil,

were examined by Dr. Joseph Pratt and his assistants, and received a strengthening of their faith through the religious services.

Worcester and McComb wrote a number of books, but probably their most important works were *Religion and Medicine*, issued in 1908, and *Body, Mind, and Spirit*, published in 1931. The Christian world and especially its ministers received their works quite controversially. Many approved, but many others believed there was an unwarranted influence from Christian Science. Although the Emmanuel Movement, as such, soon petered out after the retirement of the founders, the Christian ministry was reawakened and stimulated to greater concern for the ill.

In England, important consequences followed when the news of their work spread there. Dr. Worcester spoke at the Lambeth Conference of the Church of England,[1] an event that furthered interest in spiritual healing.

In America, after the Emmanuel Movement had shown concretely that physicians and ministers could cooperate in a common purpose, the Commission on Religion and Health was organized as a subsidiary of the Department of Pastoral Services of the Federal Council of the Churches of Christ in the United States of America in 1923.

Then, in 1924, the Reverend Anton T. Boisen became a chaplain at the Worcester State Hospital at Worcester, Massachusetts. There he had the opportunity to bring his spiritual ministry to mental patients. In 1925 he accepted three theological students to study under him and under the guidance of Dr. William A. Bryan, the hospital administrator. In this way Boisen became the father of clinical pastoral training and a forebear of this emphasis on the ministry of healing, which has increased through the years.[2]

Although this whole development might have taken place because of the discoveries of the relation between mind and body in illnesses, nevertheless, the metaphysical healing groups

[1] Carl Scherzer, *The Church and Healing* (The Westminster Press, 1950), pp. 169–182.
[2] *Ibid.*, p. 229.

have directly and indirectly acted as a catalyst in activating this concern of Protestantism.

Prayer Therapy

Concomitant with the recent interest in group therapy has been the attempt by some to evaluate the therapeutic validity of prayer. To some the study of prayer techniques, in order to produce the best extrinsic results, has sounded like the teachings of the metaphysical sects, which have been accused of trying to manipulate God.

Dr. William Parker, a Christian layman, organized the first prayer therapy group to test the value of prayer. Although he was convinced that prayer had great value, he challenged some of the orthodox views about prayer and its underlying theology.

His discovery that he had stomach ulcers precipitated his experiment. Believing that they were of psychosomatic origin and ill affording an expensive psychiatrist's fee, he turned to prayer and claimed he was cured in three months. Not content to accept the results without proof, he decided to put prayer to the laboratory test at the University of Redlands, where he was professor of psychology and speech pathologist. He began this experiment in 1951 with forty-five volunteers, all of whom were experiencing mental or physical infirmities. He divided them into three groups and gave weekly counseling to the first, which believed that psychotherapy could help. The second group of fifteen consisted of faithful practicing Christians who thought prayer could solve their problems if it were regularly and dutifully employed. The third, or prayer therapy group, applied prayer and group discussion to individual problems discovered through psychological examinations. All three sections were given a number of tests in order to locate areas of personality maladjustment, and at the end of the nine-month period of experimentation these were repeated to note progress or regression.

According to Parker, the results showed that those receiving psychotherapy made a sixty-five percent improvement; the ones using conventional prayer showed almost no progress, and in some cases, a regression; but the prayer therapy group made a seventy-two percent improvement both in tests and symptoms, including some dramatic healings.

Parker said that those in prayer therapy soon began to discuss their problems and share their experiences with others of their section. Inhibitions broke down. Each one learned to accept himself as he was, and was also accepted by the others in the group without condemnation. But each, although accepting his weaknesses, sought for improvement. Parker believed, as in his own case, that it was not the " sins of omission and commission " that caused the trouble. Of these one was aware. And normal guilt, when recognized, could help create new patterns. It was, rather, the unknown fears and hates that had been repressed in the subconscious mind. These, he believed, could be helped best through prayer therapy, and he concluded that the results proved the power was God's and due to guided prayer conducted by the students.

Some of the results Parker claimed for the individual using prayer therapy were: the achievement of the ability to relate oneself to a God of love rather than to one to be feared; the recognition that the world is not evil; the amelioration of one's condition by accepting his own faults and trying to improve himself rather than being so concerned about conformity; the awareness of the power of loving one's neighbor as oneself; the acquisition of self-confidence by discovering through prayer that one is the " image, the child or offspring of the Divine," and God, the source of help.

In the cases of those who used conventional prayer, Parker concluded their lack of improvement was because they did not seem to go beyond the broken moral laws in their confessions. They blanketed their guilt feelings by affirming they were sinners unworthy of help. He believed this gave to the subconscious only the ideas of self-condemnation and hopelessness. Their prayers were negative, and they got a negative result. He then quoted the already familiar Biblical passage in Mark: " all things whatsoever ye pray and ask for, believe that ye have received them, and ye shall receive them." [3]

[3] William R. Parker and Elaine St. Johns, *Prayer Can Change Your Life: Experiments and Techniques in Prayer Therapy* (Prentice-Hall, Inc., 1957), *passim.*

This quotation has been interpreted by metaphysical groups as the Biblical basis of positive thinking, and is the foundation of Ernest Holmes's law of affirmative acceptance. His feeling of kinship with Parker's view undoubtedly influenced him to give me a copy of Parker's book, *Prayer Can Change Your Life; Experiments and Techniques in Prayer Therapy*. In his presentation Holmes said: " That's my philosophy. It is now being proved in the colleges." Although the metaphysical healers might agree with the little fragments of philosophy contained in Parker's book, his techniques were different.

Parker's work has been received as a controversial piece among churchmen. But in spite of criticism his theories have given rise to other prayer-therapy groups throughout the United States. Notable among these are the Branches groups started by Dr. Paul Kurtz, an ordained Protestant minister of Redwood City, California. Dr. Kurtz began his work by making an adaptation of Parker's ideas. From the original prayer therapy groups others have risen bearing the names of " spiritual growth groups " or " human growth groups." The Yoke-fellow groups, originating from the inspiration of Elton Trueblood through his book *The Predicament of Modern Man* have also been influenced somewhat in their development by the Parker methods.

What about the validity of Parker's expriments? If ever proved, it is still too early to assess them properly, for one must await the results of similar investigations conducted by others. To be sure, there have been many who have participated in prayer therapy groups, but those with which I have been acquainted have augmented Parker's ideas, and some have had a shorter duration of therapy. Some have praised; others have spoken about being more disturbed afterward. But certainly a disturbance, when really understood by a person, may become the catalyst to aid one's spiritual and psychological growth. If its cause is made known, this may lead to the first facing of a reality, hitherto avoided and repressed in the unconscious, thereby contributing to one's poor mental and physical health.

One of the first to conduct an investigation of prayer therapy has been Dr. Kenneth Johnson, whose work comprised a doctoral dissertation performed at the Pacific School of Religion. For his study he used first the psychological test records of sixty persons taken at random from about two thousand who had been in the groups of Dr. Kurtz and his associates; and secondly, the records of thirteen persons who had been in his own groups practicing the same methods. If the results were not as dramatic as the reports of the Parker experiment, they still have shown personality changes that Dr. Johnson considered as spiritual growth. Since Kurtz's approach was an adaptation of Parker's, the dissertation neither proves nor disproves the results of the latter.

Interdenominational Spiritual Healing Groups

Another development in the churches during recent years has been the spiritual healing practices witnessed in some interdenominational organizations. Besides the influential Spiritual Frontiers Fellowship, already mentioned, there are the Camps Farthest Out and the International Order of St. Luke the Physician.

In 1929 Glenn Clark, a layman in the Plymouth Congregational Church in Minneapolis, first shared with his Sunday school class the idea of establishing camps where people could go for a week of spiritual renewal through prayer. Underwritten by a group of businessmen in Minneapolis, the first of the Camps Farthest Out was held in 1930 at Lake Koronis, Paynesville, Minnesota. Since then the movement has grown. Today there are forty-two such camps in the United States, Canada, the British Isles, and India. The program of the camps includes not only lectures, but meditation, prayer, and creative activities.[4] Clark's movement was aided early by Starr Daily, Roland Brown, and Louise Eggleston, all of whom have been prominent in the practice of spiritual healing.[5]

Glenn Clark was also associated with the Healing Advance, which had special camps convened annually by Dr. Clark for

[4] *Camps Farthest Out* (National Association of Camps Farthest Out, 1961), *passim.*

[5] Walter W. Dwyer, *The Churches' Handbook for Spiritual Healing*, 6th ed. (Ascension Press, 1962), p. 5.

several years beginning in 1946. These were slanted toward the formulation of basic laws of spiritual therapy and techniques of practice, in which one sees a blending of ideas from Christian theology, psychiatry, psychosomatic medicine, and from the metaphysical movements. For example, Dr. Fred Andrews, a leader of a Unity School of Christianity center in Indianapolis, was a contributor at the meeting held at Camp Ihduhapi near Loretto, Minnesota, in 1948.[6] Even though there has been influence from metaphysical sects, it would be a gross misinterpretation to infer that Glenn Clark and his enterprises were direct products of these sources.

A similar influence within the churches has been the International Order of St. Luke the Physician, an interdenominational organization devoted to spiritual healing. It was founded in 1946 by Dr. John Gayner Banks, an Episcopal priest. Since that time it has grown and become international in scope. Each year the Order holds a conference, including both clergy and laity who are interested in fostering spiritual healing.[7] Over eight thousand people from thirty-eight states of America, ten provinces of Canada, and several foreign countries, were drawn to the conference in 1961.

Dr. Banks desired to make a synthesis of healing ideas embracing the truth not only from the teachings of Jesus, the apostles, and the church throughout the centuries, but also from medical science, psychiatry, and from wherever found. He would also include ideas emanating from the metaphysical movements. Concerning " Metaphysical Healing," he wrote: " This much-abused term must be taken seriously, even though it usually arouses controversy. It represents an entirely new way of teaching and practising the elements of Christian healing as given in the Gospels."

He followed this by giving credit to the works of Warren Felt Evans and Emma Curtis Hopkins. The latter's ideas are

---

[6] John Gayner Banks, *Basic Laws of Spiritual Therapy* (St. Luke's Press, n.d.), *passim*.

[7] Dwyer, *op. cit.*, pp. 5, viii. Dwyer gives 1947 as the date of founding, but Banks cites 1946 as the beginning; cf. his article " The Order of St. Luke: the Geneology of Healing Truth," in *Sharing* (published by St. Luke's Press), Vol. 26, No. 10, Aug., 1959, p. 9.

summed up in one of the association's study courses, entitled *Truth That Heals,* published by the St. Luke's Press. Horatio Dresser's concepts of New Thought are also quoted and used by Dr. Banks.[8]

One might query whether such a liberal synthesis of healing philosophy would be compatible with the beliefs of those ministers who witness to the gift of tongues. For certainly the fundamentalism or conservatism of many in the latter group would seem far removed from any influence of the metaphysical healing sects. But the answer apparently for some is affirmative, because among the hundreds of names listed in the " Healing Directory " in Dr. Bank's periodical, *Sharing,* are those of ministers who are now promoting the gift of tongues in their churches.

The Laymen's Movement for a Christian World has also made its contribution to the subject of spiritual healing. Under its auspices in the period from 1953 to 1958, there was a series of seminars on the subject given at Wainwright House at Rye, New York. The reports and discussions, which have been published, represent contributions by clergymen, laymen, psychiatrists, doctors, and professors.

Gradually, as it became clear that illness often has a certain religious factor, other new organizations were established. For example, the American Foundation of Religion and Psychiatry, Inc., in New York, a nonprofit agency, works in collaboration with the Marble Collegiate Church served by Norman Vincent Peale as well as with other churches. It provides a clinic for analysis, psychiatric treatment, and spiritual counseling. Another feature is the healing service with the laying-on-of-hands conducted by the Reverend Dr. Howard Kew, an ordained Episcopal priest.

When the Federal Council of the Churches of Christ in the United States of America established the Commission on Religion and Health, it set forth the following aims: " 1. To show that health of body, mind, and spirit is an essential concern of religion. 2. To discover and demonstrate the distinctive function of religion in the maintenance, restoration, and improve-

[8] *Sharing,* pp. 8–9.

ment of health and emotional balance. 3. To aid in revitalizing
the Pastor's ministry to individuals in special need and difficulty. 4. To promote practical cooperation between physicians and clergymen and between other leaders of religious and
health work. 5. To improve the ministry of the churches to
those in hospitals and other institutions and to those suffering
from chronic illness." [9]

In 1956 the Academy of Religion and Mental Health began
its program in New York. It instigated a five-year study at
Harvard, Loyola, and Yeshiva Universities to develop a curriculum for mental health suitable for theological seminaries of
the major faiths.[10] Since that year the number of associations
interested in religion and health has steadily increased.

It is therefore not strange that ministers of all denominations
have had a renewed interest in the care of the sick, and many
also in spiritual healing. Because of this new emphasis, which
is in part due to the pressing claims of healing from the metaphysical sects, denominational action has now been taken by
some churches.

Interest in Spiritual Healing by Denominations

Studies on religion and health have been made by specially
appointed committees in many denominations both here and
abroad, and reports advocating the churches' concern for the
ministry of healing have been accepted and published by a
number of official bodies. Among those in England now accepting to some extent the efficacy of healing services are the
Anglican, Congregational, Presbyterian, and Baptist churches.

The Church of England took the leadership. In 1953 a Commission on Divine Healing was appointed by the Archbishops
of York and Canterbury. Its report entitled *The Church's Ministry of Healing* was published in 1958 and thereby laid down
the practices for the Church of England. The report recommends cooperation between the clergy and the medical profession, since it affirms that the causes of disease are multiple,

---

[9] John Gayner Banks, *op. cit.*, p. 11.
[10] Dwyer, *op. cit.*, p. 78.

and man must be regarded as a unity of soul and body inter-
acting upon one another. In the final analysis it holds that all
healing, whether through medicine or the spirit, is from God.
It further recommends healing services in the church, which
should be " related to its normal and regular worship and pastoral work," but also makes place for intercessory groups functioning as prayer groups.[11]

Although the Congregational Union of England and Wales
cannot be said to have an official published statement, a mimeographed document similar to that of the Church of England
was prepared by its Theological Commission at the request of
the Life and Work Committee. This was presented to the Council for distribution in 1959. The activity of the Committee had
been energized into action in 1956 when the results of a ques-
tionnaire showed that over ninety Congregational ministers
were conducting spiritual healing services with a great variety
of methods. Official study and guidance seemed to be appropriate. Therefore, after perusal of the published reports of both
the Church of England and the Church of Scotland, the Committee recommended the ministry of healing as " a normal
responsibility of the whole fellowship," which, " should be
exercised by the whole church." [12] Although willing to recommend Communion for the sick at home and the laying-on-of-
hands, the Congregationalists made it quite explicit that as far
as possible this ministry should be within the context of the
various ordinances of the church rather than at special services.

In this country the 168th (1956) General Assembly of the
Presbyterian Church in the United States of America appointed
a special committee to study " The Relation of Christian Faith
to Health." This committee, which included not ony ministers
but also medical doctors and psychiatrists, made a study of the
problem. After much correspondence and seven plenary sessions, the favorable reports of the several sections were compiled by Dr. Robert Bonthius and published as the official

---

[11] Church of England Archbishops' Commission on Divine Healing, *The
Church's Ministry of Healing; Report of the Archbishops' Commission* (The
Church Information Board, 1958), *passim.*

[12] Congregational Union of England and Wales, Life and Work Committee,
Spiritual Healing, 1959, *passim.*

statement of the church by the 172d General Assembly in 1960. The report endorses spiritual healing, but prescribes carefully the theological and ritualistic context in which it should be observed.[13]

In 1961 " A Report on Spiritual Healing " was made by a committee of the Evangelical and Reformed Church (now United Church of Christ) and sent to its member churches. In 1962 a " Report of the Committee on Anointing and Healing " was issued by the United Lutheran Church in America for its national convention in 1962. In September, 1961, at the General Convention of the Protestant Episcopal Church a Commission on Spiritual Healing was appointed to make a similar report. The Methodists have not been far behind. In the past several years seminars on spiritual healing have been held by the Boards of Evangelism of the Pacific Northwest Conference, the Southern California-Arizona Conference, the Oregon Conference, and the Virginia Conference of The Methodist Church.[14]

In general, the reports have contained the following items:

1. The growing concern about the healing claims of the metaphysical groups, and the recognition of the neglect of the healing ministry in Christian churches.

2. The renewed belief that all healing is from God, whether through medical science, psychiatry, or prayer.

3. The recognition that there is a unity of body, mind, and spirit, and that some causes of mental or physical illness may be of a religious nature for which definite help can be received through a minister and the church.

4. The belief that spiritual and physical healing may take place within the theological and liturgical framework of the church's own tradition. Besides prayer groups there may be the use of Holy Communion, anointing, or the laying-on-of-hands, depending on the traditions of the various churches.

Among the chief differences between the healing philosophy of traditionally Christian churches and the metaphysical sects

[13] *The Relation of Christian Faith to Healing* (General Assembly of The United Presbyterian Church in the U.S.A., 1960), *passim.*
[14] Dwyer, *op. cit.*, pp. 79–82.

are that the former give more recognition to a reality of sin
and of sickness, as well as to values of confession, repentance,
and forgiveness of sin, and demand that the minister should
always work in close cooperation with the medical profession.

Growing Use of Affirmative Prayer

Although the official pronouncements of organized Christian
churches have not succumbed to any direct influence from the
metaphysical movements in their healing techniques, the same
cannot be said concerning all their ministers. Among those now
engaged in spiritual healing, many are making use of positive
prayer in the form of affirmations, even though the petitionary
form is still predominant. Not only many who have been associated with the Camps Farthest Out and the International Order of St. Luke the Physician, but others too have felt there
are healing values in positive suggestions formed into affirmations. Among the extreme advocates of this type of prayer, of
course, are Norman Vincent Peale and Lewis Dunnington,
whose books make plain their positions. There are also others,
however, who use both affirmative prayer and traditional forms.
Notable among these are Louise Eggleston, a laywoman in The
Methodist Church and a member of the World Literacy Prayer
Group, whose lectures in many churches and whose printed
pamphlets on prayer and spiritual healing have been influential;
the Reverend Alfred W. Price, Rector of St. Stephen's Church
in Philadelphia, who has become well known for his healing
services, his tape-recorded lectures, and printed pamphlets; the
Reverend Alex Holmes, whose many healing services and lectures in this country have greatly fostered the ideas of spiritual
healing among the organized Christian churches; and last but
not least in this brief and incomplete list, Dr. Albert Day,
prominent Methodist minister, author, and founder of the organization called the Disciplined Order of Christ. In an issue
of its *Newsletter*, published after a retreat at the Unity School
of Christianity, appears an outline of its principles developed
at that time. While accepting the traditional belief in redemp-
tive healing, including self-surrender to God, confession, and

penitence, prayers for forgiveness and prayers of thanksgiving, the laying-on-of-hands, etc., the organization also included a belief in the power of positive and affirmative prayer as being efficacious to a science of healing.[15]

Although the suspicion of magic and of trying to manipulate God would probably be the traditional churches' principal case against the use of affirmative prayer for healing, it should be noted that all churches are constantly making use of affirmations in the meditational part of their Sunday services whenever they employ responsive readings. It is the usage, however, that makes the difference. On the other hand, even though affirmations are avoided, a positive approach is just good common sense in most cases when ministering to the ill. That which increases confidence, faith, acceptance, and reassurance is therapeutic and aids the healing process.

But the curtain is drawn; the drama is over; and so ends our odyssey among the various groups of the metaphysical movements. To some they will appear as an *avant-garde* introducing the New Age, the Aquarian Age, to take the place of a decadent dying Christianity of the old Piscean dispensation. To others they will appear as a new reformation in Christian thought transforming an outworn orthodoxy into living religion. To still others, who view with alarm their growing influence upon the Christian churches, they will seem to be a " fifth column " subverting the theology and mission of the Christian church. Yet they have made their contribution which must be recognized in the annals of American religious culture.

[15] *Newsletter*, Disciplined Order of Christ, Vol. 37, September, 1954.

Index